PAUL KELLY

THE MAN, THE MUSIC AND
THE LIFE IN BETWEEN

PAUL KELLY

STUART COUPE

hachette
AUSTRALIA

Important note: Aboriginal and Torres Strait Islander readers are advised that this book contains names and images of people who have died.

 hachette
AUSTRALIA

Published in Australia and New Zealand in 2020
by Hachette Australia
(an imprint of Hachette Australia Pty Limited)
Level 17, 207 Kent Street, Sydney NSW 2000
www.hachette.com.au

10 9 8 7 6 5 4 3 2 1

 A catalogue record for this
NATIONAL book is available from the
LIBRARY National Library of Australia
OF AUSTRALIA

ISBN: 978 0 7336 4234 0 (paperback)

Cover design by Christabella Designs
Front cover image courtesy Andrew Southam
Back cover images courtesy (*from left*): Ian Greene; Paul Kelly; Stuart Coupe
Picture section photographs are as credited. Collage of promotional images in picture section one courtesy Stuart Coupe Collection. Collage of photographs in picture section two courtesy Michael Barclay and Stuart Coupe Collection. From below left clockwise: Paul and Archie Roach; Paul; The Paul Kelly Band promotional shoot; Paul in the early days in Sydney; on tour in the late 1980s; record company celebrations; Paul Kelly and The Dots; Paul, Archie Roach and Steve Connolly; the band in Truth or Consequences, New Mexico.
Typeset in Adobe Garamond Pro by Kirby Jones
Printed and bound in Australia by McPherson's Printing Group

For Susan Lynch – honest, strong and kind.
The important things.

And in memory of Anthony O'Grady, Chris Wilson,
Chris Winter and Martin Armiger.

CONTENTS

INTRODUCTION

'That's what I would call myself – a songwriter.
That's enough. Not everyone can do it.'
Paul Kelly

PAUL KELLY'S MUSIC HAS BEEN A SOUNDTRACK TO MY LIFE for over four decades. If you've picked this book up it may well be the case for you. Maybe you came in with Paul's earliest bands, The Debutantes, The High Rise Bombers or The Dots. Heaven forbid, you may have been in the audience at Paul's first public performance at Salamanca Place in Hobart. Possibly you also wanted to be like Billy Baxter.

Or maybe it was 'Before Too Long' that first caught your attention and had you singing along. Or 'Darling It Hurts', 'Leaps and Bounds', 'To Her Door' and all those other great songs he wrote and recorded with The Coloured Girls/ Messengers.

Or was it more recent Paul Kelly? Maybe 'How to Make Gravy' or 'With the One I Love'? Or 'From Little Things Big Things Grow'. It could have been buying the *Songs from the South* compilations or *Wanted Man*. Or perhaps you bought *Nature* or *Life Is Fine* or another of Paul's most recent albums and have now decided you want to go back through that extensive back catalogue.

It's even possible you don't own any of Paul's music but have become a fan from attending his live shows. Has it become a fixture of your December to attend his How to Make Gravy shows?

In 2020 Paul Kelly is omnipresent. There's a constant stream of recordings, live performances, collaborations, books and appearances. Paul is everywhere. Part of our national consciousness. An elder. A voice of our personal and public world. An articulator of our times.

As world-renowned critic David Fricke comments, Paul is Australia's Bob Dylan, Bruce Springsteen, Neil Young and Slim Dusty. He is the most dominant and recognisable Australian song and dance man of his generation and he has already created a body of work that will be listened to and celebrated well beyond his time with us. He's worked incredibly hard to make his mark.

There are other famous Paul Kellys. For a start there's the political journalist. And one of my favourite AFL footballers, the Sydney Swans' fearless Captain Courageous, and in 2020 Deputy Chief Medical Officer Paul Kelly has become increasingly well known. But at the end of the day no one confuses them with the Australian icon that is *the* Paul Kelly.

I've known Paul since 1976 when he was with The High Rise Bombers. He was the very first person I ever interviewed. He didn't say much. He still doesn't. But he says more these days, probably because he is more confident and assured in his position.

After that initial encounter, we developed a friendship. Maybe not a close one but the comfortable one that artists and writers tend to cultivate. We both loved much of the same music and had a burning desire to hear more. To hear *everything*.

In 1984 Paul took that now legendary trip from St Kilda to Kings Cross and soon after called and asked if I'd like to meet up with him. We went to the closest pub from my office, and when we walked out a few hours later, I was Paul's manager. It was a relationship that lasted until the end of the decade and is covered in a significant portion of this book.

It was a thrilling ride for both of us — and everyone else involved. When I stepped in, Paul didn't have a record deal. His first solo album, *Post*, which was critically acclaimed but didn't sell a lot of records, came soon after. The roller-coaster really took off when *Gossip* was released in 1986 and 'Before Too Long' was all over Australian radio. Suddenly there was an American record deal and Paul and I were zooming around the globe — sometimes together, other times with The Coloured Girls/Messengers.

In between tours and recording, Paul and I talked about music and sport. Every few months he'd give me a box of C90 cassettes and ask me to record anything I was listening to and tell me to give the box back when it was full of music. Then he'd give me another box of cassettes and the process would start again. He used to say, 'Don't think about what *I* might like — just record absolutely anything you're listening to and I'll work out what I like.'

Decades later when I heard Melbourne singer–songwriter John Flanagan's song 'The Last of the Cassette Men', which is about driving Paul to a gig and discussing the world of music and cassette tapes, all those memories came back.

On my bookshelf is a first edition copy of the writings of the famous music journalist Lester Bangs. Inside my copy — a present from Paul — is inscribed, 'To Stuart — from one journalist to another — Paul'.

Paul is indeed a journalist. Of course on occasions he has written traditional journalism for newspapers and magazines – pieces on his love for Indigenous Australian music, his late band mate Steve Connolly, and a lovely piece on the great Melbourne AFL footballer Robbie Flower. But he is a broader journalist too – a chronicler of songs of our lives, our relationships, our subtleties. They are his life and they are also ours. That's why we connect so intimately with his songs and his voice. He watches, he listens, he observes and turns it all into song.

As much as Paul loves words and melodies, he also loves sport. For a number of years in the 1980s we used to play an annual cricket match. One team was made up of Paul, his band members, road crew and me as manager. We played a team of media folk. I could have played for either team but my allegiances were clear.

These cricket matches were – in theory – casual affairs. I say in theory because Paul took them terribly seriously. He wanted to win and everything about field placement, who did and didn't bowl and the batting order was done with that in mind. It's this intense focus and determination that pervades every aspect of Paul's world. Sure he laughs, can be highly amusing – if quiet – company but make no mistake: there is a singular focus and grit to everything he does. His creative life really is a matter of life and death.

Together Paul and I did good business. We had a terrific relationship with Mushroom Records and Mushroom Music Publishing. Once they realised that Paul was capable of selling lots of records, they were an unstoppable force. Paul was generating a lot of money.

At one stage the subject of Paul and money came up with the then head of Mushroom Publishing, Ian James. He said he wasn't sure how much money Paul generated but quipped, 'If Paul walked in here now and asked for a million dollars advance I'd write him a cheque.'

When Paul and I stopped working together there was no explosive breakup. We both moved on. But we had little contact afterwards. Nothing personal. We lived in different cities by then and both lived frenetic lifestyles. I stumbled into one of his gigs at Sydney's State Theatre in 1996 or thereabouts and hung in the background at a gold record presentation gathering held upstairs afterwards.

I'd first thought of a book about Paul after I finished my biography of Michael Gudinski of Mushroom Records, as Paul was a significant part of that story.

Paul had of course already written his own 'mongrel memoir', *How to Make Gravy*, which was published in 2010. It was a big, sprawling book that clocked in at almost six hundred pages. It told you a lot about Paul – and omitted equal amounts, much of which is in these pages.

So from 2015 I regularly sent emails to Paul's manager, Bill Cullen, saying I was keen to write a book about Paul, as there was so much that wasn't in his book, and that I thought I was well qualified to write it. Each time Bill said he'd talk to Paul about it. And nothing happened. Then six months later I'd send another email. And so on.

Some time passed and I phoned Bill to see if there was any progress. He said that yes there was, that he'd spoken to Paul about the idea.

'And what happened?' I asked.

'He rolled his eyes,' Bill said.

I actually considered this a good sign and suggested to Bill that an eye roll was not in fact a 'no'.

He laughed.

A few days later Bill contacted me again and said that maybe I should write a one-page outline of what I proposed and he'd send that to Paul. He explained that part of Paul's reticence was the idea of a former manager writing a book about him. I pointed out that I'd been a journalist for many years before becoming Paul's manager and that I had no axe to grind with him.

A few days later Paul sent a note to Bill saying, 'This actually sounds pretty interesting, let's talk.'

Paul and Bill talked and then Bill called saying, 'I don't believe we're having this conversation – but Paul said to go ahead, with his blessing, and that he'll sit for interviews later in the process.'

This was much more than I expected. I'd decided that if Paul was vehemently opposed to a book I wouldn't write it. I'd hoped that he'd let me do it without telling people he'd prefer if they didn't talk to me. To have his actual involvement was an unexpected bonus.

So away I went. My intention was not to duplicate what Paul had written in his own book. What's the point in that? My plan with this book has been to give voice to all the creative individuals who have been part of Paul's musical world, been there for the demos, recordings and live performances. The people who know what it's like to be around Paul.

To that end, I set about tracking down all the musicians who had been in bands with Paul since the very early days. Some sadly are no longer with us but within these pages you'll find all the other key musicians. You'll also hear the voices of collaborators, such as Archie Roach, Kev Carmody, James Ledger, Kasey Chambers, Renée Geyer and others. I've also spoken to family, friends, business associates and partners.

There were a handful of people who didn't wish to be interviewed for this book, chiefly Paul's first wife, Hilary Brown, later partner Sian Prior, and three children, Declan,

Memphis and Madeleine. Bill Cullen makes a policy of not commenting on his clients. I, of course, respect their decisions.

More than two decades since I'd last spoken to Paul, we met for a short twenty-minute radio interview when he was promoting the latest version of the *Songs from the South* compilation, and a book of his favourite poetry.

I had the lines from 'To Her Door' running through my head as I waited for him. Would this reconnection be awkward? Uncomfortable? How would we appear to each other? Would it be an easy conversation or one punctuated by silences and unease?

Needless to say it went well. It felt like old times for me and I wouldn't have been surprised if Paul had asked me what time sound check was that day. Since then we've done a number of interview sessions – backstage at the Domain in Sydney before the 2019 How to Make Gravy concert, and then a little later in January 2020 we had a long lunch together in Tamworth after Paul and his band had played with Cold Chisel the night before. We then drove to where he was staying and spent a few hours with Kev Carmody, his wife, Beryl, and Paul's partner, Siân Darling.

Over lunch that day I was reminded that I was in the presence of *that* Paul Kelly as waiters and hotel staff fawned over him after we'd been directed to a quiet table at the back of the dining area. A seemingly endless stream of staff found reason to stroll by and enquire if everything was to Paul's satisfaction.

In Sydney before two performances of *Thirteen Ways to Look at Birds* we talked again in a far-ranging conversation that took in the impact of Catholicism on his songwriting and his memories of childhood right through to him being one of the founders of The Kick, a group of Australian Rules football lovers who train twice a week and are, as at least one person has suggested, Paul's closest group of friends.

We'd planned another session in Melbourne and then coronavirus entered our lives, so instead we Skyped for two hours and continued to exchange emails and texts.

Over the years I've seen dozens – possibly hundreds – of Paul's shows. During the course of working on this book I've seen him on the steps of the Sydney Opera House, in the Domain, at a midnight band show in Brisbane during the BIGSOUND Music Conference. In Tamworth I saw him playing before Cold Chisel, singing Hank Williams songs with Lucky Oceans, and onstage with Kasey Chambers at a celebration concert for Joy McKean's ninetieth birthday.

I've immersed myself in all things Paul Kelly. Listened to every record, bootleg concert performances and cassettes, devoured an eight CD collection of rarities compiled by members of an online group known as Other People's Houses. I've re-listened to albums I'd initially not spent too much time with and realised depths and qualities that had not previously been apparent.

Ultimately I've tried to present a book about Paul through both my experiences and those who have come into his orbit. I've encouraged everyone to speak openly and honestly. This is not an officially authorised book where the subject is allowed to veto the content. It's the book I'd expect Paul to want – people talking honestly and candidly about the times when their world intersected with his.

It is indeed stories of him. And with many stories *from* him.

Stuart Coupe
Petersham, February 2020

CHAPTER 1

MITTAGONG 1985

'I just wanted you to know that we're leaving now ...'
Audience member, Mittagong RSL

THE DRIVE FROM SYDNEY DOWN THE HUME TO MITTAGONG isn't a particularly long one. Maybe an hour and a half if the traffic's good. But it can seem like an eternity if you're a comparatively unknown band heading down to ply your trade in one of the pubs, bars, halls and clubs where live music is played. Back in the eighties, the venues didn't really care who was playing. And often the audiences didn't either.

Squashed into a hired van with their stage gear are Michael Barclay, Michael Armiger, Peter 'Pedro' Bull, Steve Connolly and Paul Kelly. They are known as Paul Kelly and The Coloured Girls.

It's December 1985. A Wednesday night. The first night of a run of shows. Another drive up and down the Hume Highway playing to audiences that for the most part have little idea who the band is. It's getting towards the end of another year. Rock'n'roll stardom still seems like a distant dream.

But there is some small optimism that things might be about to change. The musicians are starting to talk about a new album they'll record the following year. Paul is saying he's thinking about it being a double album as he has a lot of songs he'd like to record.

But that seems like a long way away as the kilometres fly by. At this time they're just one of dozens and dozens of Australian bands waiting for that seemingly elusive break.

Paul has already made two albums in Melbourne – *Talk* and *Manila* – with a different band, The Dots. The albums didn't make much impression on the charts and the larger public despite a song on the first album, 'Billy Baxter', garnering some radio exposure. And although loved by music critics, the recent semi-acoustic album he made, *Post*, hasn't had a lot of attention from the general public.

So Paul and The Coloured Girls are playing gigs where they can find them. Tonight's mid-week show is at Mittagong RSL. After the show the band will sleep, two to a room, in a cheap nearby roadside motel before waking early to continue on down the Hume to Melbourne, where Paul still has some currency.

The Mittagong RSL is a big, brightly lit building full of poker machines, restaurants and a cavernous room where the bands perform. If it's packed – as it usually is on Friday and Saturday nights when big bands come to play – it's a pumping, heaving, beer-soaked, seething mass of people. When it's not, the bands performing have plenty of time to take in exactly how large it is.

The band arrive at 4 pm, just in time to grab a hamburger and chips before they wander into the club to set up their gear and do a sound check.

Things aren't going well already. The guy supplying the PA for the night has had some issues that he doesn't bother to explain but the gist of the message he's left for them at the club is that he can't make it tonight.

The supposed good news is that he's located someone who can drive down from Sydney with a PA but that person's going to be late.

Eventually the truck and PA arrive. It's a long way short of the equipment even The Coloured Girls are used to playing with. Clearly it was the last PA left in the storeroom. And the guy who's driven it down has only the barest idea of how to assemble it – and even less of an idea about operating it properly. Sound check is late, rushed and frustratingly chaotic as the sound guy takes what seems like forever to put the PA together.

The band's mood is best described as downcast with a touch of grumpy. They eat in the RSL bistro before heading back to the room where they're playing. The PA is still not properly assembled.

That it's a dud night is evident the moment they walk into the auditorium.

The number of people in the room doesn't top fifty – and that includes the band, the bar staff, the DJ, the PA operator, and the girl on the door who has taken eight dollars from each of the paying audience, which includes a group of five women, and assorted stragglers. There is no queue forming at the door. In fact no one is approaching the door at all. The venue could hold eight hundred people and still not be at full capacity.

Paul and the band drink a few beers from their backstage rider – a case of Victoria Bitter cans reluctantly supplied by the RSL club manager.

They take to the stage and start playing. The PA splutters, yelps and buzzes intermittently as they perform. The audience – such as it is – hang at the back of the room.

None of them know the songs. There is constant feedback from the PA.

The Coloured Girls continue playing and then, midway through 'Incident on South Dowling', a woman breaks away from the group she's been standing with for the first twenty minutes of the show. She walks slowly and deliberately towards the stage, eventually standing in front of guitarist Steve Connolly.

The band breathe a minor sigh of relief. At least one person seems to like what they're doing.

She beckons Connolly to come closer and he walks over and bends down so he can hear what the woman has to say. The rest of the band watch on bemusedly as Connolly stands back up and continues the song.

The woman walks slowly back to her friends and, without looking again at the stage, they walk out the door, reducing the audience by five.

The Coloured Girls finish the first of their two sets and, as they walk to the dressing room, everyone looks at Connolly wanting to know what the woman said. The guitarist is not in a good mood. None of them are. So what did she say?

'I just wanted you to know that we're leaving now and I wanted you to also know that you are the worst band I've ever heard or seen.'

CHAPTER 2

GROWIN' UP

'Kensington Road runs straight for a while before turning/
We lived on the bend, it was there I was raised and fed.'

Paul Kelly

On 13 January 1955, Paul Maurice Kelly was born, the sixth of nine children, in Adelaide, Australia. His older sister Sheila remembers the time well, 'He was just absolutely gorgeous. He had the Italian look. Even as a baby he had the black curly hair and the big chocolatey eyes. Mum would put him out in the bassinet in the backyard to have a snooze. She knew she could leave him there for hours because I would pull up a chair and sit and gaze at him, adoringly. I couldn't take my eyes off him.'

The Kellys were a large, loving and educated Irish Catholic family. 'We had a very Catholic upbringing,' Paul says. 'Mum and Dad were devout but not narrow-minded. Their Catholicism was based on Jesus and the New Testament and on the idea of "do unto others as you would have done unto you". There wasn't a big emphasis on hell and the devil and eternal damnation. It was about doing the right thing and the idea that if you've been lucky enough to have certain advantages in life, that you need to give back.

'My mother would pray to Mary and the saints. If you lost something or couldn't find something you'd pray to Saint Anthony, the patron saint of finding things. Every time we would go on a long trip in the school holidays we would say a little prayer to Saint Christopher, the patron saint of travellers. He's the guy who carried Jesus across the river. And there was Saint Jude for good luck in exams.

'Culturally I am a Catholic. I'm well versed in the bible. The Christian idea – that you should treat every person with respect, and you don't judge people – is still part of what I aspire to.'

Paul's father, John, was a lawyer who joined his own father's law practice in 1937. Paul's mother, Josephine, was the daughter of an Italian opera singer, Count Ercole Filippini. Ercole had been a leading baritone for the La Scala Opera Company in Milan and met his wife, Anne McPharland, in Australia in 1916, not long after he arrived in the country. Anne became Australia's first female symphony orchestra conductor and Ercole and Anne formed the Italo–Australian Grand Opera Company, which toured the country in the 1920s.

It's not surprising then that their daughter Josephine, and her children, studied music and the family home was always abuzz with activity and noise. Music was a constant backdrop for the Kelly children. All of them started with piano lessons. Sheila, Anne and Mary Jo were all multi-instrumentalists at various times, ranging across guitar, clarinet, piano, violin, mandolin, harp, flute and organ between them. Paul and Tony both went on to learn the trumpet. Anne taught music for several years. She also wrote a number of widely sung hymns which, as Paul points out, makes her the first songwriter in the family. Mary Jo is the only other sibling to make a career out of music, both as a singer and keyboardist specialising in Latin music for many years as well as teaching full time, running music programs, composition classes and ensembles in schools. Several of the others play guitar and sing in choirs and all are happy to sing a song from time to time at family gatherings.

All of Josephine and John Kelly's children are intelligent, high-achieving individuals with a robust social consciousness. (Their third child, Josephine, died at nine months, but all the Kelly kids consider her when counting how many children are in the family.) This is a family strong on humanitarian ideas, work ethic and practical engagement with the world. It is a family with a 'practise what you preach' mentality. It is also a family with a bloodline running thick with creativity, idealism, and romantic reverence for the poetic, musical world of the artist.

'Mum and Dad accepted us no matter what we did,' Sheila says. 'They were firm and we had to obey the rules and we got punished if we didn't, but they were very fair and very loving and accepted whatever choices we made. There was no pushing. They let us make our own choices and do our own thing.'

Mary Jo Kelly, the sibling closest to Paul in age, echoes these sentiments about her parents and says that they were a very close-knit family.

'Mum never told us what to do. Never. She'd back us up but she also told us you also had to clean up your own mess. If you got into trouble you had to deal with it. We were always encouraged as people.'

In 1968, when Paul was thirteen, his father, John, died from Parkinson's disease, aged only fifty-two.

'I remember being packed off to school the day Dad died,' Paul says. 'You just got on with it. No point hanging around the house. Of course the school was informed. In the first class the teacher made an announcement, "Paul's father died today." I don't remember a thing about that day except the house filling up with people and Dad's body in a coffin in the study. The death of a father plays out more over time.

'There were eight of us so we had each other. I think that made a difference. It wasn't like I was alone with this enormous event. And also I think you're very resilient when you're young.

'Sheila tells the story of her friend Denny picking me up from school the day that he died. I was a very quiet child and famous for not talking much, but apparently she said that I didn't stop talking all the way home. I have no memory of that.

'I also know that a couple of us went to some relatives on Kangaroo Island pretty soon afterwards. I have no memory of that either.

'You never lose your grief for a parent or sibling, or a child or close friend. It is always there but it stays down, coming up from time to time.

'When my first child – Declan – was born I had a strong wave of grief that my father didn't get to see his grandchild. I realised that Dad never saw any of his children have children and I felt a real loss on his behalf over that.

'And then when Declan had children, the same thing happened again. I thought, *I'm a grandfather now, and my Dad never had this.*'

Paul's mother, Josephine, focused on raising her eight children and, after John's death, probably for her own satisfaction as much as to keep the family purse full, she began work as a school librarian.

'When Dad died,' Paul says, 'some of the oldest children had moved out of home but we still had a full house. [My brother] Tony was only seven. Mum didn't have any help. She had all these children breaking out which she had to handle on her own.'

By all accounts an intelligent and generous woman, Josephine's devout Catholicism with a twist of paganism shaped her world view and that of her children. She was an active volunteer who would give up her time to help anyone in need. A free-thinking person with humanitarian principles, she encouraged her children to make their own paths, take responsibility for their lives, show compassion and care, and test moribund social conventions.

Mary Jo remembers this time and that her older brother Martin 'took on a father figure role for me. He was forging ahead in the counter-culture movement – the Moratorium, hunger strikes and of course I went along in his wake. And so did Paul to a certain extent.'

'It was a pretty radical family,' Paul says. 'When I was about fifteen or sixteen I stopped believing the stuff about God and Heaven and angels and I stopped going to Church. Martin and John were involved in hunger strikes protesting against the Vietnam War, and I was campaigning with a friend to abolish prefects and school captains at Rostrevor College. My sister Sheila was having an affair with someone much older than her, a doctor. We're all wearing our hair long and listening to Pink Floyd and the Moody Blues. There's strange smells … you know, funny cigarette smells, coming from the older boys' room. We were all kinds of hippies and radicals.'

Mary Jo recalls, 'Mum was very interested in everything we were going through. She listened to all the political discussions we would have and in particular about the Vietnam War and the counter-culture. She was open to things like transcendental meditation and for a while she was even going to smoke pot with us but she pulled out at the last minute.

'She was very open-minded and it's only with hindsight you realise how hard it would have been for her – she was a widow from the age of forty-five.'

Not everyone in Adelaide viewed the family freedom favourably. 'There was a little bit of ire and tut-tutting in conservative circles about us,' Paul says. 'The Kelly children are running a bit wild.'

'Mum got a lot of flak from the conservative side of Adelaide who didn't mind letting her know what they thought of her letting her children run amok and live in hippie communes,' Mary Jo recalls. 'There was a lot of stuff floating around about what the Kelly gang were doing and the line that we were a bad influence on other people's children.'

Paul was still at school at the time and was both sport and academically inclined. He played in the first XI cricket team, in the school's first 18 Australian Rules football team, and was also dux of his year. A quiet child, Paul was nonetheless highly competitive in all his undertakings.

'He was the shyest member of the family,' Sheila remembers. 'Whereas the rest of us were a bit show-offy and would perform, sing or dance or play the piano for anyone who would come around – Paul would always sit quietly in the background and just watch. He wouldn't do anything publicly. He was always watching, watching, watching. I still remember it. He was probably just taking it all in.'

* * *

Paul finished school at the end of 1971 and went travelling straight away with friends. They hitchhiked up to Darwin and worked at the Stokes Hill power station, then went to Queensland where they worked as fettlers, 'basically on a railway gang,' says Paul. 'This was my gap year before they even called it a gap year.'

In 1973 Paul started at Flinders University and enrolled in drama, philosophy and history. 'I remember our first philosophy classes seemed to be taken up with questioning all forms of authority and teaching ... I was a bit old-fashioned and I just wanted to learn philosophy and not have these debates ... I left university after a term and a half. But the friendships I formed there were crucial.'

He continued travelling, working odd jobs, and writing Arthur Rimbaud– and Charles Baudelaire–inspired poetry and prose. Initially Paul wanted to be a writer. But influenced by the friends he met at Flinders University, he began learning to play the acoustic guitar and sing. He felt like he had come to the party very late but that only made him more determined.

'I had met this gang of guys who played guitar. They were singing Gram Parsons, Commander Cody, The Allman Brothers and lots of Neil Young. So I started hanging out with a country rock gang and through them I began learning guitar. I wasn't doing my own songs yet. I was learning folk songs, Neil Young and Gram Parsons songs. The two Gram Parsons records – *Grievous Angel* and *GP* – really stuck with me.'

Among that group of musicians was drummer Tom Stehlik, whom Paul had met in February when the two were on a bus going to a university freshers' camp at Macclesfield outside of Adelaide.

Soon after, Paul, Stehlik and others would travel to the Aquarius music festival in Nimbin. 'At the time Paul was just a fun-loving hippie guy who used to hang around in football shorts and thongs,' Stehlik says. 'I was already in a band with my brother Ian. We'd all sit around and play Neil Young songs and Paul would be with us playing a pair of bongos. He hadn't picked up a guitar yet.

'After Nimbin we started a band where a group of us would drink wine and play songs on acoustic guitars. One of those events happened underneath the statue of Colonel Light, that's the reference in the song "Adelaide".

'Paul christened the band Good Enough For The Bush. Because of this he'd picked up the guitar and we showed him a few chords.'

Mary Jo has memories of Paul learning to play guitar around the house. 'He was learning something new – he'd always been pretty good at writing poems, but he was less confident about singing and playing an instrument because he didn't do that much formal training.'

'One day Paul asked me if I'd teach him a few guitar chords,' Sheila says. 'I remember sitting on his bunk bed in the boys' room and I taught him the first four chords of the Peter, Paul and Mary song "I'm in Love with A Big Blue Frog". He still says they're the four chords he uses all the time. He uses a few others too.

'When he first started playing,' Sheila says, 'I'd be laughing – "It's good Paul, you can sing, you've got a good voice – but you look like a constipated duck." He didn't know how to present himself and just waddled across the stage.'

'At that time there were a few folk clubs in Adelaide,' Paul says. 'I remember one called the Catacombs. A guy called Dave Clark used to sing there. I watched Dave Clark a lot. He was a towering figure at the time. He played "Streets of Forbes", the song about the bushranger Ben Hall. I learnt his version of it. That was one of the first songs I ever started playing.'

In 1974, almost a year after first picking up the guitar, Paul made his first public appearance at a tiny folk club at Salamanca Place in Hobart. Mary Jo says he went to Tasmania for anonymity so he could get up at folk clubs with no family or friends around. He performed two songs – 'Streets of Forbes' and a cover of a Bob Dylan song, 'Girl from the North Country'.

'After I sang I got very drunk,' Paul says. 'I had just met John Kingsmill who was from Adelaide but living in Hobart then. He took me home and put me to bed.

'When I left Hobart I travelled up the west coast of Tasmania to Savage River to work on the iron ore mines. I did that for a month or two and then ended up back in Adelaide towards the end of 1974.'

CHAPTER 3

LEARNING
THE SKILLS

'I can still see him there, with his brooding dark and
handsome, young Dylan looks, strumming his guitar
and belting it out.'

Larry Buttrose

PAUL SPENT MOST OF 1975 BACK IN ADELAIDE. HE AND
John Kingsmill both 'got cleaning jobs working outside at
the Festival Centre. It was a great job. Four hours a day –
8 am till midday.' They started a magazine called *Another
One For Mary*.

'John and I were the main writers,' Paul says. 'We had fake
names because we couldn't be seen to be writing everything.
I used the names Achelli Paolo and Kiley Pale. We tried to
get other people to write for it but we had a magazine to get
out and often it was just the two of us.'

Paul was reading a lot at the time. 'I was reading
Hermann Hesse, Jack Kerouac, Baudelaire and Arthur

Rimbaud. I was very influenced by a book of prose called *Paris Spleen* by Baudelaire. I probably got on to them via the Dylan biography by [Anthony] Scaduto but also via my friend Christopher Barnett because he knew all about Rimbaud and Baudelaire. For him, Rimbaud was the man. I gravitated to *Paris Spleen*, which was short pieces, poetic prose, and that was the kind of thing I was trying to write for *Another One For Mary.*'

Adelaide poet Christopher Barnett was one of Paul's closest friends in Adelaide in the early seventies, describing their relationship as 'brotherly'.

In *These Heathen Dreams*, Anne Tsoulis's documentary about Barnett, Paul says that Barnett was 'Neal Cassady and I was poor old stumbling Jack Kerouac trying to keep up.'

Cassady was the legendary beat generation character who did most of the driving in Kerouac's *On the Road* expeditions, usually with a head full of speed, possibly mixed with some LSD.

'It was very Neal Cassady and Jack Kerouac–like,' Barnett agrees. 'Not consciously but we were both writing. Paul had just started singing songs like "Streets of Forbes".'

The two had been drawn together by a mutual friendship with Julie Thompson who Barnett remembers as 'very beautiful, extremely bright, and phenomenally intelligent'. Thompson is the 'Julie' in Paul's song 'Standing on the Street of Early Sorrows'.

Every Friday night, for what Barnett thinks was 'a year or two', he and Paul were also part of a weekly event at Carclew House in North Adelaide, where Adelaide musicians, poets and writers would gather to perform their work.

Larry Buttrose, a bright light in the Adelaide poetry world, was one of the organisers of the weekly gatherings at

Carclew House. 'It was the usual thing, thirty or so university students and the like huddled together as we read angry, hopefully funny or erotic poems. We had a musical act as well – the same each week. It was the very young Paul Kelly, and each week he'd sing Lennon's "Working Class Hero" with much brio. He may have sung other songs but I can still see him there, with his brooding dark and handsome, young Dylan looks, strumming his guitar and belting it out.'

Barnett and Paul would also frequently go on the road – hitchhiking at various times to Sydney. On one of those visits Barnett introduced Paul to singer Jeannie Lewis – he thought it would do Paul good to spend time with her.

'She had this real sense of the world and was so extremely talented,' Barnett says. 'There was no one else like her at the time in terms of voice range and jumping genres.'

'I remember swimming in the ocean with Jeannie at Maroubra where she lived,' Paul says. 'The first time I heard reggae music was at a party at her place. "Israelites" by Desmond Dekker blew my head open. And "Stir it Up" by Bob Marley. The music sounded like nothing I'd heard before. It was electrifying!'

While Paul remembers hearing reggae at Lewis's, she recalls playing him music from Latin America. 'I still have a cassette of him singing at my place and handwritten lyrics to the songs. Some years later I'd often see The Dots when they came to Sydney; Paul was the spunky curly-haired bloke up the front of the band.'

Towards the end of 1975, Paul headed to Perth. 'I had my twenty-first birthday over there. There was a folk club called The Stables. I have strong memories of being heavily struck by bands in Perth, and I made friendships I've still got today. I remember being mesmerised by Billy Rogers, the singer with the band Last Chance Café. I used to go and see them a lot and thought they were great. They were a rockin' R & B and rockabilly band doing mainly Eddie Cochran covers and things like that. Billy Rogers would slide across the stage on his knees.

'Perth had a great little scene. There was something about Perth at this time. The bands would find a genre of music and go deep into it. There was the Zar Brothers and The Beagle Boys who played real Chicago blues.

'Jim Fisher's Outlaws, a bluegrass band, played at Mundaring Weir, just outside of Perth. I'd heard bluegrass and old-time music in the folk clubs in Adelaide, but hearing Jim Fisher and the Outlaws was really significant. This was proper bluegrass. They were very serious about the banjo and the fiddle with no drums. And Jim had a beautiful high voice. I used to see them a lot and I loved them – so it was a thrill to get Jim Fisher in the band playing mandolin for the Foggy Highway tour decades later.

'I left Perth with Last Chance Café, who were heading to Kalgoorlie to do a residency. I got a lift with them and hung around Kalgoorlie for a while before I hitchhiked back to Adelaide.'

* * *

Adelaide in the mid-1970s was an emerging creative hub that nurtured a flamboyant and experimental world. A small scene most certainly, but one that briefly burnt bright. Don Dunstan was the premier and the arts were valued. Arguably at that time, Adelaide had the biggest gay scene in Australia. It had the South Australian Film Corporation, the State Theatre Company South Australia, and Flinders University, which was radical and left-leaning. Pubs like the Buckingham Arms attracted students, artists, the transgender community and all sorts of colourful characters. Everyone mingled – everyone was accepted. Writer Nick Lainas, the godfather to Paul's daughter Madeleine, first met Paul around this time in Adelaide in 1976, encountering what he describes as, 'a callow youth without much worldly experience at all.

'The first time I saw him, he was in a backyard with an acoustic guitar on his lap, and with this shock of incredible curly black hair.'

Initially Lainas and Paul didn't have a lot to do with each other so when Lainas was preparing for a trip back to Greece, he was surprised when Paul arrived with a gift for him – a copy of Gail Holst's book on Greek music, *Road to Rembetika*.

Lainas spent the second half of 1976 in Greece, sending back travel writing and poetry for John Kingsmill and Paul to publish in *Another One For Mary*.

When Lainas returned, Paul was living in Buxton Street, North Adelaide, and the friendship developed.

'It was a notorious building at the time, a building full of junkies,' Lainas says.

'Paul was breaking free from all those conservative years of his Catholic upbringing. He was reading Henry Miller and writers like that. He wanted to disorganise his senses and extend his range of experiences, especially sexual ones.

'He had a level of determination even in those days. Paul was going to crash through. He wouldn't have lasted if he didn't have that – that iron will and focused vision. Music and songwriting became his total vision. Everything was about his ambition.'

For Paul the Buxton Street house was where he had the game changer – the realisation that he could write songs. He wrote one. Then another. And another.

'There was a piano there and I wrote a song called "We Don't Get On". It has never been recorded. At that moment I remember the feeling and the realisation of, *Oh, I can do this – if I can write one song I can write another.* I stopped writing the prose poetry and other stuff and it just became songs. Around this period I also wrote "The Going Down", this time on guitar.

'Once I began writing songs when I was twenty-one that became all I wanted to do. I didn't want to do anything else. I always had part-time jobs – cleaning jobs, and dish-washing jobs – and the dole. But all I really wanted to do was make money off writing songs. I didn't have an alternative. There was no thinking about something that I could fall back on – something like teaching or cleaning.'

It was 1976 and it occurred to Paul that it was time to start a band – and one of the people he was going to start a band with was Adelaide musician and writer Philip White.

'Paul came to my joint,' White recalls. 'It was in the middle of summer and he said, "Hey Phil, I want to start a band." We sort of talked about it. I didn't know him very well at that point. I'd been introduced to him by John Kingsmill.

'When we met I had been in a few bands that had had a modicum of success. I was a hillbilly preacher's kid, a full-on bible-bashing jerk. It was all bibles and shotguns for me. I must have seemed very exotic to Paul. I was pretty upfront. And Paul was a folk singer who hadn't really done very much. Both he and John thought they were Jack Kerouac. But I knew they weren't.'

Up until then, Paul had been drifting around Adelaide playing solo as a Bob Dylan–inspired folkie at Ginger's coffee shop on Melbourne Street and other similar places around the city but this was his first foray into a rock'n'roll band.

Paul's sister Mary Jo was working as a jillaroo on a cattle station thousands of kilometres away up in the Kimberleys when she received a letter from Paul saying, 'Come back to Adelaide, I'm starting a band.'

That band was The Debutantes. They rehearsed in a big old stable in a backyard at the top of O'Connell Street. They did more rehearsing than actual playing and there was a constant if not chaotic stream of musicians – some unknown to White and Paul until they turned up to the rehearsal.

The idea was that the band would play both Paul's and White's songs. But at every rehearsal Paul would show up with four or five new songs and it ended up being more Paul's songs than White's. White says he helped Paul work out the new songs, which were often 'three chords and a scribbled bit of paper with some words on it'.

Paul's sister Mary Jo played violin and flute and sang. She also played some keyboards. She remembers Tom and Ian Stehlik were part of it and James Black, who also played piano. Black, an accomplished musician, went on to play with Mondo Rock, Joe Camilleri and many others as well as being part of the RocKwiz television show band.

As Stehlik recalls it, Paul wanted to call the band The Debutantes but others in the band were against that. 'We were all seasoned musicians, not debutantes, so we wanted to call it The Paul Kelly Band, it was known as that as well. There were certainly elements of the Rolling Thunder Revue in it.

'We had a few extras come in. We might have added John Hyland from the Lone Rangers on pedal steel at one point, and Jo Moore was around and might have sung with us. She definitely sang with Paul on a music show on ABC television in Adelaide. I remember Paul looking so nervous and uncomfortable. She sang on his first album, *Talk*, but was sadly later killed in a car accident.

'Paul had a lot of songs. After he came back from Tasmania he'd fallen in love with Rosie Jones and all these songs started pouring out of him. "Cherry" – which is on his first album – and there was the song "Derailment" that at our very last gig Paul announced as being a song about premature ejaculation. It was very influenced by the Dylan song "Hurricane".

'The way I remember it was that we played pretty much all Paul's songs and about half of them appeared on his *Talk* album. We recorded a few songs at the Kelly family home – the Brigalow Bungalow – as we used to rehearse there. James Black offered to record the band with a Revox reel-to-reel tape recorder he had. We recorded about four songs, but James had also brought along a bag of hash cookies so things degenerated fairly quickly.'

'James Black recorded songs in the study at our home,' Mary Jo says, 'four or five songs, including "Derailment", which I loved because I got to do this funny violin solo trying to sound like a train. Paul discovered Jo Moore, who had the most incredible voice – and she started singing.'

Mary Jo says all the songs in The Debutantes were Paul's. 'That was when I realised, *Gee, he writes good songs.*'

The Debutantes played gigs at pubs like The British and The Wellington. Usually it was a shambolic mess that would occasionally become something bordering on the coherent.

'We tried to make the band work,' White says. 'Paul thought he was Bob Dylan in the Rolling Thunder Revue, and would be dressed up like him right down to wearing a scarf like Dylan did. I used to stand next to him with a white Gibson guitar wearing a white boilersuit like Pete Townshend. I soon realised he didn't want my Pete Townshend presence beside him but I thought it was better than leaving him to lead twelve musicians.'

The Debutantes played all original songs, something that was challenging and ambitious for a new band with so many members.

'There'd be a brass section coming and going,' White says. 'There was pedal steel. It was crazy. Nuts. Ian Stehlik came and went playing second lead. His brother Tom was the drummer. And then there were people like Madeline Blackwell and others coming and going as the singing girls. We'd be halfway through a song and Paul would look at a girl in the audience and say, "See that one, she's going to join the band," and the next week she'd be in the vocal section.

'It was a fricking nightmare and I had the job of trying to arrange the music – but I think we made a joyful noise. Our big anthem was a song called "Derailment". I helped Paul work it out. We'd stretch it out for ten or fifteen minutes and everyone would be dancing. It was a good knock-off song. There were, however, a lot of other songs we did that were just forgettable.'

But, let's face it, they were supposed to be 'Debutantes' after all. Although White and the others were much more experienced and able musicians, Paul was only twenty-one years old and, although he had learnt piano and trumpet as a child, he hadn't taken up the guitar until he was eighteen. There was much to learn.

Coupled with that, White feels that part of the erratic nature of The Debutantes was due to Paul's use of heroin, which White considered to be pretty serious when he lived in Adelaide.

Whether Paul's dabbling with heroin was serious or just outwardly so, White says that pretty early on he became alive to Paul's gritty determination and single focus.

'He was very easy to misunderstand because of his surly, quiet, almost receding nature but that belied a very heavy little ego and a determination which a lot of people didn't pick.'

In early 1977, Nick Lainas borrowed his father's Toyota Crown and he and Paul headed off to Sydney – with differing missions.

For Lainas, the main reason for the journey was to interview playwright Steve Spears for a feature story for *Another One For Mary.*

For Paul it was a case of – apparently without telling the rest of The Debutantes – exploring the possibility of getting a recording contract with a label. Paul and Lainas went into Festival Records in Pyrmont with a cassette of Paul's songs.

'We met with a guy in long white socks and checked shorts who was clearly listening under sufferance to this tape,' Lainas says. 'Not surprisingly there was no interest and he told us there was nothing he could do.'

Leaving Sydney the two took the coast road towards Melbourne. At one point Lainas decided to let Paul – then a notoriously bad driver – have a stint at the wheel on a comparatively quiet stretch of road.

'He almost totalled the car. He was a really careless driver who really thought he was Neal Cassady behind the wheel,' Lainas says.

Reaching Melbourne, Lainas took Paul to visit some friends of his from Adelaide, musicians from a band called Spare Change who were living in a house in Hoddle Street, East Melbourne. Paul had seen Spare Change when they were living and playing in Adelaide.

He liked what he saw in Melbourne. 'Nick and I went back to Adelaide,' he says, 'but pretty soon I decided to move to Melbourne permanently.'

The Debutantes – a part-time band at best – disintegrated, but the decision to end came out of the blue for White. He picked up the phone one day and Paul was on the line. 'He said, "You've got to come and see my new band," and I said, "What new band? What's happening to *our* band, what's going on?" And he said, "I'm not playing with those people anymore," and I said, "Well, there's fucking twelve of us – have you told them?" And he said, "Can you tell them?" And that was it. He wouldn't tell the others that it was over.'

After that the two had a tense relationship, and over the ensuing years it has ebbed and flowed.

Paul decided to travel back to Melbourne and move into the Hoddle Street house, first sleeping on a mattress before moving to an enclave under the staircase.

Some time later White paid them all a visit. He didn't like what he found. 'Fuck that was a dismal hovel of a house. I asked for a joint and they thought I was so uncool – this prick from Adelaide asking for marijuana when a bunch of them had needles hanging out of their arms.'

'I was pretty keen to leave Adelaide,' Paul says. 'But it was more like leaving the place I grew up in and wanting to see the world.'

CHAPTER 4

MELBOURNE CALLING

'The Bleeding Hearts were like young gods to me.
They didn't play music like I played.'
Paul Kelly

IT WAS 1977 AND PAUL NOW FOUND HIMSELF IN THE LARGE, rambling share house in Hoddle Street. Living in this house were the members of Spare Change – singer John Dowler, keyboardist Tony Murray, guitarists Bob Kretschmer and Chris Langman, and drummer Graeme Perry.

Like Paul, Spare Change had recently fled Adelaide. Not all the participants of the possibly mythologised Adelaide creative scene in the early to mid-1970s considered it exciting and invigorating.

Spare Change was a group of intelligent, articulate, socially and creatively aware individuals, well-read and interested in the underground film world. Greg Perano, who was part of their road crew, says, 'They would dress up,

33

glam-rock like, almost pre-war Berlin. They were very stylish and would wear a bit of eye makeup. All the guys had pretty eclectic tastes. They were like English dandies influenced by the Velvet Underground, Gram Parsons, and Big Star. They were big David Bowie and early Roxy Music fans.'

After less than a dozen gigs, Spare Change couldn't see a future in Adelaide, and they had management who reckoned they could really make things happen if they relocated to the then Australian rock'n'roll epicentre – Melbourne. The Spare Change members thought about that for a few seconds and started packing.

In Melbourne, Spare Change soon found themselves accepted into the ultra-cool Carlton music scene with John Dowler finding the scene's principal figures to be anything other than snooty and elitist. Self-aware? Sure. Self-important? Frequently. But still prepared to see what outsiders had to offer. To see if they could cut it.

'We found them very friendly,' Dowler says. 'Within a week or two of being there people were coming around to visit. They seemed incredibly impressed that we were well dressed. We wore suits and stylish clothing. The Carlton scene at the time was fairly down market except for maybe The Millionaires who used to wear makeup and costumes – but certainly groups like The Bleeding Hearts and others were determined to wear jeans and streetwear.'

So right from the start Spare Change stood out with their stage wear and deliberate leanings towards the world of the dandy.

'We were inspired by Roxy Music,' Dowler says. 'It was just about being different. We also wore makeup. It was meant to provoke people as well – which it did.'

The Hoddle Street house the members of Spare Change were living in was a large two-storey building with enough room for each member to have a bedroom and, according to Dowler, 'a lounge where we gathered every Sunday to watch *Countdown* on the TV. Just the usual rituals.'

The house also had a floating population of other musicians, roadies, small-time drug dealers, hangers-on and scenesters. Among the many people who turned up and knocked on the door of the Hoddle Street house was Paul, who had hitchhiked across from Adelaide.

'He just appeared at our door,' Dowler says. 'We didn't know him in Adelaide. We took him in and listened to a few of his songs and thought, *This guy is really good*.

'He ended up staying at our house and he slept on a mattress on my floor, mainly because I was the only one who wasn't in a relationship at the time so I could afford to have someone on the floor.'

Perano remembered seeing a young Paul Kelly at Spare Change's gigs in Adelaide. 'He was always in a black leather jacket, a real Dylanophile with a mop of black hair. He was a handsome and enigmatic character. When I first knew him he was playing acoustic folky gigs but it was obvious that he was looking for a band to play with and people to write with as well. He had the whole thing down – the Dylan look.'

For Paul, the trip to Hoddle Street Central was more than going to just another house in Melbourne. Sure, it was that era. Big share houses. People coming and going. Relationships starting and ending. Different people in the lounge every time you'd come home. Everyone was rushing about doing *something*. And that something was always very, very important. But this was a house where things really happened. At least that was the aura exuding from Hoddle Street.

In reality it wasn't all that different from hundreds of other share houses. One of those places where if you lived there and could play an instrument you were probably rehearsing in a band and trying to get gigs. If it was a house full of musicians word would get around. Other aspiring musicians would find their way there, often through the most tenuous connections or introductions.

'It was a good time,' Paul says, 'straight away I fell on my feet because I was in this house with all these guys in a band.'

The biggest of the new artists being hammered on the stereo in the Spare Change house was Television and their *Marquee Moon* album. Guitarist Chris Langman, in particular, was obsessed about what Tom Verlaine was writing and the guitar interaction between him and Richard Lloyd. He would soon share this passion with Paul who would later cover Verlaine's song 'Breakin' in My Heart' in his live shows with The Dots.

Bands would rehearse in the front room of the house and Paul continued to bed down in the makeshift room under the staircase or on a mattress in singer John Dowler's room.

It wasn't long before Paul fell into the creative, self-conscious, sometimes elitist and too-cool-for-school Carlton scene. If you've read Helen Garner's evocative *Monkey Grip* or seen the film – or Bert Deling's underground film *Pure Shit* – you'll know the world.

Everyone was doing something. Often lots of something.

Paul soaked up everything he could. He listened to The Bleeding Hearts, who rehearsed in the soundproofed front room of the house, and members of that band would later hear him in his room trying to figure out the guitar parts of songs they'd been playing.

'The Bleeding Hearts were like young gods to me,' Paul says. 'They didn't play music like I played and I couldn't work out what they did. I saw them a lot. There were other bands like The Millionaires but The Bleeding Hearts were the ones – Martin Armiger, Eric Gradman and Huk Treloar. They were only a few years older than me but looked like they'd lived for a thousand years.'

Paul also absorbed all the records the Spare Change members listened to, the way they created songs – everything about the process of making music and being a musician.

'That's what he did,' Dowler says. 'Sponging is probably a little harsh but he certainly took note of everything that was going on.

'Chris [Langman] and he and I used to have these drunken jam sessions where we'd improvise songs. In retrospect I think that Chris and I were certainly drunk – but I don't think Paul was.

'I'd do things like play him that *Shake Some Action* album by the Flamin' Groovies and a week later he'd come back with a song with a couple of little things in there that he'd obviously picked up from the album. So basically he was soaking things up and learning and folding it back into his creative process.'

'John had all his records in his room,' Paul says. 'That's where I first heard The Ramones, Jonathan Richman and Tom Petty. Being in John Dowler's room was a big musical education. The first Talking Heads album, Television, and John Cale's *Paris 1919*. John and the guys living in the Hoddle Street house were the guys who set the taste. They were the cool kids. They'd been to England. They could quote lines from French movies and knew exactly the right stuff to be listening to. I just gobbled all that up. Chris Langman loved Dylan. John Dowler did too. Dylan was obviously a big influence but so was all the other stuff.'

The relationship that really flourished in the Hoddle Street house was between Paul and guitarist Chris Langman.

'I know Chris thought all his good days had happened at once when Paul turned up,' Dowler says, 'because he was so Dylanesque, and Chris was so obsessed with Dylan. I think Chris fell in love with Paul to a large extent and they wrote quite a few songs together.'

'I'm a massive Bob Dylan fan,' Langman says. 'Massive. I think Paul over the years has waxed and waned a bit. At the time we were around each other the Dylan albums that loomed large were *Desire* and the live *Hard Rain*. The other constants were Television's *Marquee Moon* and albums by the Velvet Underground.'

Langman was a pivotal figure in Spare Change. A smart and thoughtful guy, he didn't give much away. He knew stuff but he was cool enough to not parade what he knew.

'We were close,' Langman says of his relationship with Paul. 'We had the same taste. We liked each other. Of course he was quite Dylanesque. I mean, he was a singer–songwriter with a guitar – what else can you be? And he had good lyrics and good melodies. I didn't have a problem with him being good.'

Langman's opinion of Paul being 'good' wasn't universally shared with other musicians in their circle.

'A lot of people were jealous of him when he first came to Melbourne because they could see that he was better than they were,' Langman says. 'The Carlton guys didn't fall in love with him, but I remember among the people we knew who were writing songs he was respected and John Dowler saying, "He does it better."'

'Paul and I were jumpy kinds of guys and we just liked to play. We'd play for hours and hours and hours and make up shit as we went along. I was really just a sounding board for him – and I came up with some dumb ideas.

'The thing is that he was committed. It came partly from his family. I think there was like a rolling ball of creativity there somewhere. I obviously didn't know his father but his mother was very supportive of him. And besides his family and their support, he read a lot. Like a *lot*. He read deeply and he'd read often.'

Langman recalls Paul reading 'the heavy stuff. Rimbaud and Proust.' He considered Paul as having a genuine interest and affection for books and learning, both then and now.

In these formative days, though, Paul's listening was probably even more expansive and far-reaching than his reading. There was always a huge pile of cassettes everywhere.

'He was a sponge, a bowerbird,' Langman says, 'but really, it's the only way you can do it. He just absorbed everything and he had an ability to hold everything in and remember it.'

'The thing with Paul was that he was on a mission,' Greg Perano says. 'He was very much intent on making his music his life. He could write a lyric and he was enigmatic and had a bit of mystique and style about him. He fitted in with the scene really well.'

Perano says Spare Change provided Paul with a support group and a connection to the Carlton scene, something which was invaluable when putting his own band together.

'By the late seventies a lot of the young Carlton crowd cut their hair and moved into the punk and post-punk stuff. Paul was right in the middle of the change and opened himself up to all that was happening at the time. He'd go and see The Boys Next Door and The Saints and the other bands. It wasn't like he thought the only bands that existed were the Velvet Underground and Television. He knew that there was something else out there and, along the way, he picked up elements of all that stuff. He was absorbing and learning from all sorts of music and influences.'

CHAPTER 5

THE HIGH RISE BOMBERS

'I play The High Rise Bombers tape full-blast and dance by myself, jumping high in the air.'
Helen Garner, *Yellow Notebook: Diaries*, Volume 1, 1978–1987

OUT OF PAUL'S TIME AT THE HODDLE STREET HOUSE IN Melbourne came the short-lived but much mythologised High Rise Bombers.

The Bombers had an evolving and regularly changing line-up, as well as many friends guesting at gigs. The core was Paul, guitarist Martin Armiger, bass player Fred Cass, drummer John Lloyd, guitarist Chris Dyson and a floating array of horn players, including Sally Ford and Keith Shadwick.

Like most bands of the late 1970s, The High Rise Bombers began life very, very casually.

The band's genesis was with bass player Lee 'Fred' Cass who was doing some recording with Martin Armiger from The Bleeding Hearts at a house in Parkville.

Cass was a confident kind of guy, and determined in his own way. He knew how to corral people together and make things happen. He would have made a very good band manager and, in fact, with The High Rise Bombers he effectively assumed both the role of fluid, inventive bass player and the guy you'd call if you needed to know when sound check was or where to get an amplifier repaired. He was the kind of guy every band needs in their early days.

For his part, Armiger had little interest in such practicalities. Already an admired and enigmatic figure in the Carlton music scene, the gaunt, super-intelligent, highly creative guitarist and songwriter was a central figure in The Bleeding Hearts, one of the bands he'd formed after moving from Adelaide to Melbourne. The Bleeding Hearts oozed attitude – part Roxy Music inventiveness mixed with the edge of the Velvet Underground, and the dark, threatening swagger of The Rolling Stones. Armiger was about playing, writing and arranging. All he needed to know was where he had to be and when. And then he'd be late.

Armiger had seen Paul around the Melbourne traps for a while after first encountering him at the big house on Hoddle Street. It was something Armiger recalled in great detail during a lengthy phone conversation at the beginning of 2019. Armiger was living in France and not in the best of health but despite this he was extremely generous with detailing his memories of those times. Sadly Armiger passed away in November of that year.

'It was a huge communal house and we all stayed there at various times. I'd go around there and we'd all sit up drinking and listening to old Beatles songs and other things. Paul was sleeping under the stairs in a cupboard and he was reading this really big book. It was the biggest novel I'd ever seen a rock musician read and I thought that was pretty impressive.

'But we never really talked about that much because he was a very private person. I just found him and his songs interesting.'

Around this time Paul had been singing occasionally with Spare Change after Dowler had left the band and had by then returned to Adelaide to form the band Young Modern.

'We got Paul up onstage a few times,' Langman says. 'And we did some gigs in Adelaide with him too ... It was Paul Kelly with most of Spare Change backing him. I think the Bombers started soon after that.'

As Cass recalls, The High Rise Bombers were formed because he and Armiger wanted to get a new band together.

'Buzz, the bass player I was working with, told me he didn't want to be in a band and I think that was the day Paul walked in and said he had been moving away from being a folk singer and wanted to continue developing his work with bands. I said I had a drummer, who was John Lloyd, and I said I'd play bass and we'd get Chris Dyson to play guitar, and Martin said he'd get Michael Charles and Sally Ford as a brass section. So between Martin and I we put a band together around Paul.'

Assembling a diverse array of players from their circle of musician friends was easy. Now there was just the issue of where to play.

Cass was absolutely besotted with Janni Goss, who ran the Café Paradiso in Lygon Street. He asked her if his band could play in the back garden area. 'She said yes and so we played there every Sunday afternoon for a few months. It was a real 1970s Carlton thing. A scene of hipsters and groovers,' recalls Cass. The number of people who now claim to have been at these performances would probably – just – fit inside the Melbourne Cricket Ground.

Cass also briefly set up another venue in Carlton, the Paradise Garage, which was connected to the Pram Factory, and The High Rise Bombers played a handful of Saturday night shows there. The band also played other early shows, including a party gig at the house in Hoddle Street.

'I was going to see all these cool Melbourne bands like The Bleeding Hearts,' Paul says, 'and then when I put together a band suddenly I had Martin Armiger in my band. And Red Symons from Skyhooks playing in the band at my first gig in Melbourne at The Kingston Hotel. I was just this kid who had come across from Adelaide and I was playing with these young gods. So they must have seen something in me. That stuff gives you confidence.'

Melbourne musician and person-about-town Paul Egan also lays claim to a role in the management and organisation of The High Rise Bombers.

'I knew all those guys who lived and hung around the Hoddle Street house, and when the band was getting underway I put my hand up and said that I'd go and get some work for the band,' he says.

'The Café Paradiso in Carlton was a big hang for everyone in those days so I started chatting up the woman who ran it and eventually she gave me a Sunday gig. That gig became an institution.'

Egan, a drummer, says he also organised another venue in Victoria Street, Richmond, where The High Rise Bombers played, and that he and Cass worked together on some aspects of the young band's day-to-day affairs.

'Fred helped me put up posters, but I did all the work, ran the doors at venues, and did the publicity.

'Eventually they moved out of the Hoddle Street house, and started rehearsing in the back room at my place in Alphington.

'I was trying to make ends meet like everyone in those days so we'd have parties at my place when rehearsals were on. I'd go out and get beers on my bank card and then on-sell them to the guys in the band – so I made a little on the side.'

Cass's recollections of Paul's listening habits at the time gels with everyone else. The diet was fairly straightforward – take two parts Dylan and mix with a touch of Television, then stir. The result? Rudimentary early songs.

'Paul was listening to that first Television album and whatever Dylan had out at the time – I think it was *Desire*. He was simply plagiarising those two albums, re-editing them together.

'He wrote sophisticated lyrics that none of us could understand. There was the one called "Faster Than Light", and another about a train going through a tunnel ["Derailment"]. I said, "Can you tell us what that's about?" and he said, "It's about masturbation."'

* * *

Guitarist Chris Dyson became a High Rise Bomber after – in his recollection – they'd played just one gig. He had a musician friend who knew people who lived in the Hoddle Street house. Dyson went around for a play, not really knowing anyone who lived there.

'I was playing a lot in all these bands at the time – as was everyone else, so lots of people were always coming and going. And we were all on the dole of course which helped make ends meet.'

Dyson was part of a different world, such was the geographical and cultural divide in Melbourne at the time.

'They were from the Carlton scene and I was living

in South Yarra. There was a bit of a divide in those days. Carlton was the arty, alternative area – and I'd lived there for a couple of years before – but I was involved with the Station Hotel scene. It was more country and blues – *and* it was on the other side of the river. These days it doesn't seem like much, but in those days it did.

'Carlton was near the university and a lot more intellectual. It was good to be part of that scene. Prior to the Bombers I was out in the suburbs playing rock – and we rarely got to play in the city because we were just not on the radar.'

To Dyson, this bunch of musicians in Hoddle Street felt a little different.

'Playing with the Bombers was a real eye-opener. Some bands have a particular chemistry that you can't manufacture. As soon as I started playing with them I thought, *This is going up a level for me.* It was because Martin [Armiger] was in the band. He was much more experienced and had an incredible energy about him. I learnt a lot. We did gigs at a pub in Richmond but mainly it was the Paradiso in Carlton which we did every Sunday and it was always packed.'

Dyson remembers Cass being the main organiser of the band – 'more an entrepreneur than a bass player really'.

And he found Paul extremely quiet when they first met.

'You just thought Bob Dylan when you first saw him – he had the hair and everything.'

Another core member of The High Rise Bombers was drummer John Lloyd. After studying art in Hobart, Lloyd landed in Melbourne in the 1970s and was immediately in demand, playing gigs with The Relaxed Mechanics, The Peter Lillie Band, The Cruisers, and others.

'Honestly, it felt like I was the only drummer in town.' He laughs. 'There were lots of people ringing up asking me to do things.

'I didn't know I was part of a scene, it was just happening. It was vibrant and exciting for me. I didn't even have a car. These guys who wanted me to play with them would have to come and pick me up and lug my drums. It must have been a real pain in the arse.

'I was nineteen or twenty years of age, a green-horn, really wide-eyed, like "What's going on here?".

'From Hobart I moved into a place in Brunswick Street, Fitzroy, where my brother lived. It was known as Heroin Castle. It was full of heroin addicts, cat burglars, playwrights, musicians, actors and creative people, but they were all involved with heroin. Paul got into a bit of trouble with heroin himself. It was everywhere. Paul was living in Hoddle Street where that roadie Bysshe and his partner lived. They were real sweethearts – but there was a lot of heroin around that place too.

'Bysshe was an almost motherly figure, and a road manager – but he was always out of it. He was a heavy user.'

Paul had first met Peter 'Bysshe' Stevens in Adelaide. Stevens, a knockabout, small-time crook, heroin addict, would-be manager and roadie had been part of the Spare Change crew. Stevens purportedly borrowed friends' cars so he could rob houses. He was nicknamed 'Bysshe' by the Spare Change members after the English romantic poet Percy Bysshe Shelley for reasons that probably made perfect sense at the time.

'Fitzroy was quite scary,' Lloyd says. 'Gertrude Street was *really* scary. It was really a case of don't go down Gertrude Street. There were shootings and all sorts of carry-on. The pub on the corner of Brunswick Street and Gertrude Street was *heavy*. You just didn't go there. Smith Street in Collingwood was heavy. For me, as a young kid, there was this real undercurrent of criminality. There were people with names like Felix and Shovers, all these characters.

My brother came to me one day and said, "John, I think it would be best if you found somewhere else to live." He was just trying to protect me.'

Lloyd found Paul to be an elusive, pensive person who he struggled to really get a fix on. He kept wondering, *Who is this person?* and he wasn't alone in having that thought.

'But I loved playing with him. I felt it was a real privilege. He was a serious songwriter, he had great tunes and there was this enigmatic thing about him. He was hard to get to know, but he was really interesting. I mean, he'd been dux of his school and very sporty, but he didn't come across like that at the time. I read about it later and went, "Shit, this guy has a serious intellect – and sporting prowess."

'But when I played with him he came across as this pensive, withdrawn persona. He must have been really driven. Iva [Davies] was like that. Totally driven.'

Lloyd can't recall how he became a member of The High Rise Bombers.

'All of a sudden I'm in The High Rise Bombers. I can't remember getting into the band at all. I remember being chuffed to be invited. It was, like, *Wow, all these people want me to play with them.* It was a really great experience for me.'

So there was Lloyd, playing drums under a pergola at the back of a wine bar in Lygon Street with The High Rise Bombers. And he recalls that there weren't always as many people there as now claim to have attended those gigs.

'Sometimes there were more people in the band than watching us. But we built up a following.

'People in that scene knew about Paul, pretty much from day one. We'd play at The Kingston Hotel in Richmond on a Friday night and pack it out.

'The thing was that the songs stood out. He's just got this great writing ability. There was a lot of power in his music, even then. A lot of heart and passion and power and it came through. We used to do the midnight session at Bombay Rock which was fucking horrible but it was where we really cut our teeth and developed. We did four-hour shows there.'

* * *

Sally Ford's involvement in The High Rise Bombers was very typical of the Carlton scene. She just sort of drifted into it. Inspired by watching Joe Camilleri, she'd bought herself a saxophone.

'I was playing sax in a band called Flying Tackle which was all women,' she says. 'We did gigs in Adelaide and Sydney but I couldn't really play.

'Then Paul started doing these Sunday gigs at Café Paradiso in the backyard garden. It was so beautiful. It's very hazy for me as I'm sure it is for everyone. It was a bit of a scene – Red [Symons] was playing, Martin [Armiger] was playing, Johnny Lloyd was playing, and Paul of course.'

Ford – the sister of Helen Garner – became part of the brass section with The High Rise Bombers, an ever-changing line-up called The Substitutes. The essence of it was Ford, alto saxophonist Michael Charles, John Fergus on tenor, and Chris Malherbe on trumpet.

'Michael Charles told me I should come along, even though I could barely play. The Sunday afternoons became really popular. It was *the* place to be, and it happened very quickly.'

The Substitutes really only played with The High Rise Bombers at the Paradiso, and for reasons lost to the mists of time it was only Ford playing brass at other shows the band did.

'The brass section might have been a Van Morrison thing,' Paul says. 'Or maybe a bit anti-punk. Or maybe it was because of The Saints and their record *Prehistoric Sounds* with a lot of brass on it. It could have been because of Martin [Armiger].' Indeed, Armiger said he was attracted by the horn section in The High Rise Bombers who did, 'these beautiful little arrangements'.

The High Rise Bombers' following quickly extended outside Carlton, and they ventured to Geelong and Adelaide. Ford recalls crazy shows starting sets at four in the morning at Bananas in St Kilda.

I was a huge fan of The High Rise Bombers and interviewed them for *Preview* magazine when they were visiting Adelaide in June of 1978. I'd already met them and recall inviting them around to my home. Bass player Fred Cass – ostensibly the engine room of the band – and Paul came over. Guitarist Martin Armiger may have been with them.

It was my first interview and I was nervous. No one said very much. I'm not sure I can even say Paul was my first interview as I'm not convinced he said anything. The resulting piece contained no quotes from any of the Bombers. I wrote that, 'Onstage the Bombers have a tough, pounding guitar sound that builds up and up as Paul, Martin and Fred tear up to the microphones to sing some undecipherable chorus, and Paul tilts his guitar and spits or croons out some song or other, legs apart in a stance somewhere between Gene Vincent and Elvis Costello, sometimes wimpy, other times frighteningly intense and forward.

'The High Rise Bombers play mostly original songs although Dylan's "From a Buick 6" is a regular encore. They do Armiger's "This Summer" and Kelly's "Promise Not to Tell", "I See Red", "She's The One", "If You Won't Give Me Your Lovin'", and "Cherry", Kelly's contribution to the genre of street kids love songs; it slots in with The Boomtown Rats' "Joey" and Springsteen's sagas about Sandy and Terry.

'The major problem with The High Rise Bombers is that Kelly's excellent lyrics tend to be obscured in the sound mix or by the overall sound of a big band. His lyrics are sensitive, poetic you might say, statements that have come across as secondary to the Bombers' overall sound, like Spector tangling with Cohen, obscuring his lyrics and reducing his voice to another instrument in the overall presentation ...

'Paul Kelly and The High Rise Bombers are one of, if not the best and most exciting bands working the pub circuit in this country. Playing the pubs, like [The] Sports, not because it's the only place to play but because that's where their music belongs, drinking, dancing, sweating and more dancing. They come on at a hundred miles per hour, aren't new wave or punk – modern's their word.'

Clearly I was a fan. I'd seen them a little earlier in the year, at midnight on Good Friday 1978 at the Paradise Garage in Melbourne. It was a big garage space – about fifteen square cars worth. In an article for *Roadrunner* magazine I wrote that it was, 'acoustically deplorable but a fine atmosphere decorated by the best Melbourne can offer in after-midnight hip trendies, posturing punks, and infiltrators. The PA was a collection of $50 tin boxes emitting a sound quality akin to its financial value.'

I mentioned that in Adelaide, Paul was considered a, 'Richard Clapton like singer–songwriter so his transition to loud, fast rock'n'roll promised lots.'

The Bombers played what I described as a 'tough, speedy brand of rock'n'roll' while The Substitutes filled the quieter moments with, 'rising brass sounds similar to that resplendent on the Southside Johnny and the Asbury Dukes' [sic] albums. No Clarence Clemons solos yet, just a solid wall of sax and trumpets, well arranged within the Bombers' overall presentation.'

The following night The High Rise Bombers played at Martinis in the Imperial Hotel in Carlton, and I suggested – using a bad pun – that the climax to both shows was, 'Kelly's anthem to premature ejaculation, "Derailment", a song that begins "There's a train rolling down the track" but it ends up going off the track well before reaching its destination, musically building up and up, ending abruptly and long before it should. This, and everything else in the Bombers' repertoire, is driven along by Martin's pithy guitar playing which seems predominantly responsible for their hard, fast sound – a characteristic of Martin's former association with The Bleeding Hearts.'

Armiger, as Paul admits, was like a young god and having him as a member of The High Rise Bombers gave Paul a whole cache of cool.

'Martin was king of the scene,' Paul says, 'and probably the stronger figure in that band. He was a much more sophisticated musician than I was. Arrangements – how to make songs interesting, key changes at certain points or breaking down songs in certain ways – were really important to him. He would have ideas for horn lines. And Martin would have wanted me to play guitar parts, which I find hard to do. I'm much better with rhythm. I was, and still am, a pretty basic musician. Martin taught me collaboration and musicality. I picked up a lot from him. He used to put things together in a pretty interesting way.'

But The High Rise Bombers were destined to be a short-lived project. The eventual collapse of the band came for a variety of reasons. Too many members coupled with an extremely ambitious Paul for starters.

'The demise of the band was really due to Paul's ambition and heroin,' Cass says. 'Paul wanted a band, but he wanted to be Paul Kelly supported by a band. I had a more socialist idea of how a band operated.

'In a socialist world all workers in the trenches of rock'n'roll and song are meant to be considered equal. There are no stars. But Paul hadn't signed up for my socialist band world order.

'Our first band poster was designed by a girl Paul was seeing at the time. The poster had this huge picture of him like Elvis Presley, in the middle of it, and the rest of us were just a small banner, and across it were the words "Paul Kelly and The High Rise Bombers". I hit the roof and said, "No way," so we stopped that one.'

Armiger also noticed Paul's ambition. Almost forty years later, he said to me, 'I remember the night you turned up at a Bombers gig and talked to Paul after that gig.

'I remember it so distinctly. Everything about it and how keen you were. I knew that you wanted to talk to Paul. That was okay, but I was surprised by him. We had half a plan, I think, to go somewhere after the gig and do something. Something that probably wouldn't have been good for us. But I noticed that Paul abandoned that plan to talk to you.

'This was really the first intimation for me that Paul was career-orientated. In hindsight, I guess most bands were career-orientated and I just hung around with deadbeats and losers in that Fitzroy/Carlton world ...

'I don't remember it being a conscious decision. I think we had that completely naive belief that we were in a little alternative world and if we got good enough the rest of the world would notice and then we'd have success and recognition. But I didn't know anybody who had that as an aim. That was my first feeling that night when you turned up – that Paul was thinking further than all of us on that level.'

Armiger was also starting to have some other issues with the band.

'I did have two criticisms. One was the Dylan element – the Dylan voice and the Dylan form of the songs. I love Dylan, and *Blood on the Tracks* had come out about two or three years before that and I thought it was the best songwriting ever – I liked it for Dylan, but I didn't like it for The High Rise Bombers. At the time Paul didn't want to leave that kind of song structure and vocal tone. It was too much of something else, so part of what I offered the band was to work out the songs so they weren't three chord strums and I started adding a riff here and there.

'Although the songs were phenomenally uniform and repetitious, we had Johnny Lloyd drumming, who's a great player, and a horn section. I thought, *Wow, we could do a lot here*. It felt like the band wanted me to mess around with Paul's songs more than he did. But he bore it with goodwill and it worked really well. We had terrific responses from audiences given everything. Paul was a front man. He liked to be there. It was working quite well but then he decided to change the line-up. He brought in Shaggers [Keith Shadwick]. I knew Shaggers from The Bleeding Hearts. He was a jazzy sax player. His sound was exactly the opposite of what we had put together.

'Paul didn't come to the band and say, "Do you think we need to change the brass line-up?" Instead one day Shaggers just turned up. Maybe Fred had something to do with the change too. Maybe he wasn't as fond of the dinky little brass section as I was. Anyway, it was a big change, and I realised at that stage that the band was very much Paul's thing.'

Sally Ford remembers this too. 'He [Keith] was from the hot shot jazzy world.' Ford laughs. 'And for some reason I just hung in there when he came along so it was just two tenor sax players which was kind of unusual.'

The real issue was that Paul didn't want to play anyone else's songs but his own. And that was a real deal-breaker for the other songwriting members of The High Rise Bombers.

Paul wanted the Bombers to be his band. He wanted to be the only singer and he only wanted to sing his songs. There was no room in this vision for other nascent talents who wanted their songs in the repertoire. Including other people's songs had been okay in the early days but Paul was growing in confidence and in a few short months the early days were already behind him.

'At the beginning,' Armiger said, 'I brought a few songs of my own to the band which we played, and Paul sang. Early on I didn't really get the sense that this was a problem because, like with every other band that I'd been in, if you wrote a song and you played it to the band and they liked it then you did it. So we were starting to do a few of my songs in the set and the band was just going along as you'd expect a little band to go on. We were on the booking agency books and Frank Stivala got us gigs all over the place. We went down to Geelong every Monday to play at the Sundowner. We were doing quite good. We had fun just hanging out.'

Then Paul announced that he was only going to sing his songs. No Armiger songs. No Dyson compositions. Just Paul Kelly songs. Naturally this took the wind out of everyone's creative sails. Certainly Armiger had no heart for being ostensibly part of Paul's backing band.

The lustre suddenly went from The High Rise Bombers and Armiger began disengaging from Paul and the band.

'I was hardly in the band really, I was just turning up and playing,' Armiger said of that later period. 'I can't think of anybody else in the world who would have said that. I mean, Skyhooks didn't say, "Oh, we're only doing [Greg] Macainsh's songs." If Red [Symons] wrote a song they'd do it. Or Freddie [Strauks] even, who wrote "B B B Boogie". Most of the bands were not one-writer bands – unless it was like Dragon a bit later on who had Paul [Hewson], one of the best writers around.

'That was another mark of Paul's. I don't mean it to sound critical. I'm just observing that it was a thing about him. He was one of the few people who would actually come out and express something like that.'

'Paul didn't say it like "My songs are better". It was just what he wanted to do. You could argue it from a point of artistic integrity – I can enunciate my own songs better than anybody else blah blah blah. But to me, I thought that was empty because there was so much Dylan in him. I was just astounded and I left the band. That was that. I wouldn't be in a band that was defined in that way because that wasn't a band anymore.

'Paul just had a clear idea – much clearer than anyone else I knew – of himself as a player in the big pop game. I just thought, *If that's what you want, that's what you want.* I didn't have ambition like that at that time. I didn't think, *Oh, this band is going to make me rich*, or anything like that. I just thought that I'd do what I do with whoever I was playing with.'

'Paul wanted to do only his songs,' Cass says. 'And you've got to admire him. He had ambition. I mean, you've got this thing of dope-smoking musicians in Melbourne, having a great lifestyle and getting a gig here and there, and thinking they were working hard. Paul wanted more than that.'

Lloyd says he observed Paul and Armiger clashing over songs and what they'd perform and who would sing them.

And it wasn't the last time he'd be watching those tensions unfold within a band, either.

'I can understand a lead singer wanting it all, wanting his own gig. Paul's always done that. Iva Davies was the same.'

The end was near when The High Rise Bombers did a gig at Melbourne's Bombay Rock in the winter of 1978.

'It was pretty standard in those days that sax players would sit in with another band – but not so much the other musicians,' Cass says. 'The Sports were playing after us this night and Martin said he'd been asked to do a jam with them. That was complete bullshit. He'd already decided to join them.

'By this time however Paul had said he was leaving too, so I asked Martin if he'd stay and be the lead singer. I always thought Martin was brilliant. He shouldn't have joined The Sports. He should have stayed with us and done his own songs. But he decided to join another band and all his songs got watered down and lost the fire and guts he put into them.'

In August of 1978 Armiger officially decamped to join The Sports and Sally Ford had moved on to The Kevins. She thinks that Paul sacked her. He doesn't deny that this may have been the case.

'I don't remember a "We don't want you anymore",' she says, 'but I do recall a "Fuck you then." I was inexperienced about being in a band. I remember not going to a gig and thinking, *Well, if you don't want me then see how you go without me*, and I also remember Martin ringing up and asking where I was. I told him I wasn't going to the gig and he said, "But Keith doesn't know the tunes," and I thought, *Too bad*.'

But if there was any brief bad feeling it quickly dissipated. Ford recalls Paul being shy, 'but I really liked him – it was a fun time. I just think he was slightly introverted.'

And of course the ever present spectre of heroin was hovering over the Carlton music scene and The High Rise Bombers.

Ford's perspective is that Paul was becoming unpredictable towards the end of the band and that this may have been related to his use of heroin. Certainly she believes that the band had a heroin mystique around them, regardless of whether it was exaggerated or cultivated more than a reality.

'In the Bombers days I don't think I saw Paul completely out of it – but there was some use,' she says.

According to Cass there were at least two members of the Bombers – Armiger and Paul – actively using heroin, along with their roadie.

'I realised something was up when one day the PA company rang me and said we were three months behind with payments and I said, "No, we've paid every single week." I was managing the band and the PA people insisted they hadn't received any money. I'd given the money to the roadie [Bysshe] every single time and told him to go and pay for the PA, but he was using along with the other guys. When I found out, I went, "Oh well, we'll just need to get the money from future gigs." So really the whole band paid for the heroin.'

Cass says Paul 'worked very hard but that didn't stop him using heroin, and using a lot of it'.

Guitarist Chris Dyson, though, remains unconvinced that Paul was using much in the way of heroin in The High Rise Bombers days and that his real usage came later.

'Martin was considered more of a drug fiend at the time. But we had a reputation. Everyone *thought* we were junkies. I had hung around with junkies early in my life so I could pick them and Paul wasn't ... he was a girl magnet so there were always girls around. And I don't think he washed very often.'

After Paul and Armiger had departed, The High Rise Bombers weren't quite finished for Cass and the others. Not quite. The fact that Paul was a long way from being a household name and a recognisable figure outside of Melbourne meant Cass and his fellow band mates could get away with playing without Paul being in the band.

'The Bombers were booked to go to Sydney to do a Double J live concert and about five other shows,' Cass says. 'I kept the dates as I knew Sydney didn't really know anything about who was in the Bombers. I rehearsed the band and we did some of my songs, some of Martin's and some of Paul's. We had a shit-hot rhythm section – me, Johnny Lloyd on drums, and Chris Dyson on guitar. But it didn't last.'

After a while the second Paul-less version of The High Rise Bombers crashed and burnt and Cass called it quits.

The High Rise Bombers represented the emergence of Paul as a songwriter and frontman. They had two songs included on a compilation album of Melbourne bands from the era – the Armiger composition 'Domestic Criminal' and 'She's Got It', which is credited to the whole band. Cass recorded many shows and rehearsals, releasing an array of songs on a cassette.

The band was also a manifestation of Paul's drive and determination. But it was still early days and a great period of experimentation and learning.

'I didn't feel like The High Rise Bombers was my band or my vision,' Paul says. 'It was definitely a collaboration with Martin and me – and Fred Cass wrote songs too. It was a band with three songwriters in it. Martin sang some songs. He and I shared the singing. He was a good singer.

'My time in the Bombers was about me learning how to be in a band – and learning a lot. It was a big band so it was hard to make any money. I think we became more famous after we broke up. At the time we weren't that big a band on the scene – more just a band playing around a bit and then we stopped.'

Chris Langman from Spare Change thinks he played a couple of times with Paul and The High Rise Bombers before their end. But he can't be totally sure. It was that time. Everybody played with everybody else. It was nothing serious and not necessarily meant to last. You had no thought that anyone would care in a fortnight's time, let alone decades later and that you might have been playing guitar with a future icon.

The High Rise Bombers were just another band playing around town. They were short-lived and played to small audiences. Time and the future careers of some of their members has created the mythology.

As far as Langman is concerned, saying that The High Rise Bombers disintegrated is over-stating the situation, because they never really did more than get started.

Despite the mythology that now surrounds The High Rise Bombers, Paul Egan is also realistic about where they actually figured in the grand scheme of things at the time.

'The High Rise Bombers weren't really famous. I mean they were famous in our little circle, but they didn't do any proper recording or anything like that. They came and went really quickly and to this day most people don't know anything about them. If Paul hadn't become famous they'd be totally forgotten.'

Ford would have liked to have continued playing with the assemblage of musicians in the Bombers.

'I was pretty disappointed when the Bombers ended. The Dots were too guitar for me and that's never been the sort of music that I'm drawn to.'

CHAPTER 6

PAUL KELLY AND THE DOTS

'Paul forming The Dots was like Dylan finding The Band.'
Greg Perano

WITH THE DEMISE OF THE HIGH RISE BOMBERS, PAUL didn't waste much time assembling a new band – The Dots, an outfit that quickly became Paul Kelly and The Dots.

The Dots were an extension of The High Rise Bombers in sound – they were streetwise, tough but tender, and they had just a hint of danger hanging over them. They dressed in black and if they didn't all take drugs they certainly had the pallor and attitude to suggest they did.

The Dots and later the incarnation known as The Paul Kelly Band existed between 1978 and 1982 with a seemingly endless array of Melbourne musicians passing through the ranks. And they played a lot. A real lot.

At various times The Dots' line-up numbered Chris Worrall, Michael Holmes, Tim Brosnan, Alan Brooker, Paul

Gadsby, Tony Thornton, Chris Langman, Chris Dyson, Huk Treloar, Alex Formosa, Greg Martin and others. There were a lot of Dots.

As good as The High Rise Bombers were, Greg Perano says, 'Paul forming The Dots was a bit like Dylan finding The Band. He was writing really strong songs at the time such as "Lowdown". Like Spare Change, Paul was a big Springsteen fan and like Springsteen he talked about the working man and the guts of things.'

Guitarist Tim Brosnan, who would later play with The Dots, remembers seeing what was possibly The Dots' first incarnation. Brosnan had met Paul at a pub in Lygon Street, Carlton, when Paul was playing with The High Rise Bombers, but they got to know each other better soon afterwards when Brosnan and his girlfriend went to Paul's house one night to score from his housemate Bysshe.

'Bysshe had moved into the Hoddle Street house,' Paul says. 'We got really tight. I really liked Bysshe.'

Tim and his girlfriend were both feeling edgy. That 'Will the dealer show, will he not?' feeling that accompanies pretty much every drug deal. Paul knew *that* feeling well. He'd been there.

'Paul could tell that we were a bit antsy,' Brosnan says, 'so he brought out his guitar and asked me to teach him a song that my band True Wheels were playing – "Have No Fear". Sam Shepherd wrote the lyrics. Red Symons put the music to it and Paul liked it. I think he might have done it in an early version of The Dots.

'Anyway, this night he chilled us out and made us feel really comfortable until Bysshe came back with the drugs and everything was good.'

Brosnan remembers the early version of The Dots was Greg Perano playing drums, Paul Gadsby on bass and

Paul on guitar. Greg Perano's Dot life was only fleeting, perfecting his percussive skills and going on to work with Hunters & Collectors.

Gadsby was an original Dot. The actual circumstances of him joining the band are a little foggy but the bass player thinks it might have been via guitarist Chris Malherbe who told him this Paul Kelly character was trying to get a band together. Malherbe took Paul around to the share house in Fitzroy where Gadsby was living.

'He had that inner-city cred, and the girls liked him,' Gadsby says. At a Dots gig Paul was introduced to Hilary Brown and they began a relationship that's chronicled in the song 'When I First Met Your Ma'. The two later lived in a flat on Punt Road – with a view to the Nylex clock tower and the Melbourne Cricket Ground, as mentioned in the song 'Leaps and Bounds'.

Chris Langman was there for an early incarnation of The Dots too.

'I would have been the worst player in that band. I mean, I'm okay – but Chris Worrall, Johnny Lloyd and Paul Gadsby – they're good. And Paul's a really good rhythm guitar player. But at that time, anyone who was pissed off with Paul used to call him "strummer", but he was a very good strummer – still is.'

Chris Worrall, who had previously played guitar with Captain Matchbox, The Pelaco Brothers, The Bleeding Hearts and Stiletto, joined The Dots in February 1979, replacing Chris Malherbe.

Worrall was one of the people Paul had gravitated to in his early days in Melbourne. He recalls that Paul 'sort of lobbed up in Melbourne on the tail of Spare Change who we'd all gotten to know when I was in The Bleeding Hearts'.

Around this time Worrall considers that he was a bit of a go-to guy in the Melbourne music scene. Opinionated, a tad fiery and reasonably well connected, Worrall prided himself on knowing what was going on. And with a punkish attitude he wasn't prone to taking shit from anyone and far from shy about letting people know what he knew and thought about – well – just about anything.

'I was the sort of guy who knew stuff. I had a record contract and knew managers. So there was an endless stream of people lobbing up to the place in St Kilda where I was living.

'One day there was a knock on the door and it was Paul. He had his guitar in one hand and a coconut in the other. He said, "I thought I should bring something," so he brought a coconut.

'Anyway, he sat down in the kitchen and we made a cup of tea and he played me six or seven of his songs – maybe more. They were good. They weren't great but they were on their way.'

At that time Worrall had just joined Stiletto so he wasn't available for any projects or bands but he found Paul interesting because he was a little at odds with the prevailing music scene around Melbourne, and in particular St Kilda.

Worrall also wasn't surprised when Martin Armiger left The High Rise Bombers after Paul told him he wouldn't be singing his songs and that the band dissolved soon after that. He remembers Paul and Chris Langman starting a new band called The Dots and checking them out.

'When I first saw them they had Chris Malherbe on rhythm guitar. Although initially I wasn't interested in joining them, after a few months, I said I'd really like to play guitar with them so they booted Malherbe out. The guys were pretty ruthless. I didn't really insist on that. But, nah, he was history. He probably hates my guts.'

So why did Worrall jump ship at that time when he was still a member of an evolving, hard-working and respected band in Stiletto?

'I saw an opportunity,' Worrall says matter-of-factly. 'We'd just been dropped by EMI and we were rudderless.'

The Dots' line-up was now Worrall on guitar, Paul Gadsby on bass, John Lloyd on drums and Chris Langman on guitar, 'And Paul flailing away at his Telecaster,' Worrall adds. 'We had a secret deal with the road crew. Paul liked starting the songs. He'd just start playing but he could never get his guitar in tune. It was an old 1950s Telecaster – probably worth a fortune now – but you could not tune the bastard and have it stay in tune so I used to say to the crew, "Let him do his thing and as soon as the band comes in pull him out of the front-of-house sound. Keep him in the foldback, he'll be happy with that, but lose him from the mix. At that time he really wasn't up to speed as a rhythm player. He got a lot better.'

It was also still some time before, in Worrall's opinion, Paul began writing truly memorable songs.

'I don't think he had anything very sophisticated. It wasn't until he started working with Chris Langman that his songwriting really improved. Up till that point he wrote a lot of songs that were all quite the same.

'In The Dots he came along every week with another four or five songs so we had the luxury of sitting back and saying, "Nah, that one doesn't work, that one's got potential, that one needs a new rhythm."

'It was Langman who really came up with all the bits and pieces and even if Paul didn't like it he really didn't have the knowledge at the time to come up with an alternative. And I don't think we gave him an option.'

Amid all this, though, Worrall knew that Paul was the boss, something that was being made increasingly obvious as time went on. Worrall had been around to observe the time when Paul's then girlfriend had made that poster billing 'Paul Kelly and The High Rise Bombers'. Now it happened again. Suddenly The Dots became Paul Kelly and The Dots.

'I was furious. Ropeable. He didn't ask any of us.'

Gadsby would also struggle with the band as he had desires to be a songwriter. His idea of a band was one where everyone had input into the songs. But he would soon find out that this notion wasn't going to fly in Dotsville.

'Paul's quite intransigent on certain things. He knows what he wants and if you go along with that you're okay. But if you don't, then see you later.'

Gadsby wanted to stay with The Dots, and he did for almost two years, but the songwriting thing was important to him. 'Everybody's energy contributes to the thing even if there's no formal acknowledgement of that. After a while it became clear that Paul didn't want to sing anyone else's songs. That's when I said, "See you later."'

He also had another reason for leaving: 'The smack thing got to me a bit too.' Along with other Dots members, he believes Paul dug the mystique associated with drug use, and was actively cultivating that appearance – even if sometimes the drugs were clearly controlling him.

'Having a certain mystique is probably essential for anyone who wants success. But the mystique around the heroin scene really got to me. They all seemed to think they were Rimbaud and part of some exclusive club. They'd go off to another room and act superior to us drinkers.'

As The Dots evolved and took shape, Paul found himself in a business relationship with Ron Brown, a Melbourne figure whose principal work was making music video clips along with some corporate and advertising projects.

Brown was running around in a sea of creative people that included manager Nathan Brenner and musicians Martin Armiger, Joe Camilleri and Chris Worrall.

Into that milieu came Paul, who clearly sensed that Brown had something going on that could be useful to him.

'Paul came to me and said, "You seem to know a lot about the music business,"' Brown says. 'I actually said that I wasn't really an expert on the music business – but I did know everybody who worked at the record companies. I made videos for and mixed socially with a lot of them.'

After a brief meeting, Paul and Brown formed a quasi-management relationship. Brown saw his role as looking after Paul and he stayed right out of any band politics. His gig was to further Paul's ambitions – not those of the people he played with.

'My relationship with Paul was really as his personal manager and business manager. I wasn't managing The Dots per se in terms of getting them gig bookings or anything like that. All of those things were happening with Frank Stivala and the people at Premier.

'I was actually just working with Paul – not the band. He'd come to me saying that he thought he needed management because he didn't know much about how it all worked and wasn't that keen to have fights with people and get directly into business negotiations.

'He was very strong-willed about how he sat with the rest of the band. He regarded them less as collaborators and more as sidemen.

'He seemed to have no trouble attracting people to play with him. Everyone in the scene wanted to play with him and recognised that he wrote great songs.'

Like several other people, Brown was less than taken by Paul's vocal prowess.

'I didn't think Paul was much of a singer to be honest. I told him that his strong suit was his songs. He wrote great songs and people loved his songs and they would go on to have an enormous life after him. That was my call.'

With that perspective, Brown figured the smart money was on Paul setting up a business structure to both promote and protect his songs. In other words, a publishing company. The plan was that it would be a joint venture between the two with a fifty-fifty split. Paul wrote the songs, Brown would do the business. The company was registered with the two as sole proprietors.

Paul suggested they call it Big Dwarf Music because Bob Dylan had two companies representing his songs – Big Sky Music and Dwarf Music. Paul decided to use an amalgam of the two names for his first publishing venture.

Paul and all the songwriting members of The Dots were duly signed to Big Dwarf Music. And Brown did what all music publishers are supposed to do – nurture, record and promote the songs composed by his clients.

Paul, who was living at Punt Road with Hilary by then, explained to Brown that he wrote a lot of his songs on the guitar but he also wrote on a piano – but didn't own a piano. Brown had a piano at his place so Paul went over there and recorded demos with Brown, who had done sound-engineering training prior to becoming a film-maker.

According to Brown, they recorded twelve to fifteen original Paul Kelly songs. Included in these original demos are all the songs that would be included on Paul's debut album for Mushroom Records, plus some others such as 'Leaps and Bounds'.

For a time Paul and Brown had a good relationship. Paul contributed the creativity, and Brown put in the money and did the administrative business. The band was playing a lot. Premier were doing a good job on the booking front. Brown advised Paul whenever there was something that needed to be communicated with the band members. And Brown took the songs and played them to various people in the music industry, none of whom appeared too excited about what they heard. But Brown wasn't exactly on a fervent mission. He was going with the flow of things, which wasn't always Paul's way of doing things.

'I wasn't all that ambitious,' Brown says. 'I just thought everything would flow along organically but Paul was very ambitious as it turns out.'

'Ron was around and got interested and signed my publishing,' Paul says, 'and then maybe I got cold feet. I think I was happy to get out. Nothing against Ron Brown but I just started to feel that he wasn't the right guy.'

It was a woman by the name of Michelle Higgins who would play a large role in Paul taking his next career step and going to Mushroom Records. Higgins had worked at Festival Records in Adelaide where part of her job was looking after the Mushroom Records catalogue. After coming to the attention of Michael Gudinski – her exuberant, in-your-face, take-no-prisoners approach to music she loved almost matching Gudinski's – she moved to Melbourne to work for Mushroom in Easter 1978, sharing an office with Michael Roberts who managed Jo Jo Zep and The Falcons.

As Higgins recalls it, Roberts wasn't managing The Dots but he was helping out with their bookings and general business. He's thanked for his 'assistance' on the cover of The Dots' EP, a copy of which he passed on to Higgins.

The first release from Paul Kelly and The Dots was an independent seven-inch EP which came out late in 1979. Included was one studio recording – 'Recognition' – and three live songs – 'Lowdown', 'Faster Than Light (Our Love)' and 'I See Red'. It's now a much sought-after collector's item.

After listening to it she went to see Paul and The Dots at the Tiger Lounge and had a eureka moment of some magnitude.

'I was completely and utterly blown away. I'd grown up on Rodriguez, Leonard Cohen, Bob Dylan ... I didn't know it then but that was my natural bent in terms of songwriters.

'I thought to myself, *This guy is going to be bigger than Ben-Hur – and it's going to be* tomorrow. *It's going to happen like a meteor.*

'I went backstage and introduced myself and said I worked in an office with Michael Roberts and that I just wanted to say hello. It was Hilary I first met and she introduced me to Paul, and then we all became very friendly after that because I didn't live that far from them. I lived in Collingwood and they lived in Punt Road. And I just started hassling Michael [Gudinski] and Gary [Ashley, Mushroom's general manager] about him.'

Also doing a brief management stint with Paul around this period was John Lever, who says he was encouraged by Michelle Higgins to become the manager of Paul and The Dots.

'I did feel that Hilary might have had management aspirations at the time,' Lever says. 'I remember Paul was getting into some things he shouldn't have been getting into, and I was feeling that I didn't really need it in my life and that it was going to turn into a disaster. I think I might have advised him to get rid of the band and move to America and become a songwriter. I was thinking he could become the next Terry Britten and write songs for other people.'

Higgins has vivid recollections of Paul and his relationship with Hilary. 'They were a terrific couple. They were terribly in love – they really were. That Punt Road apartment was such a moment in time. It was so terribly cold in winter and you really could see the MCG from the windows. They were totally broke.'

There are moments – often little, unexpected moments – when life can change in a millisecond. Higgins recalls that it was a beautiful day in Melbourne and pretty much everyone except her was out of the Mushroom office when she picked up the phone.

On the line was a guy called Trevor Lucas who had been a member of seminal English folk bands Fotheringay and Fairport Convention, as well as at one time being married to legendary singer Sandy Denny.

Lucas, an Australian by birth, was back in Melbourne and also producing soundtracks for films. At the time he was working on one for *Hard Knocks*. He asked Higgins if Mushroom had anyone who could write a song. Higgins said that of course they did and to leave it with her.

'I got off the phone and thought that I really should ask Tim Finn but Split Enz were off on tour. I rang Greg Macainsh but he didn't answer and I couldn't find him – nobody had answering machines or mobile phones in those days of course. So then I rang Paul and he was at home and didn't have anywhere to go. He didn't have a car but that didn't matter because Trevor Lucas's office was just along Punt Road, next to a pub on a corner and I said to meet me there and we'd have a look at the movie.'

Higgins and Paul watched the movie, then she dropped him back at his home and went back to work at Mushroom.

Half an hour later the phone at Mushroom rang again. It was Paul. He said, 'I've written it.' Higgins asked what he'd written and he explained that he'd written the song for *Hard Knocks*. So then she had to confess to Gudinski and Ashley that she'd got this guy who wasn't even signed to the company to write the song.

'I told them I couldn't find anybody else to write a song for the *Hard Knocks* movie and that I'd taken Paul Kelly to the meeting and he'd already written a song and that we had to record it. It went from there.'

Prior to this Paul was on Gudinski's radar – but only just. Other people Gudinski respected had also been talking about Paul for a while but Gudinski wasn't convinced that it was something he needed to pursue.

Before Higgins, the main person in his ear about Paul was Mary Bainbridge, who would become his trusted personal assistant for many decades. Bainbridge had been enthusing about Paul since The High Rise Bombers days, having lived at one stage in the Hoddle Street house with Paul and the Spare Change guys.

'She denies this,' Gudinski says, 'but Mary had come out from England a few years earlier and was working with Frank Stivala and my recollection is that she was the first person to play me Paul Kelly. That's who I remember bringing him to my attention.'

Also instrumental in his early awareness of Paul was Joe Camilleri.

'Camilleri was a great A & R person [talent scout]. If he'd been available to work for me in A & R I would have employed him but he had his music career going on.'

But when it came to the post High Rise Bombers version of Paul it was Higgins who ran the fan club at Mushroom Records.

Gudinski told Higgins – and anyone else who cared to raise the subject with him – that he didn't think Paul could sing.

'To be honest, I knew he was a great writer … well, I knew he had the potential of being a great songwriter,' Gudinski says. 'But I thought he couldn't sing. Bob Dylan tries not to sing but he can when he wants to, and Paul Kelly has become a great singer.'

Higgins, on the other hand, loved Paul's voice right from the word go.

'I really thought Paul was going to be huge immediately. I never thought his voice was a problem.

'I can remember sitting in Michael's office – it was early one morning – and him saying to me, "He can't sing," and I said, "Of course he can sing" … And I said, "Anyway, don't worry about that, Michael – that doesn't preclude him from being an enormous artist, people hear songwriters."

'I also remember thinking very early on about the opportunities with FM radio. It hadn't started in Australia but we were moving in that direction. I'd travelled enough in England and America – I'd been to New York several times by then and to London – and I knew what FM radio was and I knew it was going to be less Top 40-ish and that there was going to be room for someone like Paul. I thought he'd be there on day one – I didn't think we'd have to wait another five or six years.'

Despite Higgins's persistence and enthusiasm, Michael Gudinski and Mushroom Records weren't totally convinced they wanted to commit to Paul Kelly and The Dots so some demos were put together to try to establish if the songs would work on record and ultimately get played on the radio.

Those early demos were produced by Martin Armiger. Despite the way Armiger and Paul had left The High Rise Bombers, the chasm between them was clearly not deep enough to stop them working together.

'He did know that I could arrange a bit and organise a bit.' Armiger laughed. 'He was aware of that – or maybe someone else in his band drew his attention to it.

'They had a day at Armstrong's – or AAV – and of course I knew the songs from being in the band,' Armiger said. 'So we just cleaned them up, did the best we could and produced six or eight songs in the day. Then Paul took that to Mushroom and got a deal.'

But before there was any deal with Mushroom there was the small matter of Paul's existing publishing contract. Consequently, soon after the deal was flagged, Ron Brown took a call not from Paul but from Chris Langman who informed him that Mushroom were very interested in Paul Kelly and The Dots and wanted to sign a recording deal. Langman wondered if he could come over and have a chat with Brown about it.

There was a knock on the door a little later and it was Langman and Paul. The basis of the chat was that they had to get out of the publishing arrangement with Brown as Michael Gudinski was very interested in making a record with Paul and the band – but he would only do that if he owned the publishing rights as well.

It was extremely common in those days for companies like Mushroom to want to control both the recording and publishing rights. Gudinski would argue that having both rights enabled him to spend more money promoting artists and, of course, he explained that it was much simpler to have it all under the one roof. This was not necessarily the case but in those days Gudinski was adamant. It was a deal-breaker. Recording and publishing together or no deal.

Langman and Paul explained to Brown that they'd told Gudinski they already had a publishing arrangement and that Gudinski had been pissed off and told them to 'get rid of it'.

Brown saw absolutely no reason to adhere to Gudinski's demand. The whole point of forming the publishing venture was to protect Paul's songs and he didn't see why the Mushroom owner needed to have both sets of rights. The way he saw it, Paul wasn't a total newcomer to the Melbourne music scene and Gudinski and his sidekicks had been given ample opportunity to check him out and offer a publishing deal earlier.

Brown was not impressed and in no mood to roll over and be Gudinski's patsy.

'I told Paul this was a very bad idea and to keep hold of his songs and that it was in his long-term interest if he did end up doing a deal with Gudinski – and if it wasn't Gudinski then there'd be other record companies because his stuff was that good.

'Paul was ambitious, impatient and drank Gudinski's Kool-Aid basically. He believed Michael would look after him and make him famous and all the rest of it. So basically the cards were stacked against me. I held out for a while – for some months in fact – and kept saying that it wasn't a good idea. During that time I had a number of heated discussions with Paul and various members of the band. All the band members were saying they had to sign the deal and do the recordings and that was the only way their career was going to advance. They needed that recording deal and they wouldn't get the recording deal without the publishing deal.'

In other words, Ron Brown was the bad guy. He was standing in the way of Paul and The Dots' seemingly inevitable ascent to superstardom.

With matters at an impasse, Gudinski called in another of his team: Jenny Keath, who was involved in the publishing side of Mushroom Records.

Keath called Brown and said she wanted to talk about the 'whole Paul Kelly situation'.

A meeting was arranged at Brown's place in Parkville. Keath turned up with Chris Langman and, in Brown's words, 'She just hammered me for the longest time.'

Brown recalls that he threw Keath and Langman out of his house, saying that he needed to speak to Paul while reiterating his position that this was a very bad idea for the songwriter and the reason they'd set up the publishing company in the first place.

Sitting down with Paul, he said, 'What do you *really* want to do about this?' Paul said that he wanted to give the publishing rights to Gudinski, get the recording deal sorted and get into the studio and start making records.

'It really got to a very melancholic moment. We'd been working together for over a year and Paul was almost in tears and almost begging me to do this, and at that point I realised that he wasn't really listening to me. Gudinski was in his ear and he was listening to him. I said to him, "Gudinski is in one ear and I'm in the other – and you're believing him and not believing me – or for some reason you're choosing not to believe me." And at one stage I thought, *Well, if that's how he feels about it, then fine, that's what we'll do.'*

A few days later Jenny Keath turned up with some paperwork which Brown signed. It transferred Paul's publishing to Mushroom. Brown gave his fifty per cent interest in Paul's songs back to the writer so that he could do whatever he wanted with them.

'It had become obvious that it was a lost cause so I signed over what I needed to and vowed I wouldn't talk to Paul again. I didn't want anything more to do with him. I felt completely betrayed by him and that it was a very nasty outcome given that he'd come to me and I'd put time and money into it.'

Despite that, Brown went on to be the producer for Paul's 'Billy Baxter' video, something that was easy to do without any direct contact with Paul.

'From Paul's end there's probably no hard feelings because he got his way.'

Chris Worrall also remembers the Mushroom Records deal with resentment, and negatively, but for other reasons. He says Paul had 'gone and signed his publishing to Mushroom without showing us what he'd signed. It was the same bullshit standard contract that they always pulled out. I actually rewrote The Dots' recording contract with Mushroom. Gudinski thought I'd taken it to a lawyer because I'd added a few things and put in contingencies and clauses. I told Michael that I'd signed these things before with Captain Matchbox and I knew how things worked.'

The original Dots contract was signed by Mushroom Records' General Manager Gary Ashley at a cake shop in St Kilda.

'It was my favourite cake shop,' Worrall says, 'and run by these nice old Jewish ladies who had great coffee and cakes so we did it there rather than go to a pub or somewhere else like the Mushroom boardroom like every other band.'

* * *

Come the beginning of 1980, with the band signed to Mushroom Records, they released their first single for that label – 'Seeing Is Believing'/'Angel In Me', which came out in May. 'Seeing is Believing' is credited as a Kelly/Langman co-composition and the two split the royalties equally.

The catchy, ska-influenced 'Billy Baxter' was released in late 1980 and became The Dots' only national Top 40 charting single in March of the following year.

Written again by Paul and Langman, it was the second Paul Kelly and The Dots single released. A few weeks after its release, Paul and the band performed it on *Countdown* in what was Paul's first performance on TV. The song reached number 38 on the Australian charts and was Paul's first serious chart entry. Despite that, he refuses to include it on any greatest hits or compilation albums and will not perform it. It's part of his past. The past he doesn't talk about.

The B-side of Billy Baxter was 'Hard Knocks', which was the title song from the film of the same name.

The subject of the song, Billy Baxter, had been a member of the Ghetto Blasters, Big Fans of Jesus, and The Hollow Men, as well as doing solo recordings under his own name. Baxter was also a presenter on Melbourne's 3RRR radio station and is a long-time member of the Coodabeens Footy Show on ABC's Radio National.

'Paul of course co-wrote the song with Chris Langman with whom I worked at Crawford Productions,' Baxter says. 'I got to know Paul well through Chris.

'I was fairly reckless, wild and passionate, like a hurled stick of dynamite I'm told. I've never thought the song was about me per se, but inspired by more of an essence of who I was.

'I was flattered and honoured, and it did provide opportunities which may have otherwise eluded me. There were resentments too of course. "What did this guy do to deserve a song?" sort of thing. That was especially from within Paul's clique.

'I first heard the recorded version on EON-FM in a traffic jam on Punt Road, not too far from that fabulous old house Paul and Hilary lived in. Funny.

'Paul has distanced himself from the song as he's grown as an artist, and rightly so.'

Maybe it's hindsight but Worrall claims even in the early days of The Dots he could see Paul's ferocious and single-minded determination, and a desire to usurp competitors after taking from them what knowledge he needed.

'I always thought Langman was the better songwriter. Not as prolific. But really smart.

'At that time I was listening to a lot of Television – as was Chris [Langman] – and I thought that if Chris and I teamed up we could deconstruct Paul's stuff and turn it into some really good things. And we did that with a few songs. We did Langman's song "Leaning On My Car", and there was another one that the two of them wrote together called "The Ballad of Good and Evil", which is lost to the world as far as I know.

'I was there the night we wrote "Billy Baxter". It was after a gig at The Kingston. We used to all go back to Chris Langman's place and play poker with a lot of the Crawfords people that Chris hung out with.'

While Paul was focused on the band and writing songs, Langman had a job directing film and television programs at Crawfords. A job that would provide the band with after-show poker buddies and a source of income as Paul and the band got a bit of work as extras on popular television shows of the time. But the job also caused friction in the ranks of The Dots when Langman couldn't get time off to travel interstate to do some gigs.

'We all buggered off in Paul Gadsby's beat-up old Holden to do some gigs in Sydney,' Worrall says. 'We were at the Coogee Bay Hotel when Langman called saying that he wasn't coming to Sydney. He couldn't get the time off work.'

'I was going to fly up and perform,' Langman says, 'but I missed the plane and they had to perform without me. Paul got really shitty with me, and I thought, *Fair enough*. I realised I couldn't do both Crawfords and the band. So they got someone else to play the Sydney shows and replaced me when they came back.'

'I immediately got hold of Chris Dyson,' Worrall says, 'I'm not sure how – and said, "Get your arse on a plane to Sydney and do it this afternoon." I told him the record company would pay for it. Premier Artists had all these gigs booked and we told them there was no way we were going out with just one guitar. We could have, but it would have been shit. It was as rough as shit as it was.

'I was really disappointed because I thought that without Langman we would be back to Paul's stuff. And I knew that meant that Paul was going to have the upper hand in how the songs were arranged – and I was right. I was just there in my role as the loyal lieutenant, which is what I always seemed to be.'

With Langman busy with Crawfords, guitarist, songwriter and singer Chris Dyson, who had played with The High Rise Bombers, became a member of The Dots. Right from the start Dyson felt something wasn't quite right about the financial affairs.

'Put simply, there were two sets of books. One said we were in the black and everything was fine. The other set showed ten grand in debt, mainly because it was all being syphoned off and bills weren't being paid.

'I was promised a certain amount of money because I'd left another band and I had two young kids ... it was discovered that it wasn't just me, but the people who owned the van, the PA, and the lights, who were all wanting their money.'

At this stage, Bysshe was still a quasi manager of the band.

'So basically,' Dyson says, 'Chris [Worrall] and I went around to Bysshe's place to work out the money but he wouldn't open the door. The upshot was that we were ten grand in debt so we had to call all the creditors and make a case for them keeping us on the road and working, otherwise they wouldn't get any of their money back. It worked out and we did eventually pay it all back.

'My take on Paul at the time was that he was pretty much oblivious to it all. It was a case of him going, "Okay, you guys deal with it."

'So between us, Chris and I were pretty much managing the band. We'd go to Premier, who booked our tours and then I had to ring and book all the other stuff – the hotels, the hire cars and do the gig by gig organisation for the roadies.'

Dyson believes that Paul and Bysshe had a particularly close bond, which was mainly if not totally based on heroin.

'They were drug buddies. When I got up to Sydney they were in one room and the rest of us were in a room down the other end of the hall.'

During his time with The High Rise Bombers, Dyson had been uncertain about Paul's drug use but now he could see things were a lot different.

'He was totally into it and totally into the myth of it, the whole Baudelaire thing. He was one of them.

'What was happening too was that he wasn't writing much, so the band started doing a couple of my songs and I think one of Chris's [Langman] and then that became an issue for Paul because he pretty much just wanted to do his own songs.

'My recollection of the time was that I was amazed at how little Paul knew of music. He was basically a folky into

Bob Dylan and then the Velvet Underground. He was more of a literature person really, so often when we were doing songs I would put something in … and if it didn't sound like what he'd heard before he'd sort of get a bit edgy. If I put in a little riff to counter something he'd go, "Do you mind not doing that?"'

* * *

After Langman's departure Lloyd would leave and so would Gadsby, the line-up transforming into Paul, Worrall, Dyson, drummer Tony Thornton and Alan Brooker.

Tony Thornton, who had started playing drums professionally at sixteen, was involved in a number of bands playing around Melbourne. One of his band mates lived in a share house with Jo Moore, who had sung with Paul in Adelaide. Jo invited Paul over for a jam with Thornton. It was just at the time John Lloyd, who had been playing drums for The Dots, had left to join Flowers (which evolved into Icehouse) and Paul needed a new drummer. Paul offered Thornton the gig. 'A few rehearsals later and I was playing at the Tiger Lounge in Richmond with Paul, Chris Dyson, Chris Worrall and Paul Gadsby. Paul Gadsby left soon after and I asked Alan Brooker to join.'

Bass player Brooker played in the band Clean Cut with Thornton, and had first encountered Paul in Adelaide. 'I'd heard of him and he came on and played but I really didn't think anything of it. I didn't realise his prolific talent and it took a few years with The Dots to realise that.

'Even when I joined the band it took some time to get to know him. He was quite introverted. Maybe a little bit of arrogance, but that's okay as you need that to be a frontman, but let's face it, a lot of the time he was just wasted.'

Brooker remembers Paul being relatively easy to work with. It was a time when he was honing his craft and The Dots members were all learning to be better players. Everyone worked hard on the music.

'Often Paul would just come in with two or three chords and the band would mould them into some really good songs. Other times he would have more of the song developed. I guess sometimes he expected some things that he didn't get – and other times he got things he didn't expect. It was sort of professional – but it was still all about Paul.'

* * *

When it came time to record Paul's first album, *Talk*, according to Worrall, the whole experience was, 'fraught with difficulty'.

'As soon as Paul signed his publishing and recording deal with Mushroom it meant that they owned anything that Paul recorded, but it didn't say that they had to put out a record,' Worrall says.

Mushroom originally asked Cameron Allan (who went on to make his name producing rock'n'roll albums and composing film soundtracks) to produce it.

But Mushroom didn't provide Allan with enough financial incentive to do it which led Dyson and, he says, Allan to believe that Mushroom never really intended Allan to produce.

'All the discussions were between Mushroom and Paul,' Dyson says, 'but I realised when they started the process that Mushroom just wanted Paul's songwriting. They didn't give a shit about the band.

'We drove to Sydney and did a gig, then drove to Newcastle, and then drove back to Sydney and we were totally stuffed. That's when we had to go in and do a demo with Cameron and we couldn't really get it together. And Cameron was upset because he said Mushroom wouldn't give him enough money. He said he needed at least ten grand more, and that what they were offering wasn't enough. I was in a bad mood and might have insulted him as well.

'But Cameron was right. Mushroom didn't really want him to do it so they didn't offer him enough money. They wanted to give Joe Camilleri a band to produce so that Joe could be like Nick Lowe at Stiff Records.'

Saxophonist Joe Camilleri was then fronting his band Jo Jo Zep and The Falcons and had been the first person to record a song written by Paul, 'Only the Lonely Heart', which appeared on Jo Jo Zep and The Falcons' 1979 album *Screaming Targets*.

'I first met Paul at a gig,' says Camilleri. 'I liked his band. I thought, *That's a good band, I like what's going on here.* He had a few good songs. They were raw. Those years were fuelled by booze and drugs – and some people were more under the influence than others.

'What I noticed more than anything in those days was Paul's ability to write a lot of songs – and really quickly. Your first fifty songs are really easy. Your next two hundred or three hundred become a little harder. I envied the way he wrote because I was struggling to do that.

'Paul and I became friends. We didn't share the same lifestyle. I was pretty well settled in my life. I was married. He was married too – or soon to get married. But I was settled. I'm one of ten kids. I'm a provider and I knew that I had an opportunity and I wasn't going to spend my money on dope. I was going to try and make something. So we didn't share the same values on that level. But we were friends. Comrades. We respected each other and valued each other's beings and on that level we enjoyed each other's company.

'Paul and I were able to talk about things. Not necessarily always songwriting. In fact there was never much talk about that, although occasionally we might discuss an idea to add to a song. We wrote a few songs together and I'd say, "I need a little something, I'm hitting the floor hard here, you've got to lift me up," and he would put something together or he would leave a note with a few ideas.

'He came around to my house many times. He was very thin then. I remember him wearing his girlfriend's trousers. We would share a beer together.'

Camilleri had already enjoyed a degree of success at Mushroom and Gudinski respected his taste in music. Camilleri recalls that he was asked by both Gudinski and Paul to produce the sessions for the album that would become *Talk*. There was virtually no budget for the recording. 'Fuck all' is how Camilleri recalls it.

Mushroom very much wanted Paul Kelly the songwriter at this stage. There was no real interest in him as a recording artist. And then there was Gudinski saying he didn't think Paul could sing. Hardly an auspicious start to your career with your first record label. The boss doesn't think you can sing but he'll let you make an album because he thinks you might develop into a great songwriter. A real confidence booster.

It was really a way for Mushroom to secure Paul's songwriting services – throw a bit of money at him and tell him he could also make an album.

'We're recording in a rehearsal room with the AAV van,' Camilleri says. 'It's the middle of winter and I've got the flu. It was really bad. We were all trying to get the work done but we all had other things going on. All of us were playing gigs and then coming in and trying to make a record. Paul and the band would play a gig somewhere and then *after* that come to the studio to record.

'It was *really* cold. I remember Chris Dyson and Chris Worrall being pretty good, but the environment was the hardest thing. It was hostile. It was as punkish as could be, as hardcore as you could imagine.'

Everyone was out of their depth. And that was before you factored in the environment. Camilleri wasn't exactly an experienced producer then and didn't really know his way around a studio, let alone how to communicate what he wanted to an engineer. But wherever Camilleri was in terms of studio abilities he was noticeably ahead of Paul and his band mates. So it was the ever so slightly experienced leading the virtually inexperienced. Not exactly a dream scenario.

The end result was, in Camilleri's opinion, 'quite good under the circumstances – and it did yield Paul's first hit record even though he chooses not to include it on any retrospective releases.

'In many ways, as hostile as the environment was, we achieved what was required for a record company that didn't want to get too involved in it.

'I think they eventually mixed it at AAV. They gave us a few extra days in there after I said I had the flu and just couldn't do it anymore where we were. It was unbearable. It felt like they were wasting all these songs and all this energy.'

For both Dyson and Worrall the recording session was certainly memorable.

'He [Camilleri] really wanted to cut it as a producer,' Worrall says, 'and he really thought this was a chance for him – and it was.

'But unlike Martin [Armiger] who just chucks everything in, Joe took more of a layer-cake tradesman approach so everything was done in bits and pieces.

'He only did a couple of the AAV sessions. When it came time to make the actual record, Mushroom didn't want to pay for studio time so we ended up having to use a mobile recording unit operating in a warehouse in South Melbourne – a concrete box that wasn't even a studio. I mean, it didn't sound too bad. Joe was painstakingly putting it together, pretty much like he had with the Falcons, but I think we needed a much looser sound.'

'I'm not sure he had even seen us play live,' Dyson says, 'and I'm sure he wanted us to play and sound like the Falcons. They stuck us in a garage in South Melbourne in the middle of winter with one blow heater in a mobile recording thing.

'Joe was getting so pissed off that one day we turned up and all our amps were moved and he's got all the Falcons equipment there. We thought he was going to get the Falcons to do the record, but for some reason Joe thought that if we used the Falcons' equipment we'd sound like the Falcons.

'Then we did some stuff in Sydney and I did some overdubs and Joe came and wiped them all and said it was shit. Didn't ask or anything. Just said it was dreadful. When I found out he'd erased it I wanted to know why.

'The whole album got cobbled together. Maybe the "Hard Knocks" stuff sounded the closest to what we were like live.'

Dyson believes that when the first Dots album was recorded Paul was way out of his depth and didn't yet have a fix on how to work in the studio. He goes so far as to suggest that musically Paul was fairly naive – but masked it with a determination and single-mindedness.

'Paul wasn't musical in that way. You'd say to him that the band was playing well and he wouldn't say anything and then you'd hear him do an interview and he'd say, "The band's playing really well at the moment."'

One fascinating aspect of the *Talk* album is that Dyson not only gets a song on it – the final track, 'Please Send Me', but he also gets to sing it.

This would barely warrant comment if it was not for Paul's avowed desire to only sing his own songs and really not entertain anyone else in the ranks of The Dots writing songs.

'I think Paul had a bit of a dry spell,' Dyson says, 'but I don't know for sure. Maybe there was just enough people in the band saying to him that we should put that song on the album.

'I never pushed my songs but he wasn't coming up with the stuff so I said that I had a few and maybe we could try them. I knew he didn't want to do other people's songs. He'd told me that when I was with the Bombers. He'd asked me if I wanted to write songs in a way that said that he didn't want me to.'

Chris Langman has no explanation why a song penned by Chris Dyson appears on the album but counters the suggestion that Paul had suffered a heroin-precipitated writing drought. 'He had heaps of songs, at least twenty or thirty, including "Leaps and Bounds",' Langman says.

Producer Joe Camilleri was certainly very aware of Paul's increasing drug usage but isn't sure it affected his songwriting. 'I think he could have fallen over any day of the week. He was hitting the canvas a lot. I got a feeling that somewhere down the track … you hear this a lot … people pick themselves up and suddenly those missing ten years are full of songs. You don't lose all that and Paul was still his prolific songwriting self, too.'

In drummer Tony Thornton's opinion, Chris Dyson's song is one of the best songs on *Talk*. Like Langman, he doesn't agree with any suggestion that Paul didn't have enough songs at that stage, but that it was more a power play by Dyson that caused the song to be included.

'I think Chris timed it perfectly. We'd got that far into the album and I think Chris told him that if the song wasn't included he could jam it. I think there was a lot of behind-the-scenes stuff going on and Paul relented.'

From Thornton's perspective *Talk* was a botched effort that could have been a much better album if it weren't for meddling by Paul. Thornton claims that after the sessions with Camilleri the drum beds they did with him were replaced by the demo versions they did with Armiger as that was what Paul preferred. He liked the sound of imperfections, but Thornton says he wasn't listening to imperfections. It was just a bad take but Paul decided to use it anyway.

'I was mortified. Absolutely beside myself. It seemed to me that he wanted to be in control. But in the early days he didn't have the power to be totally in control. He still had record companies saying, "We want a hit, we want a hit" – so I think he was thumbing his nose at that a bit. He didn't like that slickness. "Billy Baxter" he hated.'

After the sessions with Camilleri were finished, Mushroom said that they wanted to include some of the Armiger-produced demos on the album so 'Promise Not to Tell', 'Lowdown' and 'Want You Back' were included as the first three songs. The 'Hard Knocks' song with Trevor Lucas was also included and the album *Talk* was pieced together.

Talk was released in March 1981 and sold respectably, reaching the lower echelons of the Top 50 album chart. Paul was making headway. Maybe not as quickly as he'd have liked but there was an upward trajectory. It felt like another start.

Top: Paul's parents, Josephine, the daughter of an Italian opera singer and a symphony orchestra conductor; and John, a lawyer who died too young. Paul Kelly Collection

Middle: The Kelly family sings. *Sitting from left to right*: Martin (with guitar), Tony, Mary Jo with Whisky the dog, Sheila (with guitar) and John. *Standing from left to right*: David and Paul. Missing from this photo is Anne, who is pictured *below left* playing cricket with younger brother Paul. Paul Kelly Collection

Below: Paul practising guitar outside a share house in Adelaide. Courtesy Tom and Ian Stehlik

Top left: Paul Kelly and
Stuart Coupe circa 1987
after a cricket victory.
Courtesy Ian Greene Photography

Top right: A keen fan of
cricket and AFL, Paul
didn't just watch from the
sidelines; here he strides
to the crease.
Courtesy Wendy McDougall

Middle: The same day,
celebrating the band,
crew and management
cricket team win.
Courtesy Ian Greene Photography

Left: Paul Kelly and Billy
Baxter together
on the football field.
The goal umpire is
Greg Champion.
Paul Kelly Collection

Top left: Paul at the beach in Adelaide with Tom Stehlik.
Photo by Ian Stehlik

Top right: The legendary Martin Armiger next to Paul.
Paul Kelly Collection

Middle: Sunday afternoon in Carlton, The High Rise Bombers playing in the beer garden of Café Paradiso.
Courtesy Sally Barton

Left: The Paul Kelly Band at Bondi Beach. Michael Barclay, Alan Brooker, Maurice Frawley, Steve Connolly and Paul.
Courtesy Michael Barclay

Paul Kelly
THIS SUNDAY 14

Paul Kelly and the Messengers in the

I SPIT ON YOUR GRAFIX 87 DM

THE DOTS

PAUL KELLY IN

The COLOURED GIRLS

featuring:
. Paul Kelly . Spencer Jones .
+ Billy Pommer (Johnnys).
. Pedro Farfissa + Noel Funicello (Wooloomooloosers).

HOPETOUN   WED. 31ST OCT.
HOTEL   P.S. Don't Forget!
MELBOURNE CUP DAY TUES 6TH M
LOVE RODEO
1P.M. – 5P.M.

UNCLE TOB

UNCLE TOBYS   PAUL KELLY

It is a truth universally acknowledged that when not playing, practising or writing songs, a band in search of a career has to have photos taken. *Above*: The Paul Kelly band onstage. *Below*: Alan Brooker, Tony Thornton, Chris Dyson, Paul and Chris Worrall. Courtesy Greg Noakes Photography

Paul Kelly working the phone. Courtesy Ian Greene Photography

Re-signing with Mushroom Records. *From left to right*: Paul, managers Stuart Coupe and Yanni Stumbles, and Michael Gudinski. Courtesy Ian Greene Photography

Above: Paul Kelly in action onstage. Courtesy Ian Greene Photography

Below: Paul at the city limits of Truth or Consequences in New Mexico during an American tour in the late 1980s. Courtesy Martin Kantor/Kylie Greer

For other band members, however, things were coming to an end with the band. Eventually Worrall left The Dots. He'd finally reached his limits.

'I left because of bad management and crappy deals with the record company – and I was just fed up. I was right that we were at least five or six years away from anything. Paul eventually got there but it did take him a long time.

'And Paul was becoming more and more bossy. We were doing all these shit gigs in beer barns out at places like Mount Waverley that everyone hated doing.

'The only places we got on all right was the Tiger [Lounge] and Martinis but you can't live on that. We needed the beer barns to make it work and to make a living, and I just got to the point where I couldn't see it working.

'The last straw was when we were playing this shitty little pub in Fitzroy and the half-a-dozen people who were there were clapping and wanting more. I was already tired and I said, "Fuck it. I'm not going back onstage," and Paul said, "Yes, you will," and he told me to do what I was told – ten minutes later I was in a taxi heading back to Malvern and never went back.'

Chris Dyson was the next to go, leaving the band soon after Paul teamed up with a new manager, Barrie Earl.

Michelle Higgins recalls that after Paul signed the Mushroom contract, Earl appeared on the scene as manager using the business name Mouth Piece Management.

'Philip Jacobsen and Michael [Gudinski] brought Barrie in. Barrie was right on The Boys Next Door in their early days. He'd done a lot of stuff. He'd started Suicide Records with Michael. It wasn't illogical to think that Barrie could do it. And it wasn't all Barrie's fault that it didn't happen. I liked Barrie. He was a pain in the neck but he'd done terrific work with James Freud.'

The installation of a new manager was not discussed with the other Dots. It was another early instance of Paul – and Paul alone – calling the shots. If the other band members had any lingering doubts as to their standing in the grand scheme of things with Paul then this was a further reminder that they were allocated to the back-row seats and Paul was in charge.

'It was just announced to us that Barrie was the manager,' Dyson says. 'Barrie Earl came in and started on with all this bullshit about needing good-looking players. Barrie wasn't really up for the job ... And then I got the ultimatum. It was the same thing that was said to Martin [Armiger] but I got it from Barrie and not Paul. He told me that they were happy for me to stay in the band but that they were only doing Paul's songs.

'And there was this other thing that was spelt out too, and that was that we were to do the songs the way Paul wanted them done. It was made very obvious that this was the way it was going to be.

'I didn't mind not doing my songs, but when a guy comes in with three chords and just strums ... you can't just go with that. And you've got to be careful with clichés. They do become problematic. When you're playing five or six nights a week you don't want someone telling you to do the same solo in the same place in the same song night after night. And having to remember to do that. That's just not the way I play.'

Looking back on the time, Dyson wonders if Paul felt threatened by him because he could write songs and play guitar pretty damn well. Was there the threat of a palace coup within the ranks of The Dots?

'From Paul's perspective, I think he might have thought that I was trying to take over the band. He has this thing about controlling everything.'

As far as Dyson could see, Paul had little knowledge or insight into the machinations of his band. Maybe he didn't even care. Everyone was replaceable. Except him.

'I honestly don't think Paul had any inkling of what we went through. I mean Chris [Worrall] just walked offstage and never spoke to Paul again as far as I know. We were constantly cleaning up the mess.'

When Chris Worrall exited the line-up, Dyson played one more gig with The Dots at the Sentimental Bloke in Bulleen on a bill with the Models. He enjoyed being the only guitarist in the band.

Despite his departure, Dyson's relationship with Paul didn't sour.

'I wasn't really sacked. I was a bit pissed off. Paul's a friend of mine. He's been good to me since and given me work – but I don't think he'd really recall much of that time given the state he was in.'

But again, despite the state he was in, Paul still seemed to have his head focused on the main game. He knew what he wanted, even if his lifestyle was a constant threat to derailing this.

'Paul was always totally focused on himself and his own career. He had this philosophy of being true to yourself, which basically meant ignoring everyone else.

'Eventually he got there even though he had some pretty dark days on the way.'

CHAPTER 7

MANILA

'It's a *bad* place.'
Chris Thompson

IN LATE 1980, GUITARISTS TIM BROSNAN AND MICHAEL Holmes replaced Dyson and Worrall in The Dots' line-up.

The two guitarists had been playing together in a band named The Squeaky Girls and when that folded Paul appeared on the scene and said that he had two guitar spots available in his band. Both passed the audition and became Dots.

Holmes remembers that, when he joined, The Dots were still out playing to promote *Talk*.

'I can place it because I was playing that fucking horrible song about wanting to be like Billy Baxter. One night the crowd kept calling out for it and we played it three times in a row. But after that we never played it again. That was the last time.

'I'd done that song on television, on *The Don Lane Show* with Paul – and Billy Baxter came on. In the rehearsal I remember they had Billy do all these jokes and when it went to air, Don knew all the punchlines but Bert [Newton] fucked up every line and made Billy seem like an idiot.'

Although Holmes fancied his skills as a burgeoning songwriter, he knew better than to try to push that within the ranks of The Dots. That was Paul's turf and it wasn't wise to tread on it.

'I knew right from the start not to try and write. I dabble in writing songs. I wrote the music to "Don't Go to Sydney" by The Zimmermen and I write in the band I'm in now. But I knew then not to try. It was the same when I was in a band with Eric Gradman. He wouldn't have done a song I wrote. Singers are like that.'

In those days The Dots were touring a lot, playing consistently in Melbourne, Sydney, Brisbane, Adelaide and Tasmania – and all spots in between where the booking agent could find a venue to take them.

'We were like a band of brothers,' Holmes says. 'Sure, we'd have a few differences, especially when you're locked in the van for all those hours, but I thought we all got on well. Paul came across as part of the band even though he was the frontman, the singer and the songwriter – and it was his record deal.'

At their peak Holmes recalls they were doing up to nine gigs a week. The Dots members were on a two hundred dollar a week retainer whether they played or not. A common week would involve a show every night from Sunday through till Thursday, and then two shows on each of Friday and Saturday night. Sometimes there were also lunchtime or afternoon gigs at universities.

'At that time you had to. You're hiring a PA, a truck, lights and two roadies – and all that has to be paid before you get a cent. Then there're five of you in the band so there's another thousand dollars a week so you had to be out there working constantly to cover everything – plus putting money away for when you're not on the road. Every band I was in from that time was doing that.'

In charge of everything was Barrie Earl who Holmes remembers as being an 'old school' manager, part of the Gudinski/Stivala camp where they looked after each other.

Despite some of the problems that others had with Earl, from Holmes' perspective he did what he was meant to do.

'We needed him because he was connected and he would fight for the best gigs for us.'

And also from Holmes' perspective the relationship between Paul and Earl was largely a good one. That was probably because Earl was getting things happening for Paul, dealing with Mushroom and keeping The Dots on the road.

'You smell a rat but you know you need that rat to get where you're going.

'When I joined, Paul and The Dots were Barrie's only band. I was with them for two years so maybe after the first year he took over the management of The Runners as well. We got a bit annoyed as we thought he was going to start giving them some of the best gigs but he managed to look after both bands pretty well.'

During this seemingly endless touring, Paul was growing in confidence. He was for the most part delivering fine, passionate live performances and had a sense that things were on the way up.

The Punt Road flat where Paul and Hilary Brown were living was also changing. It was pretty rundown and decorated with various bits and pieces, including a couple of Holmes' paintings.

'He had this ratty place,' Holmes says. 'It was actually a beautiful old apartment with high ceilings, big windows, one large room that was a dining room and kitchen with a tiny kitchen.

'But it was pretty grotty.'

Hilary was pregnant and, according to Holmes, when she went into hospital to have the baby – a boy, Declan – the 'whole band hit the joint. We put all the furniture away, got the rollers and painted the whole place white and made it look great for when she came home.'

Brosnan was part of the crew too. 'I was there – but I didn't do much painting. We'd finished a gig at about three am the night before and the guys started painting at ten am the next morning. I was just blitzed. But Paul was really touched. He wasn't often open with his emotions to us.'

There was only one black spot in this period.

Paul Kelly and The Dots had scored the national tour with Dire Straits from late March into April 1981.

On the face of it, it was a coup to tour with Dire Straits, but due to the costs of the planes and accommodation, The Dots had to play extra gigs every night in each city after they'd played the Dire Straits show.

'We hardly saw Dire Straits,' Holmes says. 'We saw a couple of gigs but most nights we'd be loading the stage gear out straight after we finished and into the van and head off to do another gig.

'Barrie wanted us to become friends with Dire Straits so we stayed at all the same hotels as they did, which cost us much more money than we had. We did become mates with the band – but I think we saw [Mark] Knopfler once.

'I remember that we were given a slab of beer as our rider. With five guys and a two-man crew we would drink that in a second.

'So after we'd do our set we'd go backstage and wait until Dire Straits went on and then we'd nip into their band room where they had a bathtub full of Heineken.

'About five nights into the tour Mark Knopfler came into our room and asked how it was going and if we were getting everything we needed. We mentioned that we were only getting one slab of beer a night and that two would be nice so after that we got two every night – but we still drank their Heinekens.'

The tour was going well until an April night at the Regent Theatre in Sydney when The Dots were due onstage but Paul was nowhere to be found. Holmes remembers it vividly.

'The worst thing was that the whole band was backstage, tuned up, guitars ready. We're thinking, *He might just come, he might just come*, and then we hear the voice over the PA saying, "Due to unforeseen circumstances Paul Kelly will not be performing tonight." The whole crowd goes, "Yyyyaaaaayyyyyyy" – it's not what you want to hear.'

Holmes is uncertain what happened the night Paul didn't make the show in Sydney and thinks they were lucky they weren't kicked off the tour. 'Rumour has it he OD'd at a hooker's flat.'

Alan Brooker also has his take on Paul missing the show.

'We did five shows in Sydney with them but we were meant to do six. He just went out and got on the gear. Barrie Earl – our manager then – found him late that night or maybe it was the next morning. Paul answered the door and said, "I'll just get my guitar," because he thought Barrie was picking him up to go to the gig.

'The presumption was that he went somewhere, had a little taste, then had a nap as you do, and then woke up and had some more. And time goes by so he missed the whole show.

'I remember Paul being a bit sheepish about it, as anyone

would be. That shit happens if you take drugs. He didn't miss any shows after that.'

Guitarist Tim Brosnan has a better idea about what happened. 'He fell asleep in the bath. He was with this stripper who hung around bands. David Dawson, the journalist, wrote a story where he said Paul was with a notorious woman. Hilary saw it and was straight on the plane to Sydney.'

Paul himself explains it simply: 'I missed a show on the Dire Straits tour after being up all night with a woman taking speed. I fell asleep at her place sometime during the day and completely missed the show. I never felt so bad as when I woke up and realised what had happened.'

'It's lucky that he didn't fucking OD and die,' Holmes says. 'We were more worried about that than the tour. He got messy with drugs. But he was for the most part discreet about it. He was good at hiding it.'

According to Brosnan, Paul's heroin use in the early 1980s was significant – particularly as he appeared to have a dangerously low tolerance for the drug, at a time when its potency was high. Brosnan was certainly around on a number of occasions when Paul overdosed.

'He wasn't afraid of the needle. I saw him drop a couple of times and we had to bring him back. The OD potential was pretty high ... But everyone was into it back then.

'There was a lot more smack around and it was stronger in those days. We would use together. Not all that often but from time to time. I think Paul used less than we did.

'He had writer's block at the time and the earth was moving under his feet a bit. He wasn't getting any support from Mushroom.'

This was a rather seedy environment and typical of the time.

'Sometimes they had dope around, other times they went out and scored,' Brosnan continues. Declan [Cooney], Paul's close friend and later sound mixer, was around and had done chemist busts and was a pretty committed dope user. But it wasn't an everyday priority for any of us. I used it for a bit of down time. We were working a *real* lot because Barrie [Earl] needed to keep his end of the deal up. He was richer than any of us but we were getting good money – two hundred dollars a week was a fair bit of cash, and with the dole on top. We didn't save anything of course. We spent it all on restaurants and cabs and food.'

Alan Brooker noticed the drug-taking as well. 'In those days I would say he [Paul] was using a lot – and hiding it. I was a bit naive and it took a month or two before I even realised what was going on. It was just one of those things. People would come up and say, "Oh God, he's just about falling asleep onstage or nodding off." He was using consistently, but in periods. Certainly in the Tim Brosnan days as Timmy was a big user too, and then Declan [Cooney] came on board and learnt to do sound so you had an outfit of junkies. The Dots had a bad name as pretty much all of us ended up using at one stage or another. I dabbled too.

'Smack was everywhere, and lots of guys in bands with wholesome images were using, so image is really what it's all about, and image can be a lie – but in Paul's case it wasn't.'

Paul always had the reputation as a heroin user, and it was a hard one to shake, if, in fact, at this stage he was even interested in doing that.

'Paul had gone with Hilary to a Mushroom Records do,' Brosnan says, 'and he was out of it, so from then on he was a junkie as far as all those people were concerned. But he probably wouldn't have gone out of his way to dispel that image.'

Sometimes it just all got out of control. Such as a night in Geelong at the Eureka Hotel when the brain surgeon in charge of disseminating the band's drugs of choice got it all very wrong.

Holmes was one of the outsiders in the band as heroin wasn't a drug for him. 'Each to their own. It didn't worry me. Some nights were pretty ragged like the one at the Eureka where the band accidentally mixed up the drugs. Instead of the speed they usually did before the gig they took the heroin which was for afterwards. I just laughed and had another beer – I'd seen it all.'

Brosnan says of the Geelong night, 'I remember Paul saying, "This stuff is pretty mild for speed," and then we realised it was smack. Poor old Alan Brooker had to sit on a chair to play his guitar and was constantly getting up and going to a corner to vomit. The place was packed.

'We drove back to Melbourne at about twenty miles an hour because Paul was so stoned. I was terrified a cop car was going to stop us and we were all going to get busted.

'We took a lot of risks in those days. Especially when we were in Sydney, staying at the Bernly next door to the fucking Manzil Room. But after a while the fun went out of it because it became such a hard grind.'

Many of the band agree that Melbourne was bad for drugs, but Sydney was much worse. When they were away from home there were no checks and balances except turn up and play the gig. Sydney in the late seventies and early eighties was a city on fire – with all the good and bad aspects. of such a time and place.

'Sydney was shocking,' Thornton says. 'We had a sound engineer who I shared a room with. One night I walked into the bathroom and he'd nodded off – standing up – with the pick still stuck in his arm.'

Brooker, like a couple of other band members, has cloudy memories of the nights that The Dots did at the Manzil Room in Sydney's Kings Cross. 'I used to love playing the Manzil Room. We'd play Clash covers, "Breakin' in My Heart" by Tom Verlaine and every so often we'd jam on some Lou Reed song that wasn't part of the set.'

I was in the audience one night when the artist Brett Whiteley walked into the venue and stood close to the stage. Paul walked offstage, went over to Whiteley, knelt in front of him and played 'Alive and Well' before getting to his feet and walking back onstage to continue the set.

It wasn't just heroin and the other drugs that were at the centre of the early 1980s good times. There was also the sex.

'To get to the nitty gritty,' Brosnan says, 'Paul and I were pretty sexual guys. We had some wild parties and got up to some pretty serious mischief. I can't remember half the stuff I did.

'He was a classic bad boy in those days — but he wasn't cruel or an arsehole to anyone.

'Paul would always get the girl. He wasn't obvious about it. I just noticed that at the end of the night he was going off with the best-looking girl.'

Brosnan insists that Paul's drug of choice at the time was speed, much more than heroin, and that he'd often stay up for days on end, like when he missed the Dire Straits show.

Drummer Tony Thornton felt at odds with the core of The Dots because of the heroin use and also because he felt they viewed him as intellectually inferior.

'I tried heroin a couple of times and I didn't like it. I was a weed smoker and I used to drink excessively because, believe it or not, way back then I was extremely insecure socially and all of a sudden I'm playing with all these people who I considered very intelligent. University people. I mean,

I left school at fifteen. And here I am hanging around with this mob because of my drumming skills. No other reason. So I used to drink and hide in the corner and that affected a lot of things. It was scary for me. It was the intelligentsia of Melbourne and you met them en masse at every gig. You'd go to a party at Paul's after a gig and the queue of intellectuals was pretty deep.

'I remember I was playing a gig at Inflation with a band called The Real McCoys and Paul turned up and sang a couple of tunes – a couple of Elvis songs. After the gig we were all sitting at a table. Paul was with someone and I heard them lean over to him and say, "The one across the table – the light's on but nobody's home." That sort of thing happened all the time. If you couldn't hold a strong intellectual conversation you weren't there. Hence the drinking. There's a lot of things that I'm disappointed in from that period because of the drinking. I'm sure Paul would have been disappointed also but maybe with the drugs he didn't notice.'

At one stage Thornton found himself seeing the angry side of Paul – once again over the subject of heroin.

'One day we were doing a gig supporting Mike Rudd and The Heaters at the Sandringham. I got to the gig to do the sound check and Paul was absolutely furious. If looks could kill I'd have been dead on the spot. I couldn't for the life of me work out what was going on. But what had happened was that someone I knew who was living in a share house with Mary Jo Kelly [Paul's sister] had quite flippantly or naively mentioned to her that her brother was using smack. He'd been trying to keep it a secret and apparently it was my fault because I'd told someone who'd told someone who'd told someone. The truth of the matter is that I hadn't but that unleashed some stuff and it took a long time to get over that. I just couldn't convince him that I had nothing to do with it.'

* * *

A band can be like a family, the closeness bringing camaraderie and friendships, but also inevitably some tensions.

As things progressed, many of The Dots were getting pretty upset about the financial state of the band.

'I was sick of getting ripped off,' Thornton says. 'I asked Barrie Earl to look at the books. There were things like "miscellaneous − $10,000" − what's this? Meanwhile I'm working as a doorman at Bananas, on the dole and he's living in a mansion in East Malvern and dining out every night.'

Although Earl may have been living the high life, things weren't exactly that bad for the band at that time. The Dots were working constantly and the band members were being paid two hundred dollars a week which was fairly reasonable for the time.

Paul and Barrie Earl travelled to Asia early in 1981 on what could best be described as a fact-finding mission. Sherbet had done an Asian tour and there had long been discussions in the music industry about how to establish a live touring circuit in Asia.

So Earl and Paul headed off for a look-see. Other less charitable observations about their reasons for the trip suggest that Earl was also particularly keen on finding an Asian bride.

While there, they found a stash of unbelievably cheap Gibson and Fender guitars. Earl and Paul couldn't believe their luck. They decided to take as many as the guy offering them could supply and then sell them to instrument shops and fellow musicians for a tidy profit. They planned to offer each of the guitar players in The Dots a free one before they off-loaded the remainder. There was even a Fender Precision bass for Alan Brooker. The only thing missing was a new kit for Thornton.

When they returned, Earl called a band meeting at his place. He and Paul were planning to have a dinner and chat about the future. Everyone would be in a great mood because they'd have a new Gibson or Fender guitar as a gift from the manager and singer.

The band arrived to find the passageway lined with these guitars. It was Thornton – a drummer – who started laughing first.

'I was the one who first pointed it out. We've gone to Barrie's for dinner and they've lined these Fenders up and down the passageway. I've walked through the door and gone, "Wow, these are great," but as soon as I picked one up I knew they were bodgy. I nearly cut my finger off on a fret board. I said, "These aren't real," and they said, "What do you mean?" Paul and Barrie didn't have a clue. When the drummer points out that you bought bad guitars you know that something is up.'

Thornton speculates that the guitars were taken to a music shop and sold for twenty dollars each – sort of what they were worth.

While in Manila, Earl and Paul had found a studio, which they figured was not only cheap but exactly what they wanted. They could go to a foreign country and record an album for a fraction of what they would spend in Melbourne.

Gudinski didn't like the idea one little bit, despite the suggestion that he might have secretly welcomed the potential financial savings.

'I wasn't comfortable with it at all. I didn't like the idea of him going there – and not just for the obvious reasons.

Barrie had a passion for Paul Kelly. He was also the person who started Suicide Records. I thought it was a strange combination. And at the time, the idea of an artist going to fucking Manila to make an album … that was just insane. But as it turns out, it was really just a statement!'

Paul and Earl wanted Tony Cohen – then the emerging and in-demand hipster engineer in Melbourne – to go with them but Cohen didn't want to leave the country so they approached another young engineer and Cohen's friend, Chris Thompson.

Paul, the band and Thompson hammered out demo sessions of all the songs considered for the album quickly at Richmond Recorders, an Eastlake design style studio that was very popular, particularly in California, in the late 1970s.

'The Eagles and all those sorts of bands would record in these quite dead environments with this standard-shape designed control room and recording space,' explains Thompson. 'There were dozens of these studios built all over the world – all virtually identical.'

According to Thompson the demos were sent to Gudinski who couldn't hear any potential singles in what was submitted. That in itself is fascinating given that one of Paul's now most anthemic songs – 'Leaps and Bounds' – was already written at this time.

Still, Gudinski agreed to commit financially to the recording of a second album. Thompson thinks the budget was around twenty thousand dollars – not a lot of money by the standards of the day. And small enough to convince Earl and Paul that they could stretch it a lot further by recording in Manila.

In Earl's mind the way to go was head to Manila, hire a studio for a quarter of the price of what it cost in Australia and, as Thompson put it, 'give the boys a holiday in an exotic location where there're lots of bar girls'. Thompson pauses. 'It's a *bad* place.'

Towards the end of 1981 Paul and his band travelled to the Philippines to record. In the entourage were Earl, Paul, wife Hilary, the very young Declan, Brosnan, his partner Katie, Michael Holmes, Alan Brooker, Tony Thornton, Chris Thompson and lighting guy Scotty Duhig, who was taken along as a thank you for his hard work.

Mission Manila was underway.

Expectations were high. They were all young, in many cases leaving Australia for the first time.

Earl got the studio and airfares paid for from the budget and what Thompson describes as 'a vast amount for entertainment expenses' left over.

The studio they were going to use looked impressive. Thompson had seen a brochure and thought it was up to par.

What could possibly go wrong?

Lots.

'So we get there and we look at this studio they've got for us – and it turns out that it's a jingle studio in a place called Greenhills,' Thompson recalls. 'It's out in the suburbs and hasn't even got a drum booth or any good microphones. Sure, it's got a tape recorder and a console. That's good but there's nothing else there that you'd need to make an album.'

So much for the brochure. Thompson wasn't at all happy.

'I told them straight away that we couldn't record there and Earl said, "Well you find us another studio then – we've fucked up but if you think you know better then do something about it." So I literally got the Yellow Pages and looked up recording studios.'

Thompson found a studio in a compound which was owned by Jose Mari Gonzalez, a Filipino movie star from the 1950s who had made a fortune and owned a huge estate with a recording studio.

And guess what? Gonzalez's studio was an Eastlake design. It was identical to Richmond Recorders in Melbourne. Only in the middle of a hundred-acre estate in Manila.

Thompson discussed recording there with Gonzalez who – not surprisingly – was delighted about the prospect.

'He goes, "Yeah, sure, you come and record at my place. I make you famous."'

But there was one condition. Thompson had to also record Gonzalez and his brother singing a version of 'Johnny B Goode'. Just because.

'He was obviously a gangster,' Thompson says.

Gonzalez explained to Paul and Thompson that, as they'd be travelling backwards and forwards to the studio at night, they would need some assistance – and he handed Thompson a pistol. 'If a taxi driver looks to be going off the route or taking a strange road,' he said, 'you show him this and tell him to get back on the right road.'

'This is our second day in Manila,' Thompson says. 'We've got no budget. We're now living on really cheap per diems. But the studio is quite good. It's just that the owner was a bit dodgy.'

Still, there was one small problem. At the time the studio wasn't actually working properly. It was broken so everyone had to wait for an engineer to come across from Hong Kong to fix it. Then Thompson and the band were told that while it was fine to use it – they could only have it on weekends – this meant that all the rhythm tracks were done in two weekends.

Only being able to work on weekends left the band members with far too much time on their hands to get up to all sorts of mischief in Manila. Girls and bars. Girls and bars. More girls and more bars. They were away from home and this was an invitation to run amok – big time.

But for those weekends, Thompson was sitting in the big chair, thousands of miles away from home embarking on his first production job – with Paul as his co-producer.

'I got the gig because Paul and Gudinski loved the sound of the demos that we knocked over in two days. And I still think to this day that some of those demos are better performances than what we got in Manila.

'The main problem was that everyone was completely distracted in Manila. For starters Paul brought his wife Hilary with him, and their baby. Declan was really young but they both came with Paul.'

'Manila with a young baby – what were we thinking?' Paul says now.

'The band were just cutting loose,' Thompson continues. 'There're girls and booze everywhere. They're having a great time.'

But it was a turbulent time to be in Manila. Martial law was in place. Arriving to see police standing on street corners with serious guns was an eye-opener for the young Australians.

And the icing on the cake was the semi-gangster, ex-actor owner of the studio who joked about his connections.

'He would make jokes about it, saying, "I can't see you tomorrow, I have to go off and have dinner with the Marcoses."'

At one stage it was suggested that Paul and the musicians could also meet President Ferdinand Marcos but they declined.

Thompson and the band were living on two hundred pesos a day (roughly fifteen dollars in today's money and probably not too bad at the time).

While Earl, Paul, Hilary and baby Declan stayed in comparative luxury, as did Brosnan and his partner Katie, the rest of the band and Thompson were plonked in a rundown hotel in the heart of the red light district in Manila.

'We were in the Tower Hotel,' Thompson says, 'right in the girlie bar area of Manila, and next to Makati, the financial and business area. Right outside our hotel there were bars with girls everywhere, and all sorts of other strange things that we hadn't seen before – like shops that would sell worms in a burger – worm burgers!'

Nothing went to schedule. Nothing at all. The only constant seemed to be the regularity with which certain members of The Dots were ending up in the casualty department in hospital. The original plan was to be in Manila for a month but the recording stretched out to eight weeks because of the limitations on when they could use the studio.

Manila at the time was also not a place where it was easy – or advisable – to try to score the sorts of drugs that fuelled The Dots in those days. As a substitute they turned to cough medicine containing hydrocodone, which they chased with San Miguel beer.

'The cough medicine had this weird effect,' Thompson says. 'It sedated you but also made your heart go faster. Shocking stuff.'

'Paracodin was freely available,' Paul says. 'Junkies took it when they couldn't get heroin. Lots of codeine in it.'

'Three times we had to drag Michael Holmes out of the hospital,' Thompson says. 'We'd finish a session and he'd go off, have some cough mixture and we'd get a call at four in the morning saying he was in emergency again.

'Michael was pretty sickly. Pale and thin. He'd take the cough medicine and fall unconscious and end up at the hospital. I remember on one occasion going and getting him from the hospital, driving him to the studio so he could do some guitar parts and then back to the hospital.

'Tony Thornton went into hospital a couple of times. They'd just swallow a whole bottle of this stuff. That was really the only drugs we had available. Even trying to score marijuana was really hard. In Manila we eventually got some, but it wasn't easy.'

Thornton was sent home after acting up one day in the studio. Paul kicked him out and told him to go home. Thompson was okay about it – the drummer had done all his parts for the album.

'It was a big stink. Tony exploded in the studio one afternoon. He had a big argument with Paul and Barrie. He ripped his shirt off and Paul told him to go home. Barrie left pretty soon after.'

Thompson explains that Earl had 'a whole floor of a hotel with three girls with him. He only lasted two weeks. He got so pissed and had so much sex that he literally wore himself out and went back to Melbourne. He couldn't see any reason to hang around Manila.'

Thompson and Paul worked well together, especially given the situation they'd found themselves in.

As Thompson recalls it was during this time that both Paul's world view and listening habits became increasingly broad.

'When we were recording in Manila he went through a big Clash period,' Thompson says. 'Their *Sandinista!* album heavily influenced his writing on the *Manila* album. He was becoming aware of world issues and the brutal and inhumane politics of the day, and throughout history. The Clash were singing about social and political injustice, and it was affecting Paul's songwriting.

'Paul's a very clever man. A great writer who was very interested in history and events.

'I remember one night, it was after his birthday when we were recording in Manila. It was just me and Paul in the studio. We did some overdubs and we were sitting at the grand piano with a bottle of rum, just talking.

'He'd just had a huge fight with Hilary and it was his birthday. He was worried about his drug use and other things. We ended up sitting up all night.'

* * *

When the band eventually returned to Australia with the multitrack tapes they still had to be mixed.

'The studio set-up over there in Manila was very similar to the one in Melbourne,' Thompson says, 'except that it didn't sound any good.

'It didn't have any of the speakers that I liked to work with and I couldn't really make a decision on the mixes, so in the end I just did some reasonable rough mixes and gave them to Gudinski.

'When we returned to Melbourne we went back into the same studio that we did the demo in a year before and mixed it again. The same songs. And the take-home for Thompson about the album?

'*Manila* would have been a fabulous record if we'd stayed in our hometown with our wives and girlfriends and babies where you only had to catch a tram to the studio.'

And probably where the drugs were better and no one needed to drink cough syrup.

* * *

Bass player Alan Brooker had been deflated by the decision to record the second album in Manila. He personally wished that if Mushroom were happy to send them overseas they'd have chosen New York and asked Lou Reed to produce it. He figures that was more in keeping with the band's musical influences and leanings at the time.

The other mistake he thought with *Manila* was the lack of a really experienced producer. Between Earl, Thompson and Paul there wasn't a depth of knowledge about production techniques.

'I really liked *Manila* but it was a dark record and had that feel it probably wasn't going to be a commercial success given what was on the radio at the time. But I loved playing those songs.

'Our first single from that album was "Clean This House" which radio wouldn't play. I remember one comment that it was too sexist. That made me laugh because it was about drugs. But the radio dickheads thought it was sexist and about Paul telling his wife to clean the house because it was dirty.'

Despite being a strong album *Manila* also didn't sell the sort of quantities Gudinski and the Mushroom accountants would have hoped for. Not by a long shot. Not even a contribution to the soundtrack of Gillian Armstrong's film *Starstruck* – a song called 'Rocking Institution' – helped their profile. A little later, in 1983, Paul would also contribute to the Cameron Allan–produced 'Love is the Law' to the film *Midnite Spares*.

Soon after returning from Manila, Paul had his jaw broken in an incident in Richmond when he and Declan Cooney were returning from an early Hunters & Collectors gig for which Greg Perano had put their names on the door. This meant that the album release had to be delayed, which didn't help.

'Declan and I were walking and we just got king hit out of the blue,' Paul says. 'There was no lead-up, no provocation, no "What are you looking at, mate?" I remember going into a bathroom and there was blood coming out of my mouth. I think I went to hospital straight away. I can't remember Declan's injuries but I don't think they were as bad.

'I didn't see it coming, I didn't see the person, and it turned out – I found out later that this guy had been generally aggro before we came along – that he was from a very famous Richmond family and no one was prepared to do anything. I couldn't identify him and nor could Declan, and to press any charges they needed witnesses and no one was prepared to come forward.

'My jaw was shattered into small pieces. I can still feel it to this day. There's still a bump along the jawline. It was a bit of a mess.

'I had to suck on a straw for a couple of months.'

* * *

Thornton survived the Manila experience but the rift between him and Paul wasn't going to be repaired easily and he felt like it was time for a change. He figured that if Paul was ever to have any serious success it wasn't going to happen anytime soon. And at this time he was right.

Thornton also wasn't reticent about coming forward about his contributions to Paul's songs. As far as he was concerned any input from the band members should be credited.

'I was always hassling about it. "Forbidden Street" came out of a jam we had and then Paul added some lyrics and said it was going to be on the record. I said, "Well, hang on a second – we all created that song and I want a slice of the action," and that's when he credited us all with that one song.

'"Leaps and Bounds" is my groove and I am proud of that.'

Thornton decamped to another band and Barrie Earl also moved on. Peter S Davies became the new manager and is credited on the *Manila* album.

After Thornton left the band, Paul reconnected with Huk Treloar, whom he'd met back when the drummer was playing with The Bleeding Hearts. But it wasn't destined to last long.

'I was on speed and he was the other way around,' says Treloar, 'so that didn't gel all that well.'

Eventually Treloar lost interest in playing – and the playing he was doing wasn't all that great.

'Paul rang me one day and said that he had to talk to me. I said, "It's okay, I know I'm not cutting the gig anymore." I knew what he was going to say because I was just playing like crap again. Too many drugs.

'But it was a lovely band. Nicest band I've ever been fired from.'

Soon afterwards Alex Formosa took over. Formosa didn't know a lot about Paul, just that 'Billy Baxter' had been a bit of a hit and he had an album called *Manila* coming out.

'I was good friends with the Cold Chisel guys and I remember talking to Don Walker who really loved Paul back then and thought he had great potential. Don was with Jenny Brown, of course, who was Paul's sister-in-law.

'Don told me I should go for it [the drummer role] and that it'd be really good – so I did and I got it and Paul and I got on really well.

'At the audition Tim Brosnan and I also hit it off. We were like blood brothers. So I played with The Dots for about a year and a half.'

Gradually Formosa and Paul developed a good relationship. As with any interaction with Paul, it took time.

'It took a while for me to get to know the guy but eventually the floodgates opened and we got really close. I was still living at home with my family and he was coming over a lot for dinners. Being part Italian, of course, he got on really well with my mother and father. I remember when he was really sick and he couldn't eat because his jaw was wired, my mother made him purees to drink out of a straw. I'd take them into the hospital almost every day.'

With Peter Davies as manager, there was a lot of work booked once Paul was able to sing again.

Formosa remains bemused as to how Davies managed to work with such an addled bunch.

'He was very straight. Really clean cut, a very well spoken man. I don't know how the hell Peter could manage us as he was so opposite to Paul and the band.'

But Davies managed, along with the Premier Artists booking agency, to find the shows and put together the tours. Arduous, unglamorous touring up and down the east coast of Australia with occasional forays to Adelaide and surrounds.

'Eight people in the van, bass, drums, two guitarists, Paul and two horn players – all in an eight-seater Tarago,' Formosa says. 'Massive long tours in that little Tarago. Lots of trips to Sydney, staying in the hotel next to the Manzil Room.'

The touring seemed endless during this time and Paul's drug use also seemed to spike. Maybe it was the intensity of the road and the relentless schedule. The band in a bubble, in their own crazy world.

Formosa recalls one night at the Manzil Room.

'Paul got the microphone and started banging it on his forehead and blood started gushing out. Afterwards I asked him what that was all about and he said, "Oh, it's called theatrics."

'He didn't need stitches, but there was a bit of a wound that eventually healed. I remember thinking, *What the hell is this all about?* ... I thought maybe he was pissed off because he couldn't hear himself or how the band was playing, but no – he said it was theatrics.

'Paul was doing all sorts of strange things at this time. His heroin use was pretty heavy in those days. It was a combination of heroin and speed and all sorts of crap.'

When they weren't touring, the band were rehearsing and making demos. Formosa was involved in the demoing of songs, including an early version of 'You Can Put Your Shoes Under My Bed' which would surface on the *Post* album.

'The recordings weren't very good because pretty much everyone was really out of it. No one was really with it.

'There was a lot of writing going on at the time. When Paul got his jaw broken he was living in Punt Road and because he couldn't do much he would invite people over and have big music binges. We'd all sit around and he'd put the tape player on and record us jamming. That was how he would write songs. We'd all jam and play along and he'd use that as a writing tool.'

Despite some crazy antics and the drugs, Paul still appeared very much in control of his perceived destiny. And he was captain of the ship. Formosa saw a man who was very singular about where he wanted to go, someone who knew who was boss and wasn't entertaining sharing that role with any of his band.

And if Formosa had any ideas of contributing more to The Dots than just playing drums that idea was quickly knocked on the head. One night he was in a room at the Bernly Private Hotel, sharing with Paul, Brosnan and another band or crew member. Everyone had some form of drug in their system so they were restless and sleepless. They talked.

'I remember it vividly. I was trying to bring up some stuff because I hated the production on the *Manila* album. The feels were quite good and I kind of liked the grooves and I thought some of the songs were okay, but I thought the production was really bad. I said to Paul that I thought we could improve some of this, and that we could also play around with some of the arrangements. I thought I could bring something more to the table. This was also around the time that I'd just started writing songs.

'But he made it really clear that he was the boss and that he didn't want any of that. Instead he wanted to be like Springsteen and the E Street Band – and he wanted to be the Boss. At that point I decided I wanted to pull out. I'd already had a belly full of the punk scene. I wasn't really into it.'

Not long after their late-night confessional, Formosa found himself at a party in Adelaide.

'It was just a massive self-indulgent orgy of drugs ... I remember Joe [Camilleri] was there and he turned to me and said, "Do you really want to play with these guys?" and I immediately thought, *No, I don't want to keep doing this.* I handed in my resignation the next day.

'The band didn't want me to leave. Paul was calling me day after day asking if I was sure I wanted to go. Despite the darkness there was a great chemistry there.

'Tim really wanted me to stay too but there was no way they were ever going to listen to me about pulling their fingers out and getting clean. And that wasn't up to me.'

Time to find yet another drummer.

'The night Alex Formosa left was essentially the night I joined,' says Greg Martin, the last of Paul's drummers in The Dots.

'A typical road story. I was touring the east coast with some band and I wasn't very happy and had decided to leave as soon as I got back to Melbourne.

'So we're in Sydney and did what we always did when we finished a gig which was to head to the Manzil Room. On that particular night Paul was doing the headline spot which meant the band started around two am. There was a good crowd as all the musos were there having finished their own gigs.

'It was one of the most amazing shows I've ever seen, and in many ways for all the wrong reasons – especially for Alex. It was shambolic, teetering on the edge of disaster. Paul and Tim were clearly whacked and it sounded like it was going to fall apart.

'Tim was going off on all these amazing tangents, like he did. Paul looked like he was going to fall off the stage. But it was also great. It was loose and I was just mesmerised by it. I must have known Alan Brooker so, after they finished, I was chatting to him at the bar and saying it was one of the best edgy fucking shows I'd ever seen. He told me that Alex had had enough and was leaving. I told him I was about to leave the band I was in and he said to call him when I got back to Melbourne.'

Back in Melbourne, Martin went to a rehearsal and got the gig. He joined the band at a tough time for The Dots. They were touring to support *Manila* and nothing much was happening.

'They all seemed like they were trying to get off heroin. Paul was on, off, on, off with it. I became one of the guys who would come to Paul's rescue at pubs when someone tried to pick a fight with him, or if he collapsed if he went off it for awhile because he had a low tolerance.'

But there isn't darkness without light, and many shades in between.

'There were lots of laughs. Great gigs. Bad gigs. Gigs to empty and full rooms. We were certainly more popular in Sydney than Melbourne.'

Martin also recalls Paul being extremely generous with his band mates.

'We were backstage one night before a gig and Paul walks in and starts handing cash to everyone. We asked what was going on and he told us that he just got his APRA cheque that day and that the band deserved to share in it. It was something he didn't need to do.'

But by this stage, the lifestyle was starting to catch up to many in the band.

'For a time we played every single day,' guitarist Tim Brosnan says. 'We might have one day off gigging every couple of weeks but we had to rehearse as well. At least seven gigs a week but often doubles and triples.

'A triple would be a lunchtime gig, then a night gig and then somewhere like Bananas really late. That was often the best gig because we'd be tired and not give a fuck and it was such a wild place so we'd often go down a treat.'

And like many before him, Brosnan was feeling frustrated with what he perceived to be Paul's refusal – or at best reluctance – to properly acknowledge the musical contributions of those around him.

'We did a lot of fleshing out of the songs. I remember saying, "If you want a loyal band, mate, you've got to cut them in, they can't be sidemen, they've got to be your band, your brothers."

'I think our friendship had got a bit broken in Manila and back then I was too wimpy to express my actual feelings.'

Brosnan 'wouldn't turn up for sound checks and I was really moody. I have this thing where if I'm not in a really good frame of mind I'll choke when I get onstage. Incredible volume will cover that. There were some great nights when we were really on, but we were inconsistent, I think mainly because of our huge workload.'

Eventually the grind of touring and a sense of not making progress wore Brooker down too. He didn't have a falling out with Paul. He'd just had enough.

'We didn't have a record deal. Paul had a lot of great new songs but I was just sick of it and thought I could do something else. That was stupid of me. If I'd known I was going to get a couple of tours around the world with him I wouldn't have left. But you're not to know that.'

The end for Michael Holmes came when Paul succumbed to the symptoms of Hepatitis C.

'Paul was laid low by Hep C and we went off the road for about three months.

'I said to my girlfriend at the time, "If I can't put my own band together I'll go back and play with Paul." He recuperated at his mum's place in Queensland [she had moved there in 1978] and when he came back he rang me to tell me and I said, "Sorry, mate, I have my first gig with my own band tonight – I'm leaving.'

Holmes is adamant that Paul's heroin use continued unabated well after he left The Dots.

'After I left the band I didn't see Paul play for a long time. Eventually I went along to a solo show he was doing at the Continental in Prahran. People said he was clean but he walked out completely pinned, smacked off his tits. He did the show, no problem, but he was smacked. And I thought that he shouldn't be doing that – he wasn't Lou Reed.'

* * *

Despite being a powerful album *Manila* didn't yield any hits and sales were disappointing. Gudinski and Mushroom decided they didn't want to continue with Paul as a recording artist. 'We had really made a big deal about him,' Higgins says, 'and then it seemed like we had more records returned than we had pressed.'

Talk and *Manila* are like a baby's first steps. There is nothing steady about the process. It's fraught and always teetering on the verge of collapse. But as imperfect as these albums are, they are nonetheless big achievements and necessary ones that set Paul further along his life's trajectory. So it is perplexing that Paul has done everything in his power to eliminate the existence of *Talk* and *Manila*. They can't be bought new on CD or vinyl, or digitally on iTunes, nor even be listened to on Spotify. The video clips from that era have been removed from YouTube. 'Billy Baxter' is not included on any of the three versions of 'greatest hits', *Songs from the South*, nor is any other material from those two albums. Paul wants the world to believe that his career began in Sydney with the release of *Post*.

For most artists withdrawing material they personally don't like from the marketplace would be impossible but in a rare (and generous) move, just before selling Mushroom Records' assets to Rupert Murdoch's business interests, Michael Gudinski handballed some key artists the rights to portions of their back catalogue. He didn't need to do that and it was a risky gesture in terms of his commercial negotiations.

The typically frenetic conversational style of Gudinski reverts to a soft, intense, pause-filled whisper when reminded of this.

'Do I regret it?' Gudinski ponders. 'A bit.' Long pause. 'A little bit ... because you just don't do that. But it meant so much to him and he really had a thing about those albums.

'He didn't want those two albums around. He just wanted them *DEAD*. But they're a part of his history.

'Would I do the same thing now? It's a different world now. Probably not. But if I remember back then it was because he couldn't listen to those records.'

Alan Brooker feels that Paul has disassociated himself from *Talk* and *Manila* because he is embarrassed by them.

'I guess he's not happy about the production or the arrangements on those records. He may not be happy about how the band played, but I think the playing is pretty good on a lot of it.

'It was a bit like playing in the sand pit and then suddenly going to high school. He didn't want to know about the sandcastles anymore.

'I think the best song on *Talk* was the one we did with the Fairport Convention guy [Trevor Lucas] – "Hard Knocks". I think that's got far better production. We were in AAV studios and relaxed and we didn't have a producer telling us we were shit. A lot of having a producer is them being encouraging and teaching. Making people feel comfortable and getting the best out of everybody.

'Much later I was working for AUSMUSIC and wrote this little textbook for high school and primary school kids about how to play bass guitar without learning to read music. AUSMUSIC wanted to use something from The Dots days to promote and publicise the book but Paul wouldn't let them. He just doesn't want to be associated with those records.

'Paul has his reasons and he sticks to them but it's disappointing for his musicians because these songs and albums were part of our craft, our history.'

Music writer David Fricke suggests, 'It may be that they represent a period in his life that he doesn't want to go back to. Lou [Reed] had no problem talking about drugs if you addressed it in an intelligent way, but most people don't do that and I'm sure with Paul that it was a very difficult period in his life.

'Why would you want to go back and revisit songs that tell me about a person you didn't really like?'

To the suggestion that Paul possibly dislikes who he was in those days and anything that reminds him of that, Joe Camilleri isn't sure.

'There may have been a bit of that but there was a joy in those years too. I knew him as a strapping lad who was sensitive and had a lot of heart.

'Unfortunately the gear got to him, but he had a beautiful wife, she was a beautiful girl. But when someone's on the gear or loaded and you're their friend and you try to say, "Listen, man, you don't need this shit, you're better than this shit, what are you doing?", it doesn't really do anything because they will only stop when they want to stop.'

Camilleri's opinion is that, even if Paul doesn't rate *Talk* and *Manila* as albums, 'You still have to own it.'

Drummer Alex Formosa is straight to the point when asked why he thinks Paul wants to forget that period of his career and has attempted to bury his first two albums.

'My theory is that he hates that period of his life. I think he might look back and see himself as a bit of a stupid junkie who didn't really appreciate anything around him so he's trying to forget that time. And he had a very volatile relationship with Hilary too.

'I think it's wrong to hide your past. It is what it is, and people can and do change.'

Like Tony Thornton, Paul Gadsby says he doesn't mention to people that he used to play with Paul because everyone always wants to know what he's like and all he can say is – 'I really don't know.'

'I don't bring it up. But I'm not bugged by him ignoring those first two albums. It's just the badmouthing of them that gets to me.

'Eno has this theory about how, while artists take all the credit for their creations, their art actually arises out of the world they're living in, the scene.'

'It would be great if *Talk* and *Manila* were still available though,' says Billy Baxter. 'There was some cracking material there.'

'*Talk* and *Manila* had a good run,' Paul says. 'They were available to buy for around sixteen years but they didn't sell. When I gained control of my work in the late nineties I simply chose not to make them available anymore. It wasn't the fault of the bands on those records. It was me. I don't like the songs or the singing on them. They're embarrassing to listen to. I remember hearing a story about Elvis Costello being in the studio and listening to the playback of a record of his and just hating himself and hating the record. That really made me feel quite affectionate towards Elvis, that he could feel that. I know that feeling.'

For his part Chris Langman, now a busy and successful film and television director, still maintains a friendship with Paul but wonders why Paul attempts to suppress the early recordings, the ones that include his contributions. 'Okay, so not all the songs on the albums are great – but they shouldn't have disappeared. I am sure he has his reasons.'

A firm friend, Langman is matter-of-fact about Paul's drive and ambition in the early years in Melbourne and his evolving and sustained success. 'There are some people who feel like Paul left them behind. But he doesn't owe them anything. And at that time he never gave anyone the impression that it was ever going to be any different than what it was ... if they did feel left behind, they were naive to his ambitions.'

Michael Holmes remains proud of being part of The Dots.

'We were a fucking kick-arse live band. Timmy [Brosnan] is one of the best guitar players in the country. Alan Brooker is one of the best bass players in the country, and Tony [Thornton] was a really solid fucking drummer. Paul had a hot band, a *really* hot band.

'And we had a great time. We knew we could go on and blow other bands offstage because of our ferocity and passion. Paul was a passionate singer, and a great commentator, and made people pay attention to him and fucking look at him. So it's not just his songwriting but his presence as well. So yeah, it was great. And we worked bloody hard.

'And Paul has given a lot of people a leg-up. He's been very generous to people, a good Irish boy to the heart. In The Dots days he worked his fucking arse off. Every band in those days did.'

CHAPTER 8

FROM ST KILDA TO KINGS CROSS

'The Hopetoun was like a big shining light. We used to drive past ... and it always had lights blazing and was packed. It looked like a big party ship.'

Paul Kelly

IN 1983, AS THE DOTS GROUND TO A HALT, PAUL PUT together an outfit known as The Paul Kelly Band with musicians including Michael Armiger on bass, Chris Coyne playing saxophone, Maurice Frawley on guitar and Greg Martin on drums. Later Michael Barclay took over as drummer and Graham Lee did some shows playing pedal steel guitar.

By 1984 Paul and Hilary Brown's marriage was in disarray and she had moved to Sydney. Paul decided to break up the new band and relocate to Sydney too – he and Brown could share child-rearing responsibilities and, frankly, he needed a change of scenery.

The songs were coming slowly and intermittently. There was no new record deal. His health was not exactly fabulous. Melbourne didn't seem to offer much beyond the constant reminder that things were not going so well on any level. It was time to move on. Start afresh. Leave the old days behind. Head north. Buy a bus ticket and settle into a thirteen-hour trip from St Kilda to Kings Cross – read, doze, stare out the window, think and watch the white lines pass on the long drive up the Hume Highway.

Paul, of course, had made numerous trips to and from Sydney at this stage, often driving as well as on the bus. After he had alighted from the bus in Kings Cross on one of those visits he made his way to the home of Cold Chisel songwriter and keyboard player Don Walker and Jenny Hunter Brown.

'My first awareness of Paul was as Hilary's boyfriend or husband given that I was living in quite a long-term relationship with Jenny, Hilary's older sister,' Walker says. 'So it was very much, "This is Paul, he's a nice bloke and he writes songs."

'I knew some of the people that Paul was playing with in earlier bands I knew because they had been in bands in Adelaide. But I never met Paul in his Adelaide days.

'When we met he had a deal with Mushroom but he wasn't really having much success outside the arty kind of Melbourne inner-city scene.

'He made a couple of albums and things just weren't working – not only professionally but personally. He was two albums in. He made the album in Manila and things started to bottom out with everything. But then suddenly something clicked with his writing, at least to my ears, and he started pouring out the songs very rapidly, the songs that appeared on *Post*, while he was in the process of moving his life up to Sydney. I got to see that at close range because our spare bedrooms were part of that whole transition phase.

'Initially he was staying with Jenny and I but that was not for long, never for more than a few nights, and then he moved into an apartment with Paul Hewson up in Ward Avenue which was half a block from Jenny and my place in the Cross. They lived there – from memory – for quite a long period, maybe six months, and it was during that period that Paul made *Post*.

'The songs for *Post* were written during his move. My memory of "From St Kilda to Kings Cross" is Paul getting off the bus over by the Koala Motor Inn and walking with his guitar case to our place. He came in the door really excited and saying, "I've got this song," and sitting there playing it on his guitar and me thinking, *Holy shit, this is really good. There's something really good going on here.* In his book [*How to Make Gravy*] Paul says he remembers writing this song on my piano – but I don't recall my piano having much to do with it.

'I was encouraging to Paul because he was kind of an in-law but then suddenly he's coming up with these songs and it felt like I didn't need to be. It was pretty clear from the songs that he was not a young guy who would like to be a good songwriter, he *was* a songwriter and it was happening here right in front of me.'

The considered person he is, Walker chooses not to speculate about the specific reasons for Paul's split with Hilary and his decision to move to Sydney. But he concedes Paul wasn't in the best place and things didn't look to be going well in either his professional or personal life.

'All the things that you add up to make a sustainable life were failing for him but he was lit up by this thing that was happening inside him.'

Walker was close to Paul in those early days in Sydney and is surprised at the suggestion from one person that Paul and Ian Rilen [from Rose Tattoo] shared living quarters at any time during that period. He has no doubt that all sorts of 'shenanigans' went on in the flat that Paul shared with Paul Hewson, the fabled Dragon keyboard player and songwriter – and it was highly likely that Rilen would have been involved in many of them.

'Ian was one of the gun writers of the time and everyone wanted to know him. Paul was younger but coming up and everyone realised – especially with the *Post* stuff – that he was a good songwriter. *Post* remains my favourite record of his.'

Early on in Sydney, Paul wanted to record some demos of new songs. He approached Tony Cohen, the legendary producer who had been his first choice to accompany The Dots to Manila, to record some demos of these new songs.

Cohen was an incredible talent with an unorthodox, anything-is-worth-trying approach to recording, and a lifestyle that may as well have been called Fear And Loathing Wherever Tony Is. Cohen knew his way around drugs – and sometimes how to control them.

Cohen was the studio engineer of choice for Australian artists who wanted the daring, edgy approach to the studio that accompanied him. Artists like The Birthday Party, The Go-Betweens, The Moodists, Models and Hunters & Collectors sought him out.

At the time Cohen was doing some work in a small studio in Sydney with little more than a reception area, a tiny recording space and a cupboard for microphones, cords and other gear.

One night he had a session booked with ska band The Allniters, but to squeeze in a session with Paul, Cohen feigned a migraine attack and sent the band home early. As soon as they left – so the story goes – Paul emerged from the small cupboard where he'd been hiding and the two started recording.

Paul was particularly keen to demo the song he and Paul Hewson had written about Olympic gold medal–winning weightlifter Dean Lukin, but while at it the two also recorded a bunch of other acoustic demos.

* * *

Having decided to make Sydney his home base, Paul was focused on establishing himself and got on with the business of writing many of the songs that would appear on *Post*. It took time to find his feet with live work. There were solo shows and gigs with drummer Billy Pommer, when he wasn't busy with The Johnnys. There were also duos with Steve Connolly, a guitarist Paul knew from Melbourne who relocated to Sydney towards the end of the year.

'I met Steve through my friend Ronnie Reinhart who is dead now,' Paul says. 'He went to school with Steve. They went to one of those progressive schools. Ronnie said, "You should meet my friend Steve – you guys would get on well and you should play together." He took me to see Steve's band The Cuban Heels. Spencer [Jones] was in that band. They were playing at a bar in Richmond and I liked them straight away. I thought, *I should get to know this guy.* Ronnie introduced me and we had a quick chat that night and followed it up a little while later and then we started playing together.'

Connolly was a marvellously inventive, understated guitarist, a determined, opinionated individual and the perfect foil for Paul. 'Paul and Steve shared a lot,' says one of Connolly's two sisters, Sharon. 'It wasn't only their knowledge of music and music history, but their love of poetry. Steve was incredibly well read for someone who was formally un-educated.'

'I met Steve at the right time,' says Paul. 'He was very opinionated … He probably had a stronger pop sensibility than me. He turned me on to ABBA. I thought they were just rubbish on the Top 40. Steve told me that their songs were really good and played me "Dancing Queen". We used to go and see Bjorn Again. We loved them. They were like ABBA but they rocked.

'Another great thing was meeting Steve when I was getting into writing shorter, sharper songs. Steve would always cut the flab off a song if I was hanging on too long between verses. He really taught me about being concise.'

These Sydney gigs with Connolly were often augmented by the voice and percussion of Michael Barclay, a fresh-faced surfer with drumming skills and an angelic voice. Barclay had been in Paul's orbit both on and off the stage in The Dots days and, together with Connolly, they had hung out in Melbourne, singing the songs that Paul was writing at the time such as 'White Train' and 'Little Decisions', which would appear on *Post*. Paul was creating a different style of music from what he'd been writing and recording up to that point.

Before the move to Sydney, Barclay remembers finding himself with Steve Connolly at a late-night party at Paul's Wellington Street house in Melbourne. There were longnecks of beer, acoustic guitars and a singalong. There was chemistry. A chemistry that would eventually propel him to follow Paul to Sydney.

* * *

Now in Sydney, in the ultra-vibrant year of 1984, people came and went. Bands broke up before they formed, everybody seemed to be in seven different outfits and would profess that each one was their priority. There were gigs aplenty and an audience for just about all of them.

The suburban beer barns were at their zenith, but around inner-city Sydney, where Paul started plying his trade, there were numerous hole-in-the-wall pubs to play and a motley, shady army of hard-drinking, often drug-addled, music aficionados to attend them. For those years in the early eighties Sydney was what Melbourne had been in the late 1970s – the place to hang out.

Paul says, 'My memory of some early shows in Sydney was doing a Sunday residency at the Strawberry Hills Hotel with Steve [Connolly] and Michael [Barclay] ... We couldn't get booked at the Hopetoun. That pub was like a big shining light. I remember we used to drive past it to get to our gig at the Strawberry Hills Hotel and it always had lights blazing and was packed. It looked like a big party ship. But we would head on past it to the Strawberry Hills where there'd be about thirty people, and we'd do our thing.'

It would take the formation of a new band – with luminaries like The Johnnys members – to attract the attention of the booker at the Hopetoun. Amid the acoustic gigs, Paul put together a band he decided to call The Coloured Girls, inspired by Lou Reed's song 'Walk on the Wild Side'.

The very first appearance by The Coloured Girls was at the now iconic Hopetoun Hotel in Sydney's Surry Hills on Wednesday, 31 October 1984. While acoustic Paul wasn't seen as a big drawcard, the presence of two members of The Johnnys and amps would have tipped the scales in his favour.

Billed as 'Paul Kelly in The Coloured Girls' the first incarnation of the band featured Paul, Spencer Jones on guitar, Billy Pommer on drums, Pedro Farfisa (aka Peter Bull) on keyboards and Noel Funicello on bass.

Jones and Pommer were able to play because their regular band, The Johnnys, were taking a brief break from touring. The others were just hanging around.

'It was pretty incestuous with musicians playing with each other around Surry Hills at that time,' Pommer says. 'You could form a band and then break it up a couple of weeks later and then get other people to play. That's what Paul was doing.'

The band rehearsed during the afternoon, running through a selection of Paul's songs – some old ones and other more recent compositions that would be on the *Post* album – along with a handful of cover versions such as 'Venus in Furs' by the Velvet Underground.

'I was hanging out with Paul a fair bit in those days,' Pommer says. 'He was writing and demoing a lot of new songs. We did a few gigs as a duo at the Strawberry Hills Hotel near Central. It was Paul singing and playing acoustic guitar and me on a basic drum kit. I recall he had a booking for four "off" nights – either a Thursday or a Sunday.

'We played a lot of songs that would be on *Post*, plus Paul was doing a cover of Culture Club's song "Karma Chameleon".

'I also used to go around to where Paul was living with Paul Hewson, in a flat behind the Sebel Townhouse. He was doing demos on a four-track recorder there.'

Pommer says that the first incarnation of The Coloured Girls played just one other show together before The Johnnys went back on the road, and Paul headed up to Townsville with Steve Connolly. The show was a nuclear disarmament fundraiser at Selina's at the Coogee Bay Hotel when Peter Garrett was running for parliament.

Keyboardist Peter 'Pedro' Bull who played in those early Coloured Girls gigs was firmly in the mix of players who would play other gigs with Paul, as was, briefly, Rick Grossman, who went on to play with the Divinyls and Hoodoo Gurus.

Bull remembers Paul being quiet. Not withdrawn but reserved and plain talking. Nothing was complicated.

'We didn't really talk a lot. We just started playing his songs and letting arrangements fall into place.'

One of the short-lived projects that Paul involved himself with during this transitory phase in Sydney was an outfit known as the Absolutely Five Believers, a play on the Bob Dylan song 'Obviously Five Believers' from his *Blonde on Blonde* album.

The band line-up – which contained in fact six members – was Toby Creswell (keyboards), Joe Breen (drums), Jolyn Burnett (vocals), Mark Callaghan (bass), Tim Gooding (guitar) – and Paul playing guitar, singing and playing harmonica.

This band gave just two performances – one at the Hopetoun Hotel and another at the Clovelly Surf Club.

'We played all Dylan songs except in the car on the way to rehearsal,' Toby says, 'Paul said with a smile that he'd like to do a Bob Dylan–like song that he'd just written. It was "Darling It Hurts". Paul knew every song backwards and played the harmonica solos perfectly.'

* * *

It wasn't long before Paul realised that he needed someone Sydney-based to take care of business for him.

Paul and I had kept in contact. We'd hung out a little at Luna Park in Melbourne during the party festivities following Mushroom Records' tenth anniversary concert, I'd go to gigs, and had reviewed both *Talk* and *Manila* extremely favourably for *RAM* magazine. I considered Paul a friend – not a close one but close enough, in the way that journalists and musicians have friendships.

In 1983 I'd stumbled into band management after the Hoodoo Gurus approached me to assume that role for them. That gradually evolved into full-scale management of the naive kind until our relationship ended after an ambitious and gruelling US tour covering forty-two shows in forty-five days.

The conclusion of that relationship was barely finalised before Paul Kelly phoned my office – Gidget Management – in Victoria Street, Kings Cross, one afternoon wondering if I wanted to have a beer and a chat.

Paul and I met in the front bar of the Green Park Hotel, the closest pub to the office. We chatted about Paul's relocation to Sydney and his plans. He explained that he'd saved $1500 and was intent on making an acoustic single. There was no firm commitment from Mushroom to continue their relationship with him.

There was no two ways to look at it – *Talk* and *Manila* had been commercial failures. Critically well received, sure, but the ledger looked decidedly grim and Michael Gudinski had moved on to focus on other label priorities such as Split Enz, The Sports and Jimmy Barnes. The only person really waving the Paul Kelly flag was Michelle Higgins.

From the pub Paul and I moved on to my home where I played him Chris Bailey's 1983 acoustic solo record *Casablanca* and Johnny Thunders' acoustic *Hurt Me* album from the same year.

I suggested that an acoustic single probably wouldn't make much of an impact but an acoustic album – now that was a statement. A real statement and the best possible chance to resurrect his already flagging career. Paul also asked if I was interested in becoming his manager. And that's how I became Paul Kelly's manager, something I did with my then partner Yanni Stumbles.

The first order of business was to work out how to revive Paul's career. It was hard to imagine Mushroom Records releasing an acoustic Paul Kelly album, but it was the era of independent labels and someone might take a punt on it.

Paul managed to assemble a line of credit and approached former Sherbet member Clive Shakespeare about producing an album.

'He was recording it at Clive Shakespeare's studio after hours,' Don Walker remembers. 'Sometimes they'd be going in and doing a song at two o'clock in the morning.'

The resulting album, *Post* – dedicated to Paul Hewson who died of a heroin overdose in January 1985, just before the album was released – contained the songs 'From St Kilda to Kings Cross' and 'Adelaide', which are still part of Paul's repertoire.

The core performers on that album are Paul, Steve Connolly and Michael Barclay, with additional performances from saxophonist Chris Coyne, Ian Rilen on bass, Peter Bull on keyboards, along with contributions from guitar and dobro player Graham Lee, singer Toni Allaylis and piano accordion player Jimmy Niven.

'When I hear songs from *Post* it makes me want to run and hide,' Paul says. 'It's just the voice. Even [the later] "To Her Door" also seems to me very samey all the way through. The further away the records get the harder it gets to listen to them. I don't really like the sound of my own voice all that much.

'I've done enough recordings that I can judge when something is the best performance I can do of a particular song at that moment. With some songs I know that in five years I might be singing it better or I might find new things in it.'

We wanted to sell *Post* via mail order but Michelle Higgins, Gary Ashley and other staffers at Mushroom Records continued to advocate for Paul and managed to convince Michael Gudinski to get involved. *Post* was released on their newly formed White Records offshoot.

* * *

Just before *Post* was officially released, Paul and Steve Connolly travelled to Townsville to do an extended residency at the Townsville International, a hotel better known as the Sugar Shaker because of its appearance. They spent seven weeks honing their performance skills there.

'Going to Townsville was a pretty crucial time,' Paul says. 'We'd just made *Post*, and via a friend we got a job playing there. Steve was adventurous and up for it so we headed up. We played a lot of Gram Parsons, Beatles and Stones. We started to get this gang from James Cook University coming down to see us. Initially it was just the suits coming in after work. We'd be playing things like "Dead Flowers" by the Stones and lots of other covers, and slipping in the *Post* songs without saying anything. I learnt very early on that you don't say, "And now we're going to play a new – or original – song," as it'd clear the dance floor. It was a really good training ground, and after a while we noticed people coming down who weren't businessmen.'

John Watson, who would go on to become one of Australia's most successful music managers, worked part-time in a Townsville record shop and after work every Thursday for two months in 1985 he and Gary Hunn, who ran Wavelength Records, would close up and wander over to the Sugar Shaker to watch Paul and Connolly do a couple of sets.

'It was super exciting,' Watson says. 'Because of seeing these shows, when *Post* came out, we knew a lot of the songs. It was quite possible too that they were working out some new songs that would later appear on *Gossip*.

'The set-up was *very* basic. A little PA with a small speaker on each side of the tiny stage. Usually there were maybe ten people at tables watching. Nobody knew who he was. He'd had a minor hit with "Billy Baxter" so you'd be walking up thinking, *I hope he plays "Billy Baxter"*. They did a lot of pretty cool covers. I remember an *amazing* version of "Your Cheatin' Heart".'

Jon Schofield was also in Townsville at the time, playing bass with Jeremy Oxley's soul band, Chinless Elite.

'I thought I'd be playing guitar as that's what I was doing in my previous band The Grooveyard,' Jon says, 'but I rolled up to rehearsal and Marcus Phelan was playing guitar and he was a much better guitarist than me. Jeremy said I should play bass, but I'd never played bass before. Marcus offered to lend me one, so he went and got it and I plugged it into a Marshall amp and started learning to play soul songs, and it was so much fun.'

Oxley wanted to get out of Sydney during a freezing cold winter so Chinless Elite headed north where they found a residency at the Seaview Hotel in Townsville. Paul and Connolly were in town doing pretty much the same thing but Schofield says it wasn't just the weather that attracted Paul to that part of the world, he also wanted to get healthy and save money to pay off some debts.

'Why else would you be playing to American businessmen who weren't listening?'

And there were no hard drugs to be found in Townsville at the time. It was earn money and get healthy time.

'They were going nuts and so was I ... Anyway, Mark Fuccilli, the sax player in the Chinless Elite, had an advance cassette of *Post*.

'I wasn't a big Paul Kelly fan. The Dots used to come over to Adelaide a week after bands like Jo Jo Zep and The Falcons and play the same venues like the Tivoli. The Falcons were as tight as hell and disciplined, and then Paul and co turned up acting a bit too cool for Adelaide. They were a bit rough around the edges and I just didn't get it.

'But I heard *Post* and it blew my mind. Before I knew it, I knew every song. And Paul and Steve were the only other AFL fans in Townsville and it was footy season. I didn't have an AFL team at the time as there was no Adelaide team. But it didn't take long to become a Bombers fan like Steve as they won two premierships on the trot. Paul and Steve invited me to come and sit in with them – and vice versa.

'They came to see us on their day off. There was nothing else to do. I sat in and played bass on blues covers they were doing and played everything from *Post*. They were doing three or four sets a night.

'Then the Chinless Elite moved to Magnetic Island. There was some benefit show at the racecourse on Magnetic Island and Paul and Steve came over and played on the bill.'

'We used to go and see Chinless Elite who were at the Seaview on our nights off,' Paul says. 'I can still remember them doing "Love and Happiness" by Al Green. They did a great version of it, totally killed it. They were a great soul band and I loved them.'

By this time Schofield, Paul and Connolly enjoyed each other's company and knew they could play together.

* * *

At the end of their run at the Sugar Shaker, Paul and Connolly headed back to Sydney and Paul called Barclay about doing a tour. Without hesitation Barclay threw his drums on the next train to Sydney. 'I got to Central Station with five bucks in my pocket on a steamy summer's night and asked someone which way it was to the Hopetoun. Paul was playing there that night with the Five Believers and I walked into this packed, heaving inner-city Sydney pub and it was fantastic.'

Weddings, Parties, Anything songwriter and singer Michael Thomas recalls seeing Paul playing with Steve Connolly in Melbourne around this time. He thinks Michael Barclay jumped onstage and shook a tambourine and sang a few harmonies and Alan Brooker played double bass.

'But it was basically Steve and Paul. *Post* had just come out and that was the first time I remember thinking, *He's better than just good, this is really something else.*

'I remember someone saying to me, "Paul's taking this really seriously." The reason being that Paul had walked into a venue carrying a briefcase. He was running the band.'

Despite *Post* not selling particularly well it was well received by music critics and Michelle Higgins believes it was a credibility breakthrough for Paul.

'God, it was the breakthrough with the media. Journalists all jumped on it.

'I asked Bill Page at SAFM in Adelaide, "Are you playing it twenty-four hours a day?" He said, "No, but we are playing it after 6 pm," and that was enough to get Festival really excited and put the album in the stores ... In those days Festival was the only label that had warehouses in every state so they had a big staff compared to other record companies and a lot of those people started to really like Paul as he started to tour. In South Australia, when *Post* came out with the song "Adelaide" on it, and Festival there really got behind it, he got proper FM radio play.'

Higgins still has specific memories of Paul's reluctance when it came to interviews, despite the fact that many in the media had fallen for *Post*.

'I remember Paul saying early on that he didn't want to talk about his songs and I said, "Paul, this is Mushroom Records – home of Shirley Strachan, Ted Mulry, Dave Warner – what are you going to talk about if you won't talk about your songs?" Before that I'd worked with Phil Judd [of Split Enz] who *really* didn't want to talk about his songs either.

'Paul was *really* uncomfortable. Really shy. That's all it was. Everyone in his family is very eloquent. And so is he. He's just very shy.'

CHAPTER 9

THE COLOURED GIRLS

'I was never so angry with anybody as I was with the world until Paul Kelly got airplay.'

Michelle Higgins

IN THE SPRING OF 1984, PAUL AND STEVE CONNOLLY WERE living in a huge flat on Coogee Bay Road in Sydney's eastern suburbs. Declan Cooney was also in residence and Tim Brosnan seemed to be there some of the time as was his partner, Katie, after the couple had decided to join Paul in Sydney.

Connolly and Brosnan appeared to hit it off, and Brosnan suggests that Connolly was influenced by his playing on *Manila*.

'Steve said to me that they listened to all the out-takes from *Manila* and he'd borrowed my solos. I was flattered by that. There's been a bit of revisionism. You wouldn't hear Paul say, "I stole that from John Dowler" or anything like that. Everyone steals in one form or another. The genius is being able to disguise it and make it something of your own – and he did that. Paul often acknowledges that he steals – but not often does he admit to doing it from his own musicians.'

Brosnan recalls that heroin was an extremely prevalent drug in Sydney at that time, and despite their intentions to try to modify their usage, everyone in their circle was rarely far from the temptations of their previous lifestyle. He remembers Declan Cooney carried a couple of ampules of Narcan around with him in case someone overdosed and he could shoot them up with it and bring them back.

Emotional and physical baggage from Melbourne followed Paul, Cooney, Brosnan and others. Friends would visit from interstate and offer temptations, or newfound acquaintances in Sydney would assume that nothing had changed from the old days in Melbourne and invite the newish kids in town to venture into old habits.

Michael Barclay meanwhile found himself some floor space, went to the beach every day and played drums whenever there was a gig. He was a happy guy. When that living situation fell apart, another building was found near Alison Road in Coogee. Paul and Cooney had a flat down one end of the floor, Barclay and Connolly had a flat down the other. It was across the road from a church and the bells would ring when there was a wedding or to herald an auspicious event.

'They were slightly out of tune,' Barclay says. 'We used blankets on the windows and had a mattress on the floor. There was nothing much else there. It was spartan.'

Next stop was a move across to Surry Hills. Paul and the two Declans – his son and his sound guy – moved into a share house in Collins Street, Surry Hills, a stone's throw from the Hopetoun Hotel, while Connolly and Barclay took residence upstairs at the Hopetoun. The band played a gig there every Wednesday night, which covered the cost of the rent. This would allow Connolly and Barclay to concentrate on playing music instead of working at menial jobs to keep a roof over their heads.

The Hopetoun headquarters was furnished with whatever Essendon Football Club memorabilia the pair could lay their hands on. They even had a little shrine to the team facing south on the TV.

Accordion player Ron Blake was part of the group of musicians living upstairs at the Hopetoun and a member of a short-lived band that Paul put together, The Wandering Hands, which comprised Paul, Blake, Connolly and Barclay.

'It was sort of an a cappella styled band,' Blake says, 'but with Connolly on guitar and me on accordion. We supported Los Lobos at Selina's in 1985.

'We were mainly playing Paul's songs from *Post* and some that he was working on that would appear on future records. We played quite a bit and were fairly busy but certainly it didn't last for more than a year, probably not even that long.'

Blake auditioned to be a member of Paul's pre–Coloured Girls band as bass player but the position went to Michael Armiger.

'I think the main reason I didn't get the gig at that time was because I was using too much smack.'

Looking back, Blake claims that he didn't detect anything overly remarkable about Paul at the time.

'I didn't find him determined or anything out of the ordinary. He was just another guy that I knew who used heroin and played in a band.'

Blake, who's been clean for more than three decades, considers Paul's heroin usage to be unusual. He believes that when Paul moved from Melbourne to Sydney his habit changed from being a heavy user to that of a professional dabbler. That's not the way these things usually play out.

Billy Pommer also observed that Paul was working hard at getting his life back on track – writing constantly and maintaining a comparatively healthy lifestyle.

'He'd turned over a new leaf. He was getting healthy and a bit later he went down and joined the Sydney East's AFL footy club and played a couple of games in the reserve grade at Trumper Park in Paddington. When he moved to Sydney he'd made a decision to turn his life around and to get fit and healthy, and that's what he did.'

* * *

Paul seemed comparatively content with life at this time. Hilary was living nearby and Declan would move between the households.

'Paul used to have big dinner parties,' recalls Irene Karpathakis, who was living at the Collins Street house when Paul and the two Declans moved in. 'Every time he got money he would go out and fill the house with food and have a huge dinner party out the back. Chris Bailey from The Saints, Michael Thomas, Ron Peno from Died Pretty – they'd all be there. There was lots of music. I used to play DJ. It was fun.

'Later when Paul got his first money from his record contract he gave thousands of dollars to a youth centre I was working at in Redfern. And he came over and played pool with the kids. One of them recognised him and said, "That looks like Paul Kelly." He hadn't said anything.

'And he paid for everyone in the house to go and see opera. We saw *Don Giovanni* at the Sydney Opera House. He had a very kind, generous side.

'Early on I remember him having a job chipping bricks at a construction site. I felt so bad for him coming home after doing some really hard yakka.'

But despite outward appearances to the contrary there was still the spectre of drugs around. 'There was a lot of heroin at the house. Everyone – except me – used. Paul and Declan Cooney used together. I remember one night watching the two of them, they were so funny.

'But Paul functioned. The thing is that he always got up and took Declan to school. He was on.'

The early full band days at the Hopetoun led to the true birth of The Coloured Girls. There were a few names in contention for the band, including The Wandering Hands, before The Coloured Girls took hold.

The band playing at the Hopetoun was Paul, Barclay, Connolly, Michael Armiger and Peter 'Pedro' Bull, the latter having played that first gig at the Hopetoun with The Coloured Girls back in 1984.

'There was never a big plan,' Bull says. 'It was just a case of doing what we did and getting better at it. We started playing the songs better and the arrangements got tighter.'

After a year of gigging in Sydney and around the usual traps, Michael Armiger decided to call it quits after Paul, Connolly and Barclay embarked on an acoustic tour opening for Australian Crawl and The Motels. A few people were auditioned for the bass-playing position but Jon Schofield, who Connolly and Paul had connected with in Townsville, got the job. It would be this line-up of Paul, Connolly, Bull, Barclay and Schofield that would tour constantly for the next seven years and go on to make the albums *Gossip*, *Under the Sun*, *So Much Water So Close to Home* and *Comedy*. For many fans, they are the cornerstones of Paul's career and a special combination of people.

'We gelled quickly as a band,' Schofield says. 'I knew Pedro [Bull] from The Flaming Hands and was a fan of that band.' Schofield also enjoyed playing with Barclay. 'The first time I played with Michael Barclay I just thought, *I want to be in a band with this guy – I don't give a fuck who the hell's singing*. He had a great sense of humour and beautiful angelic harmonies and I love the way he drums. And there was this surf rocker thing and Beach Boys aspect that counteracted the serious inner-city Melbourne side that was there in the band.'

The Coloured Girls initially played around Sydney, with occasional forays outside the city limits where often there was a crushing reminder of their place in the whole scheme of things.

Michael Barclay recalls a gig booked at the Doyalson RSL on the Central Coast. 'We arrived and there were maybe two people there,' he laughs. 'We were guaranteed $1500 to play and the venue manager offered us $900 not to play – he said this was better financially for him than opening the doors that night. Paul insisted that we'd play until he upped his offer to $1200 – and we'd already made a dent in the drinks rider, so we took the money, turned around and drove home.'

The band also did the three-set grind at the Manzil Room and inner-city and suburban pubs, but there was no huge demand for them. It didn't matter, as Schofield says that there was an unstated feeling between them all that this band could go places. They just needed to record great songs and get them on the radio.

* * *

Post hadn't exactly set the world on fire sales wise so things were again tenuous – at best – with Gudinski and

Mushroom. And then Paul told me that he wanted his next album to be a double album. Yep, a double album. Two records. Straight after three single albums that hadn't sold.

Double albums weren't common, even from super-successful artists and certainly not from those struggling to maintain their relationship with their record company.

Maybe Paul wanted a double album because of Dylan's *Blonde on Blonde*. Maybe he just had a lot of songs. Possibly he just figured ... who knows? But I'd already learnt that when Paul announced a decision it came after he had given it a lot of thought and the chances of changing his mind were not good.

As manager it was my job to try to sell Gudinski on the idea of Paul making a double album as his follow-up to *Post*.

I set up a meeting with Gudinski at his office in Dundas Lane in the Melbourne suburb of Albert Park and – still a comparatively inexperienced manager – prepared to try to sell this concept to the larger-than-life, hyper-fuelled 1980s version of Gudinski.

I managed to stammer out the words 'Paul Kelly ... new album ... double album,' before Gudinski exploded.

'YOU'VE GOT TO BE FUCKING JOKING. Get out of here. I'm not doing a fucking double album.'

Gudinski in that mood is almost impossible to talk to. You just soak it up and try to throw in a few counter jabs. You feel like a young, vulnerable boxer thrown into the ring as sparring practice for a belt-wearing champion. You walk in exuding tentative optimism ('Critics loved *Post*') only to be hammered into submission by a formidable figure ('Yeah, but did anyone actually buy the fucking thing').

'I'll give you a sixty thousand publishing advance – now, get the fuck out of here,' was what I can remember of how the rather short meeting went.

Gudinski was standing up behind his desk and barking. He gave good bark. He was intense, in-your-face and arrogant. Very arrogant. But this was a breakthrough.

If I heard him correctly he was saying that he would put up money that Paul could use to record album number four. Not a lot of money. (In the 1980s artists were regularly spending several hundred thousand dollars making albums.)

The money wasn't even coming as a recording advance. Gudinski and Mushroom weren't interested in that. The sixty grand was a publishing advance. The upside to that of course was that there was actually no commitment from our side of things to release the completed recordings on Mushroom.

I managed to come back at Gudinski: 'Okay, we'll take the sixty thousand and give you a double album. If we do and you release it we want you to agree to sell it for the price of a single album.'

Gudinski snapped back: 'Okay, now get out.' Meeting over.

* * *

I arranged a meeting between Paul and producer Alan Thorne at Trackdown, a rehearsal studio out the back of a keyboard shop in Bondi Junction. I'd encountered Thorne when I was managing the Hoodoo Gurus and had enjoyed being around him while he produced their debut album *Stoneage Romeos*.

Thorne was a calm, methodical, easy-going guy who didn't seem intent on forcing his sound onto artists. Not that I knew that much about how this record-producing caper worked but I thought he and Paul might hit it off.

After the meeting Thorne went to see the band play. He loved the songs and wanted to work on the album. He knew that Paul wasn't a big priority for Mushroom and that there wasn't a lot of money to play with.

'The way I understood it was that Mushroom and Gudinski thought that Paul wasn't going to sell a lot of records but that he wrote good songs and that they'd put up some publishing money – and if he elected to use it to make a record that was his business,' Thorne recalls.

'The budget wasn't big but I thought we could do it. We discussed getting the band set up in the studio and getting as much down from the rhythm section as quickly as we could and getting the feel of the band down.'

Initially Thorne had expected that Paul and I were talking about a single album. After all, with three commercially unsuccessful albums it was hard to imagine any other scenario.

'I'd been thinking that the budget was enough to maybe do a single album with what he had. It wasn't a big budget but I thought we could get there. Then Paul said he wanted to do a double album. I said, "Okay, let's make it work." I knew Trafalgar as a studio pretty well and knew that I could work quickly there.'

Not only was there little money from Paul's end but Thorne had to work another day job to pay the bills. So it was a case of making the album when everyone could be in the same place at the same time. Not an auspicious start for what would become a landmark Australian album.

'At that time I had a day job at Film Australia which was taking up a lot of my time. I had a young family so I had to earn a constant income.

'I told Paul I could only do evening sessions, and weekends. He was happy with that. So we'd start at six o'clock in the evening and go till midnight, or maybe one o'clock in the morning. On weekends we'd have long days. So that's how we did it – I'd do my day job and then head to the studio and work with Paul and the band.'

And without the budget to book extended time in Trafalgar Studio, Thorne, Paul and the band had to take whatever they could get. If Trafalgar was pre-booked they had to go elsewhere. The rhythm tracks were all completed at Trafalgar but later overdubs were done at various other studios.

'I'd never made an entire album before,' Schofield says. 'I thought it would take a while but before you knew it we had a double album finished. It was very quick and easy. We were gig-fit from playing around Sydney and we went in and did them pretty much how we were playing them live and then embellished them with lots of bells and whistles.'

Thorne recalls that Paul was extremely focused on what he wanted to do with the album.

'He was shy – but confidently shy. He knew what he wanted. And I think that's part of what Paul's personality is. We hit it off really well. Once we got to work we had a fantastic time. I liked working with Paul and we worked well together and the band were great.'

Thorne thinks that Paul had a very clear perception of the songs. He knew what he wanted in terms of structures and arrangements. Things were defined before they began the recording.

But Thorne observed Steve Connolly playing a significant role in this.

'Steve was pretty instrumental in the song structure. He played a big part in arranging a lot of Paul's songs and he had a pretty good handle on it.'

The hardest song to get a recording that everyone was

satisfied with was the initial breakthrough single, 'Before Too Long'.

'It was a hard one to get right. Initially the guitar parts in the song were a lot lighter. It wasn't such a full-on kind of rock song.'

'"Before Too Long" felt quite clunky at first,' Paul says. 'I never had a sense of it being a single early on.'

In fact it was the one song on *Gossip* that just wasn't feeling right. But as time marched on it needed to be completed.

One night, late in a session, Thorne and the band decided to revisit the song and see if they could make it work. Thorne suggested stripping everything right back – and almost starting again, building it back up to see if he, Paul and the band could find a way in.

'I said, "Guys, let's just put a good acoustic guitar down in this thing and then build it up." We'd had all these bits and pieces and jangly guitar parts going on in it. So we took all those out and put in a straight acoustic rhythm guitar, and then we double-tracked that and made a big wall of acoustics and then we thought, *Let's throw some organ on it*, and that hadn't been part of it at that stage. So we had this Hammond B3 there and we put that down. Then we put this heavier guitar riff through the song and it got built up from there.

'That was one of the songs that did stray from its original musical arrangement. It went in a very different direction. But that was an exception – I think the majority of the tracks were pretty much worked out before we started. We recorded it as the band played live, with obvious embellishments. But the way the band played live was how it went down.'

As the night progressed, it was obvious to all in the studio that something special was going down with 'Before Too

Long'. Thorne recalls that even then – that night – there was a feeling that they might have created a potential hit record. Of course no one could know but there was a niggling, tingly sense about that song – especially as it had been the hardest to record.

'That song pretty much came together that night,' Thorne says, 'and Paul said, "I'm going to put a vocal on this now." It was getting late but we were all so excited about it, and it was sounding so good, so he went in and did a vocal.

'Then I said, "Let's double-track the vocal." Paul wasn't that keen on double-tracking but I thought, *This will work on this track*, so it was double-tracked.'

* * *

With no firm deal on the table for an album release via Mushroom, Paul and I started shopping *Gossip* around and met enthusiasm from Martin Fabinyi and his successful independent label Regular Records, who – like Mushroom – were distributed by Festival Records.

Regular was a hipster label with their ear to the ground in Sydney. They concentrated mainly on Sydney artists and viewed Mushroom as a Melbourne-centric, behind-the-times independent label that was starting to seem a little tired and out of touch.

With few exceptions Mushroom had dealt almost exclusively with Melbourne artists until 1980, when they established a Sydney office and subsequently signed Sunnyboys. It may have been a coincidence that this happened not too long after Regular opened for business and started attracting the cool and interesting new artists from Sydney. Despite being three albums down the track,

Paul was becoming a hipster figure in the inner-city Sydney scene and ticked most of Regular's boxes.

It would not have been lost on Fabinyi and his partner Cameron Allan (who had briefly been considered as a producer for Paul) that it might be kinda fun to take a relocated Mushroom cast-off and throw in a touch of Regular hipness.

Fabinyi was very keen. Unlike anyone from Mushroom, he visited the studio when Paul and the band were recording and clearly wanted the deal. Terms were agreed and a signing party organised. It was all too straightforward: album on Regular, publishing with Mushroom.

Enter Michelle Higgins, whom Gudinski now considered one of his most valuable staff assets. She'd heard the news about Paul signing to Regular and she didn't like it. Not one bit. She loved Paul and those first three albums, believing that it was only a matter of time before he broke – and broke big.

Higgins recalls that she called Gudinski to ask what his understanding of a new contract for Paul was.

'He said, "There are just a few things to sort out," and I said, "THEY ARE ABOUT TO SIGN TO REGULAR."'

Higgins doesn't believe Regular would have been the right label, even though both they and Mushroom were distributed and marketed by Festival Records. And she's not convinced that Regular's Martin Fabinyi really wanted Paul; she thinks maybe he wanted something that he thought Gudinski might want.

By this stage I had played Higgins the potential single 'Before Too Long'.

'You came over and we sat in the foyer of the Harbour Agency on a rainy day. And I rang Michael and said, "He's got a hit record. HE HAS GOT A HIT and we need to move on this. We need to do something – and now."

'It seemed like a big departure for Paul,' Higgins says of the song, 'but it wasn't really. It was very Billy Baxterish. He was really going back. He'd gone full circle.'

The next day Higgins came to meet with Paul and me at my management office in Victoria Street, Kings Cross. She walked in, burst into tears and said to Paul, 'You are not leaving Mushroom.'

She then went back to the Sebel Townhouse in Elizabeth Bay and called Gudinski, telling him that she was staying at the hotel – on his dime – until a deal with Paul and me was sorted. Despite the length of her stay being exaggerated, and growing by the year, Higgins recalls it being a matter of three days.

'But I wasn't going anywhere until it was sorted. I was so pissed off that they could be so careless as to let something like that go. I was also cranky with Paul. I thought we'd been through enough together and that he knew me well enough that he could have called me and given me a heads-up. There was no reason for him not to call. I think he thought I knew more than I did.'

If anyone less indispensable to Mushroom had made Higgins' move they would probably have been fired on the spot – if they'd even had the audacity to try such a play on Gudinski in the first place.

Nothing about Gudinski's attitude before this betrayed even the slightest enthusiasm for Paul and his music, beyond his being a potential good earner for Mushroom Publishing as the composer of songs for other artists to sing. As far as Gudinski had been concerned, Paul had had his stab at recording success with Mushroom and now he and Paul were no longer dancing together on that stage. If it hadn't been for Michelle Higgins it would almost certainly have stayed that way.

Naturally, Paul and I knew we had the upper hand in the negotiations as Gudinski's respect (and need) for Higgins was so great. Gudinski and I talked and negotiated deal points. Eventually, and with what still appeared to be a great reluctance from him, a deal was hammered out. 'Tell Fabinyi to shove his party pies,' he said on the day we agreed to terms, which was also the day Paul was scheduled to sign the Regular deal. It was that close to the wire.

I sensed that Gudinski wanted a victory over the precocious rival independent label in Regular and Fabinyi more than he actually wanted Paul. And he wanted Higgins to be happy. Her passion was important. Gudinski may rarely trust his own judgement on these matters but he is swayed by the passion of those around him who he respects.

'Michael bared his bum in Bourke Street for that deal,' was how Higgins explained it soon afterwards. The new contracts were signed at Festival Records in Pyrmont with Gudinski, and Festival's general manager, Jim White, in attendance.

Gossip was released in September 1986 and Gudinski was true to his word, the album retailing for $14.99, the then price of a single vinyl album. And, as history attests, it was Paul Kelly's breakthrough record, reaching number 15 on the national charts and going gold, with over fifty thousand sales. The first single, the extremely catchy 'Before Too Long', became a radio staple and reached number 14 on the national charts. It was followed by 'Darling It Hurts' and 'Leaps and Bounds', which was released as one side of a single, along with 'Bradman', a seven-and-a-half-minute song about the cricket legend. Suddenly Paul and his band The Coloured Girls were big business.

To accompany the Bradman song Paul and I spent a night with cricket historian Jack Egan at his home in Bellevue Hill watching all existing footage of the Don. We sent the video compiled from this footage to Bradman, who wrote back saying that he remembered Paul's father, the two having been friends in Adelaide, and that while he didn't understand the attention given to him, he was flattered by the song. Bradman explained that he didn't own a VHS video player but would watch it when next he went to Sunday dinner with his daughter who did own one.

With *Gossip* getting a lot of attention, the crowds at the shows grew quickly. At one point Frank Stivala, the head of Paul's booking agent, the Gudinski-owned Premier Artists, called me up and told me he was taking me out for dinner at his favourite Italian restaurant. I asked why. 'You and Kelly have just grossed three hundred thousand dollars in the last six weeks,' he said. 'The least I can do is take you out for dinner.'

Literally before too long, Paul Kelly and The Coloured Girls were a major live drawcard around Australia. Gudinski was now a Paul Kelly fan. He was a believer. Always had been. He started turning up at Paul Kelly gigs. Briefly. A typical Gudinski night out in those heady days was for him to race around Melbourne, dropping in to up to ten shows. There'd be a whirlwind of energy as he barged backstage during a break between sets (he always seemed to know when that would be) or after a show, slapping everyone on the back, dispensing Gudinski's version of enlightenment and then he was gone.

Gudinski says that making the double album 'was a critical call that you made – and also that I made by agreeing to sell it for a single album price.

'That album made such a statement. That's what you and Paul were after ... It also showed what an incredible songwriter he was.

'Why did it work? I think we did an amazing job.' He laughs. 'Back then there was Triple J, who would have been supportive, but you could also get new commercial songs on commercial radio like the Triple M stations and we got quite a bit of airplay which we'd never had with him in the past. "Before Too Long" was a simple and catchy song. We understood it, and it really started the rise of Paul, and his confidence. He started to believe in himself.

'In the early days Paul was introverted but he was keen to learn and progress. He didn't have the confidence. I think deep down he loved what he was doing but he didn't actually know where it was going to go, which is fair enough. But he had some real grit and determination.

'I was smart enough to never yell at him, and I'm glad I didn't because it would have freaked him out. There was a lot of passion around that album. And the decision to do that double album – whether it was you or Paul, or both of you – was very critical in his career.'

Higgins adds, 'The time was right ... Album radio people had come on board. Billy Pinnell and his ilk around the country were there for *Post* and most certainly *Gossip* whereas they hadn't been there for *Talk* and *Manila*. It was just the right time.'

Higgins agrees that the idea I had for Paul and The Coloured Girls to play a show in the loading dock at Festival Records for the staff of the company, particularly those in the warehouse, was a master stroke. A set from Paul and the band and sandwiches (provided by us) meant we knew that when record shop orders came in from around the country *Gossip* was going out first and as a priority.

'That would have totally turned it around with those people because no one did that.'

For Higgins, who was soon to decamp to New York permanently, this was the breakthrough she'd worked so hard for – and wanted so desperately.

'I was never so angry with anybody as I was with the world until Paul Kelly got airplay. I'll never forget with "Before Too Long" – we'd been through all this and I was at my desk one day and the song had gone to radio. We'd done that and [influential radio figure] Lee Simon came up the stairs to see Michael and I said, "Well, did you add it?" and he said, "Add what?" I said, "DID YOU ADD PAUL KELLY?" and he said yes. It was such a great moment.'

Paul and The Coloured Girls had been in a car heading to a gig when they heard the song on the radio for the first time. Game on.

CHAPTER 10

GOSSIP AND BEYOND

'What was so noticeable was how quickly it went from forty to six hundred people. It was staggering.'

Michael Barclay

WITH *GOSSIP* OUT AND DOING SIGNIFICANT BUSINESS, Paul and The Coloured Girls began touring constantly, increasingly developing into an even more cohesive band.

Michael Barclay has a more practical take on it.

'We were five people who could actually sit in a Tarago together pretty much all year and not go mad. We all got on. It's a stupid thing to say but it is hard to find five people who can do that.'

The band members had their own personalities but it somehow worked – onstage, in the studio, and on the road. Make no mistake, they all had their moments. There were moods and tantrums – but they passed quickly.

Paul and Connolly had the most intriguing relationship, one that could be both intense and respectful at the same time.

'Steve worked well with Paul because Steve was one of the few people who would stand up to Paul and say if he thought something was crap,' Barclay says. 'Paul liked that, I think. He certainly respected it. Steve would tell him to cut the flab in a song, tell him that he didn't need something in a particular part of a song and to get rid of it. And Steve would argue it for an hour if he needed to.'

With the success of *Gossip* in the late part of 1986, and the income that started flowing from having a hit single in 'Before Too Long' and the resulting escalation in crowd numbers, The Coloured Girls started reaping some of the early benefits of rock'n'roll success. And what were those benefits for The Coloured Girls? Nothing glamorous, just the usual things that bands in their situation could now do – get off the highway as flying to some gigs became an option, and get single hotel rooms.

'Getting our own room meant we got some time to ourselves if we needed it,' Barclay says. 'In terms of the touring, it meant less time on the Hume. We also stopped playing what are known as "doubles" – two shows in the one night. What's a double really? It's a double drinks rider. Double the drinks meant we did a few shabby second gigs so we agreed – enough of that.'

What Paul Kelly and The Coloured Girls also experienced was that sudden escalation in popularity. With a hit single, the band went from zero to one hundred in an incredibly short period of time.

'I remember playing at Promises in Sylvania,' Barclay says. 'In my memory it seems to be about six weeks before "Before Too Long" was a hit – and we played to about forty people. The next time we played there we set the house bar record. What was so noticeable was how quickly it went from forty to six hundred people. It was staggering.'

The Coloured Girls turned into a super-versatile, road-fit rock'n'roll band, capable of – thanks to the power of mainstream radio – pulling significant crowds right around the country.

Still, the band never became slick and overly structured. During their time together they played without a set list. They'd know the first three songs each night but after that Paul would just call the songs and off they would go.

* * *

During the mid to late 1980s Paul Kelly and The Coloured Girls toured a lot. A real lot. That was what Australian bands did during the 1980s. It was a heady, frenetic time, not only for Paul but other outfits he and his band would develop an affinity with – chiefly Hunters & Collectors and Weddings, Parties, Anything.

Michael Thomas from Weddings, Parties, Anything says that 'soon after The Coloured Girls started appearing as a thing, they came to a show in Melbourne as a band to check the Weddings out and that was really exciting. I thought, *This is what bands are supposed to do, they're supposed to turn up at other bands' gigs.'*

It turns out that Paul and the band weren't just checking out Weddings, Parties, Anything, Paul had an agenda. He was well aware of Thomas's band and he had a song for them. One he had on a cassette in his pocket.

'Paul said hello and said he had a song he thought I might be interested in, and he handed me a cassette of "Laughing Boy". We thought that was just *the* most amazing thing.

The two things that were really pivotal to Weddings at that very early stage were *Post* and Billy Bragg's *Talking with the Taxman About Poetry.*

'We used to play every Thursday at the Jika Jika bar in Northcote and we'd always go back to this house for a party and they were the two records we'd play constantly. It's just a weird thing – because neither of those records had rhythm sections so we could play them late at night because we all lived in share houses and there was always someone asleep.'

Thomas has always been attracted to songs located in place and time, but there was something else that attracted him and his band mates to *Post*.

'It was really a blues record. Although there is some joy, it has a fair bit of pain in it. With not having bass and drums on it, it felt like a really bold record. Particularly in that era, it felt like a really bold thing to do.'

The relationship that developed between Paul and The Coloured Girls and the members of Weddings, Parties, Anything during this period was particularly close. There was a respect and admiration for traditional folk music, a punk rock ethos, a passion for consuming large quantities of alcohol, and a love of sport. They bonded over all these essential and important tenets of young rock'n'roll bands of their ilk.

'It was usually hotel room sessions, just sitting around playing songs,' Thomas says. 'Parties at houses and in the rooms at the Prince of Wales.'

Thomas and Paul had a good relationship – one that, as with many of Paul's relationships, didn't involve a lot of talking.

'He's never been effusive, but he was always very respectful and helpful. I remember really early on The Coloured Girls had a New Year's Eve show, probably at the Venue, and we thought Weddings were on and then we didn't get the show. Our manager at the time, John Sinclair, told me to ring Paul, which I didn't want to do – but I did and I told him how we'd had a really tough year and that some things were falling down for us and Paul was really good and said he'd get us on. We ended up getting up at the end to sing something.'

By the late 1980s a bill with Paul Kelly and The Coloured Girls and Wedding, Parties, Anything was extremely common.

'I think the two bands just really hit it off – maybe a bit too much for Paul's liking and sometimes it became too much of a party, a bit too loose.

'I remember one gig – I think it was at La Trobe University, and there was some fuck-up with the PA and some unreasonably long period between us and them going on, and Schoey got pissed and then Steve was giving it to him, on Paul's behalf. I think Stevie had assumed that role for Paul in the band.'

The connection between the two bands also became more Sydney-focused, with the Hopetoun Hotel in Surry Hills being central to that relationship. 'Our first real success in Sydney was at the Hopetoun. People always ask me what our first gig outside of Melbourne was and it was the fucking Hordern Pavilion opening for Stevie Ray Vaughan. I think we did two shows at the Hordern and then a Sunday night at the Hopetoun and I just thought, *This is heaven – this is like the perfect pub.* By then The Coloured Girls were living upstairs. But as they were deciding to move out, we decided that we should move to Sydney, and Marcus [Schintler] took up residence.'

Thomas spent a few weeks living in the same house as Paul in Collins Street, Surry Hills, before Paul moved out and Thomas moved in with his then girlfriend.

Playing a lot meant even more exposure to other emerging musicians on the road. Singer Deborah Conway first encountered Paul when her band Do Re Mi went on a tour with The Coloured Girls in the period between the release of *Post* and *Gossip*.

'I remember making some joke about the good, the bad and the ugly as we were all lying around the pool,' she says. 'I'm not sure he liked that.

'Prior to that, though, I remember thinking, *I'm really interested in seeing this guy. He seems really interesting, I like his work, and he might even be good boyfriend material.* I remember that thought going through my head.' Paul was a good-looking guy.

But it wasn't only his looks, of course. 'I was attracted by his lyrics – things like "You Can Put Your Shoes Under My Bed" on *Post*, and the original version of "From St Kilda to Kings Cross". I thought they were very down-to-earth and direct songs, and very immediate ...

'When we got to know each other Paul and I enjoyed a lovely, warm and close relationship and I became part of the family because Alex [McGregor, Paul's cousin] and I were a properly bedded down, living-together couple for five years.'

* * *

Early in 1987, with *Gossip* doing very well, I had a meeting with Michael Gudinski and Mushroom's general manager, Gary Ashley, to discuss all things Paul. They had a great idea. A really great idea. Remember, it was the music business in the 1980s. They thought Paul and I should go to America for four to six weeks.

'To do what?' I enquired.

'Just drive, travel around,' they replied.

While the idea sounded attractive enough – both Paul and I loved many, many things about America – the rationale seemed kind of suspect, not to mention that adventures like this cost money.

'Don't worry,' they said. 'We'll pay.'

In retrospect, I realise they were hoping Paul would be inspired to write songs about locations other than South Dowling Street and Adelaide. He might begin to drop references to American cities and therefore increase his marketability as a songwriter when it came to Mushroom shopping his publishing catalogue internationally. It didn't work. It would be some years before songs like 'Cities of Texas' came along. But we weren't to know that then.

In Nashville we stayed at Shoney's Inn, right in the centre of Music Row. We heard that George Jones was doing a radio concert that night. Paul had been telling people that if anyone covered one of his songs, George Jones would be his ultimate wish. We needed to go to this performance.

Somehow we managed to get in and watch a short set from Jones and his band in front of a couple of hundred people.

As the show ended, I briefly lost sight of Paul. When I spotted him again he was over by the side of the stage, near the door where Jones and his band had exited. He was clutching a cassette tape he was obviously hoping the security guard would take and give to Jones. Paul returned without the cassette, so mission accomplished. George Jones never covered a Paul Kelly song – but it wasn't because of a lack of trying on Paul's part.

In Nashville we spent time with Steve Earle and his manager Will Botwin, an enthusiastic, ambitious, cheery type who went on to run Sony Music in New York. At the time he was managing Earle, Rosanne Cash, Rodney

Crowell and some other artists in an impressive roster. He was keen to be involved in the North American management of Paul.

One day we went down to the studio where Earle was finishing up work on his *Exit 0* album. They were mixing the great song 'The Rain Came Down' when we arrived. I decided to hang in the studio and watch the process. Earle wasn't that interested and he and Paul decided to head off for a few drinks.

They went to a bar which was a favourite hang of Nashville old-timers. The two songwriters settled in for a session that extended until both realised that they actually had no money and there was a bar tab to settle. Apparently this particular bar had a tradition that if you couldn't settle what you owed them you could clear the tab by getting up and singing three songs. I missed the Steve Earle and Paul Kelly clear-the-bar-tab performance.

Despite years of hard drug and alcohol abuse Earle still recalls that afternoon, the beginning of a long-standing friendship with Paul.

'He just wanted to see downtown. By that stage the Opry had moved to Opryland so it wasn't there anymore but we went and walked around the Ryman Auditorium that was empty at that time. And we went to some of the bars around there and sat in. We played a few songs which I don't think I'd done ever. We both sang some songs. I showed him the Row. I'm always keen to show people the history of places and explain what happened and what buildings used to be home to what.'

Asked about what he thinks makes Paul stand out, Earle doesn't hesitate.

'The closest equivalent over here is Bruce Springsteen, simply because Springsteen became the singer–songwriter of his generation. Springsteen came out of having a bar band but he was born to be a songwriter. Paul's background is essentially in punk rock when it gets right down to it, and a moment in Australian rock'n'roll where a lot of things were happening.

'Lyrics are the only reason rock'n'roll becomes an art form in the first place. I really do believe that Bob Dylan is who we have to thank for us having a job. Otherwise it'd just be songs about girls and cars.'

Paul and I also found ourselves in Memphis during the trip.

This was my second visit to the city and on the previous trip I'd made a pilgrimage to Graceland which I'd found fascinating. I dragged Paul along for a second visit but he seemed bored and keen to leave. Not that he didn't like Presley, maybe more the barrage of memorabilia and the commercialisation of the place didn't impress him.

I had a vague relationship with Tav Falco, an underground cult figure and musician based in Memphis, and called him up. He and his girlfriend collected Paul and me and took us to what seemed like the middle of nowhere and a classic, now legendary southern juke joint, The Green Room.

It was everything I'd read about such places. Sawdust on the floor, long tables full of people drinking beer from jugs, a bluesy combo playing at one end. After a few minutes it dawned on me that our quartet were the only white faces in the room.

At one point I went to the bathroom. As I came back I saw Paul on the dance floor, his slightly built figure clutching for grim death to the hips of one of the largest women I'd ever seen as she propelled the hapless Paul around the dance floor.

At the end of the song he came back and sat down. 'What the fuck happened there?' I asked.

Paul whispered, 'She came up and asked me to dance – I was too scared to say no.'

Driving from Memphis towards New Orleans, largely on Highway 61, but taking some quiet Blues Highway roads to avoid freeways, we encountered two young-looking kids hitchhiking down the road, one carrying a rabbit on a skewer. It was the stereotypical backwoods, southern American scene. With a twist.

Paul decided to pull over and offer them a lift. When they approached the car window a look of abject terror appeared on both their faces and they ran quickly down the road, getting as far as possible away from the car.

Momentarily stunned I then realised we were two white guys on a back road pulling up and offering two African American kids a lift. They must have been terrified. Welcome to America.

* * *

By this stage American record executive Steve Ralbovsky had fallen in love with *Gossip* and wanted to work with Paul.

Ralbovsky had come to Australia on a talent-scouting mission a few years earlier. Gudinski met him at the airport and set about educating him about Australian music, particularly the artists he had an involvement with. After all, in those days most Americans didn't know much about Australian music beyond the names AC/DC and Men at Work.

Gudinski believes it was his instigation to play Paul's album to Ralbovsky, who he knew was about to take up a position at A & M Records in Los Angeles. Gudinski had a close relationship with A & M and I was also comfortable with Paul being signed to A & M as, through my previous work managing the Hoodoo Gurus, I had relationships with a lot of key publicity and marketing people there.

Eventually Ralbovsky moved across to A & M and relocated from New York to Los Angeles. His first signing was Paul Kelly.

One morning, on a later trip to Los Angeles, Gudinski picked me up outside my hotel in a convertible. I hopped in and he zoomed off in the direction of A & M, lifting an arm in the air and screaming, 'I love LA.' He had a new horse in the American game. This colt was named Paul Kelly.

Gudinski introduced me to everyone I didn't know. He knew the company in ways that no other Australian did – and he wanted Paul to be embraced by the company.

Despite Paul's strong protests, *Gossip* was cut back to a single album for the American release. A & M correctly thought that an unknown artist debuting in America with a double album was crazy.

The American release also omitted the songs 'Adelaide', 'I Won't Be Torn Apart', 'Going About My Father's Business', 'The Ballroom', 'I've Come For Your Daughter', 'So Blue', 'Maralinga (Rainy Land)', 'Gossip' and 'After the Show'.

On Ralbovsky's suggestion a number of songs were remixed by Scott Litt who he had a close relationship with. Litt was a hip young producer on the rise and would make a name for himself, chiefly through an extended period working with R.E.M.

For the American version of *Gossip*, Litt went to work remixing 'Before the Old Man Died', 'Tighten Up' and 'The Execution'.

Then there was the issue of the band's name. The record label insisted that the name be changed. The Coloured Girls was, of course, a homage to the line in Lou Reed's song 'Walk on the Wild Side' but it wasn't washing with A & M.

'You want to play down South?' one executive asked in a meeting with Paul and me, 'Well change the name or forget about playing down there.'

There wasn't any argument from either of us. Paul, speaking more recently, says, 'The Coloured Girls was an off-the-cuff name we came up with which we thought was ironic and satirical. It wasn't long before the name didn't sit right with me. Lots of people didn't get the joke and it was a bad joke in the first place. I knew it was time for a change.'

He agonised about what to rename the band. At one stage The Terraplanes – a nod to Robert Johnson and his 'Terraplane Blues' – was strongly favoured but eventually he settled on The Messengers.

* * *

In the Sydney winter of 1987, Paul met Kaarin Fairfax, who was appearing in a production of *A Lie of the Mind* at Sydney's Belvoir Street Theatre. At the time Hilary Brown was working at the box office. Paul's cousin, Alex McGregor, took Paul to see the play and he met Fairfax briefly after a performance. A week later Paul called Fairfax – using Brown's phone – and asked her out on a date.

The 'date' was in fact one of Paul's gigs at the Freezer Nightclub on Oxford Street in Paddington. The first song he played that night was a version of James Reyne's 'Reckless'.

'I took about twenty people with me,' Fairfax says. 'I thought, *This is a gig, I'm not going by myself.* Afterwards pretty much everyone left and it was just Paul and me, and the rest really is history.'

At the time Paul was living in the Collins Street, Surry Hills house with the nearly seven-year-old Declan there frequently.

Paul and Fairfax eventually married in 1994 and she became Paul's second wife.

* * *

Paul now had stability on the home front and with the deal in America and the band name changed, he and The Messengers were busier than ever with a run of dates opening for Crowded House's 1987 American tour just at the moment their popularity was escalating.

On the American tour with Crowded House, Michael Barclay recalls, 'They were playing "Better Be Home Soon" as an encore but it hadn't been recorded yet.'

For that tour The Messengers' line-up was augmented by harmonica player Chris Wilson. Wilson's onstage prowling and seemingly menacing appearance threatened to overshadow the rest of the musicians.

'The next time we went back on tour in the States everyone said, "Where's the Big Guy?" – that's the one they all noticed,' Barclay says. 'He had such a presence.'

It seemed like overnight that Paul Kelly and The Messengers were really living the rock'n'roll dream. This was the stuff that *every* young artist dreams of – hit songs on the radio, international deals, touring the globe. For this ratbag assembly of Australian musicians the endless slog of small gigs evaporated quickly and Paul and his band went straight into playing two thousand to three thousand seat theatres and some amphitheatres with Crowded House. Sure the mundane slog would come later but as an opening gambit, this was pretty hard to beat.

The biggest thing up to that point for them had been a year earlier when they had opened for Bob Dylan and Tom

Petty and the Heartbreakers at the 12,000-seat Sydney Entertainment Centre.

'I remember thinking that I'd ticked that box, walking onstage and standing where I knew Dylan would stand,' says Jon Schofield.

'But we got in trouble for eating some of Dylan's rider before the show. No one told us not to go in a particular room that was meant to be exclusively for Dylan, so we did and we ate a few sandwiches which were for him and his band. We weren't allowed to go out of our room at the time he would be walking down the corridor to go onstage. Then a few years later he was giving Paul a really cool belt buckle as a present.'

'My recollection is that we were a pretty lucky band,' Barclay says.

As the touring intensified and the shows grew longer, frequently the band would perform a song or two during the set without Paul, allowing him time to get a beer, go to the loo or just take a breather. Connolly would often play the Buggles song 'Video Killed the Radio Star', Barclay's love of The Smiths would surface in a rendition of their song 'There Is a Light That Never Goes Out', or Schofield would perform the classic 'Nobody Knows You When You're Down and Out'. Peter Bull would from time to time sing Iggy Pop and James Williamson's 'Johanna' and, after spending time in Mexico and falling in love with mariachi music, he would break into a Mexican standard. In the early days, Bull would pull out his trumpet too.

Bull also remembers a night at a hotel in the inner-west of Sydney where the band played a show that contained pretty much every single song they knew. It was a marathon that lasted three and a quarter hours.

'We might have missed a few but we played every song that we liked and were likely to play at a show. It was exhausting – for the audience and the band – but everyone got through it.

'It was a point of pride that we didn't have a set list and that Paul could call any of those songs and we could play them. It was one of the aspects of the live show that kept it fresh and edgy.'

Not all the shows they did were to paying fans and in support of big names. Even before *Gossip* came out and the band's profile lifted, Paul was approached to play in Long Bay Jail, which led to a later run of shows at other Australian jails.

The first jail show was at Long Bay on Christmas Eve 1985, and subsequently early in 1987 came a number of shows at Long Bay Remand Centre, Long Bay's Central Industrial Prison, Parramatta jail, Bathurst jail, Orange jail and also the women's prison at Silverwater where they performed behind a cyclone wire fence to separate the band from inmates. In other prisons there were no barriers.

'Long Bay was first and that was a weird experience,' says Schofield. 'I've never wanted to get out of a place so fast in my life. It was stinking hot and the guard on the boom gate was pinned to the eyeballs. All the screws were stoned. It was heroin central.'

The first show at Long Bay was a remarkable experience. It was a hot summer's day and the band and crew loaded in all the gear and PA equipment and set up to play outdoors. There was a palpable sense of excitement and anticipation from the prisoners.

Paul and the band, still known then in Australia as The Coloured Girls, started playing and after the first song there was polite but mild applause. The same thing occurred after the second song. By the third many of the prisoners were starting to drift away and walk around the yard or work out.

I asked one of the guards if something was wrong and he looked at me incredulously before explaining what to him was incredibly obvious. 'Mate, what do you think is wrong? You come in here advertising yourselves as Paul Kelly and The Coloured Girls – and there's five ugly blokes up there. What do you think is wrong?'

They were tense shows with everyone being searched before entering – and leaving – the performances.

'At one of the shows one of the prisoners told me he really liked my sunglasses,' recalls Peter Bull. 'They were sort of like the ones John Lennon wore in one of those famous photos. He wondered if I'd trade them and he opened his palm and he would have been holding half an ounce of nice black hashish. I thought, *Imagine being arrested for trying to smuggle hashish* out *of prison.* That wouldn't have been a good look.'

'When we played at Pentridge Prison we went and had a swim with the prisoners in the pool inside the jail,' recalls Bull. 'It was a hot day and they didn't mind.'

* * *

After the success of *Gossip*, Alan Thorne was asked to produce the next album, *Under the Sun*, in 1987.

Most of the rhythm tracks for *Under the Sun* were put down at Alberts Studios in Neutral Bay. Some of the other recording, overdubbing and mixing was done at Trafalgar, Thorne recalling that the band were happy to get back to the studio where they'd recorded *Gossip*.

'*Under the Sun* was a much more concise recording. I didn't have a day job by then and was totally free to work on the album. Nothing much had changed with the band. They were pretty excited about the fact that *Gossip* had done so well, and it felt a bit more financially comfortable. During *Gossip* we were all watching the pennies. No one was flush with funds but by the next album they knew money was coming their way so it was a bit more relaxed – but they hadn't changed in themselves. Paul was still the same.'

As with the previous album, Paul, Thorne and the band went to a smaller studio and put the songs down quickly.

'When I heard "To Her Door", I remember saying to someone – maybe you – that I'd do the album just for that song. It was such a great song and I thought, *This is going to be a hit.*'

'To Her Door' was a hit and reached number 14 on the Australian singles chart.

* * *

In 1987 A & M flew Paul and the band to America for a week to make a video for 'Dumb Things' which was slated as an upcoming single in North America.

Then back they came to Australia to tour to promote *Under the Sun*, then back to America to tour in support of the album's release over there.

In 1988 there were more frenetic tours in quick succession. After that first American trip for Paul, he and I were back in America, staying at the Roosevelt Hotel on Hollywood Boulevard. *Gossip* had just been released in North America. We had a long night. Drugs were almost certainly involved. It was Los Angeles, the 1980s and cocaine was my drug of choice.

The next afternoon I came to consciousness and looked out the window to see Paul in the hotel pool swimming laps. A little later, he rang my room. He didn't seem happy. 'Come to my room – now,' was all he said.

I started to wonder what might have gone down the night before that my foggy brain wasn't yet processing. I dutifully went to Paul's room and knocked. He opened the door and still didn't look particularly happy. 'Sit on the bed,' he said.

At best I figured I was about to get a lecture about my drug intake. But no. Paul sat on the chair in the room, reached for his guitar and sang the words, 'How many cabs in New York City, how many angels on a pin ...'

He had a new song. It was called 'Careless'.

* * *

By the second half of the eighties, 'everything was just happening for us,' Bull says. 'Stuart Coupe had a lot of contacts and networked really well to get us the A & M deal and all that stuff. It was an exciting time and about to get more exciting because we were getting to record an album in America.'

Despite their success with producer Alan Thorne, Paul and The Messengers found themselves being encouraged by A & M Records to make their next album in Los Angeles with Scott Litt producing. The decision to record the album in LA was, in hindsight, a naive attempt to bolster the North American enthusiasm. The thinking was that if an album was done in Los Angeles then A & M records could feel invested and involved. Key staffers could hang in the studio and feel part of the process. Of course no one did.

When The Messengers finished a North American tour with The Smithereens, they did a few dates of their own before finishing up in New York. While the rest of the band returned to Australia, Bull and his partner Ailee Lynn Calderbank travelled to Mexico, with everyone reconvening again in Los Angeles in February 1989 for the recording of *So Much Water So Close to Home*.

Respected journalist Richard Guilliatt had been following Paul's career since The High Rise Bombers days and travelled with The Messengers through Texas in the latter part of the 1980s. He also attended a show at the Bottom Line club in New York City, a show that Raymond Carver's widow, Tess Gallagher, was also at.

'I remember that show because Paul dedicated a song he'd written about Kaarin to Tess – I think it was "Big Heart" – and Kaarin was livid. I just remember having this sense of how hair-raising it could be being Paul's muse.'

In Guilliatt's opinion this was a period when A & M Records were really going after success for Paul.

'There was a big feature in the *New York Times* with his photo. It was about him and John Hiatt – mature-aged songwriters. It was in the Sunday Arts section so they were really trying to break him.

'But then I think a key guy who was a fan of Paul's at the company got shafted and I got the impression the wheels feel off pretty quickly after that.

'Around that time Paul was thinking that he was about to go to the next level. I remember him thinking he had a song that Aaron Neville could record and was hoping that the label could get it to him. He really wanted to get a foothold in America.'

Paul and The Messengers were at this stage still being treated as a major priority by their label. They all lived in an apartment building and everything was taken care of. Of course, pretty much everything lavished on them would go on the recoupable side of the ledger and be repaid from future royalties, if they ever eventuated, but at this time no one was thinking of such minor and annoying details.

'A & M were throwing money at us,' Bull says. 'We had three hire cars which was funny. Paul had one and he doesn't really like driving. We were in flash apartments with cleaners dealing with everything.'

The recording took place on Sunset Boulevard in Hollywood at the legendary Ocean Way Studios, a nondescript building that is central to so much of the history of recorded music that came out of Los Angeles.

'We were in the second room which was where Frank Sinatra recorded a lot of stuff with Nelson Riddle so it was pretty flash,' Bull says. 'It was suitably old and you could feel the history dripping off the walls.

'Aaron Neville and Linda Ronstadt were in the big room at the same time, recording the duet they did. I was a *big* Neville [Brothers] fan but I was too scared to say anything and they were pretty unapproachable.

'And there was an LA heavy metal band in the third room. For the *whole* time we were there they worked on the *same* bass line – for eight hours a day. And they never got it right.

'We had a lockout in the studio so it was there any time of the day or night that we wanted to record. We drove in from the Hollywood Hills to record. Steve Berlin from Los Lobos came in to play baritone sax on "Sweet Guy".'

When the recording was finished, the band returned to Australia, leaving Paul and Litt to finish the album in a studio up in the Hollywood Hills.

In Bull's opinion the collection of songs that became *So Much Water So Close to Home* hung together nicely, but contained no obvious hit singles.

For Bull this was when he started to sense that The Messengers might be nearing the end of their time with Paul. He began to feel as though he was getting a bit stale.

'I don't think the songs had the sharpness and the directness of the batch of songs that were *Post* and into *Gossip* and even *Under the Sun*. There wasn't a "To Her Door" on it. Nothing with a distinct story on it.

'Paul was starting to write songs that were going in a few different directions. And maybe I was starting to get interested in other things as well.'

Paul and Bull also had a significant falling out in LA, possibly over musical direction.

So Much Water So Close to Home did well in Australia and reached platinum status with sales in excess of seventy thousand. Recording the album had been a *very* expensive undertaking though, with the recording costs clocking in at over three hundred thousand dollars. That – on top of the (largely recoupable) tour support for The Smithereens they'd already put in after the *Under the Sun* album release in America – meant that Paul was significantly in the hole to his American label. The budget also meant that, contractually, the American label owned the master recordings of *So Much Water So Close to Home*, which was subsequently licensed by them back to Mushroom for its Australian release. To this day the ownership of that album is a bone of contention for Paul as, while he found a sympathetic – if generous – ally in Michael Gudinski when it came to the rights to his earlier albums, A & M consistently refused to budge on granting back the rights to this album; a position that is unlikely to change.

The sweetener for Paul and the band was that the deal meant royalties in Australia and New Zealand were quarantined from being recoupable against A & M's outgoings. So while the American company was losing money, Mushroom and Paul were doing very nicely from the record in this part of the world.

Paul, Connolly and Barclay returned to America for a promotional tour after *So Much Water So Close to Home* was released at the end of 1989. They visited what must have seemed like endless radio stations as well as playing a few stripped-back shows in between but there was no proper band tour to support the new album.

It is a very fine album – containing songs such as 'Careless' and 'Sweet Guy' – but one that everyone realised could have been made in Sydney with Thorne for a fraction of what was spent.

Despite the album selling very well in Australia and the band having previously opened for The Smithereens in America, the album just didn't connect with the American public and media. A & M made a decision that they'd given it their best shot but it was time to cut their losses.

Despite Ralbovsky's best efforts, the relationship between A & M and Paul had never really gelled. A & M had enjoyed a lot of success and had grown extremely quickly. There was a lot of prioritising and Paul never really found himself anywhere near the top of the queue.

Gudinski certainly used all the clout and muscle he could inject to make it happen, but concedes, 'In some ways – and in hindsight – it might have been better if we'd tackled England first.'

Gudinski also believes that Paul's Australianness made his acceptance overseas more difficult.

'I'm very proud of the guy and his Australian focus but, as many other great superstars and writers – English, Australian, American – know, that identification doesn't always necessarily translate in other countries. I think Paul, through everything, was a true Australian who loved footy and cricket and Australia, and people overseas had that sense and didn't embrace him in the way we'd all hoped.'

Around this time, I stopped managing Paul and The Messengers after my relationship with Yanni Stumbles ended. Stumbles, a visual artist, is best known for her cover design of the Hoodoo Gurus' debut album, *Stoneage Romeos*. She also designed the album sleeves for *Post*, *Gossip* and a number of Paul's posters. Stumbles would look after Paul until he found a replacement.

Michael Barclay says Paul didn't want to go down the obvious road and get an experienced insider music industry figure who was cosy with all the other major players. On many levels that would have been the expected thing to do, but Paul already had a reputation for not doing what others expected.

So Paul settled on Rob Barnham, who had been his tour manager for some time. He owned a PA and truck and was a highly experienced nuts and bolts organiser. He had an old-school, no bullshit, direct and lacking in subtlety approach and knew how to say no – loudly and frequently if it meant getting what was required for Paul. It could be argued that he was exactly the right person for Paul at the time.

'From the time he left Melbourne for Sydney, Paul always had the right guy at the right time, always,' is Barclay's take on this.

When Rob Barnham took over the reins, the eighties was at an end and The Messengers were about to be too.

Paul and Fairfax would also decide to end their days in Sydney and move to Melbourne, but before they did that in 1991 and started their family, Fairfax had a few other things to do first.

In the early days of their relationship Paul wrote many songs with Fairfax in mind. As time progressed he would also write songs for her to perform. Fairfax had always enjoyed singing and had been in bands with her former partner Terry Serio. She could cut loose from her acting with singing. With the help of a few of her creative friends, Fairfax combined her loves and talents and Mary-Jo Starr was born. Fairfax started to perform just to amuse herself but with encouragement she recorded a demo and sent it to Jenny Hunter Brown, who was then working in A & R at Mushroom Records, and along with Michael Gudinski they decided they wanted Mary-Jo Starr to record an album.

Steve Connolly was enlisted to produce the album, with Paul writing five of the twelve songs that were recorded with a band, which included Connolly on guitar and Jon Schofield playing bass. Paul plays acoustic guitar on just one song, his composition – 'Don't Say I'm No Good'.

The album, *Too Many Movies*, was released in 1990 and sold respectably well, and much better than Fairfax was expecting. For a moment in time, the cult of Mary-Jo Starr threatened to become much more than a fun part-time gig in between acting work.

'Mary-Jo Starr really took off and I wasn't ready for it,' Fairfax says. 'She got a lot of attention. The thing was, I made up a story about her life, and it was a pretty tragic story. As Mary-Jo became more popular I had to commit to the story knowing it was all made up. I just hated talking about it. I think I freaked myself out, partly because it was doing so well and because people believed the story.'

* * *

The Messengers and Paul seemed – at least to outside observers – to be the perfect combination. It was hard to imagine a time when there wouldn't be a Paul Kelly and The Messengers.

But that time came sooner than most of The Messengers expected, in 1991. Maybe there was a little inkling of change, a feeling of disconnect between band and leader – but nothing that would have prepared them for Paul breaking the news that the end was approaching.

With *So Much Water So Close to Home* having effectively flopped in America, Paul decided to make the next album, *Comedy*, in Australia – back at Trafalgar with Alan Thorne – and then call it a day with The Messengers.

'Paul spoke to them,' says Barnham. 'It wasn't up for discussion. He'd made his decision. Paul had also done a big solo tour before then, which he'd never done before. I think he did it to financially set some things up and it was a huge success. He played the whole country – from one hundred and fifty people in Cunnamulla, to places that averaged four hundred to five hundred. He wanted it to be intimate.

'At the same time, The Messengers had been out playing as a band without Paul. They played as Michelle Shocked's band and also opened those shows as the support band.

'It was feeling as though Paul wanted to work with other people and not just The Messengers.'

Bull wasn't surprised by Paul's decision to cease working with The Messengers.

'I thought that we weren't moving forward and developing. I think we'd run out of musical ideas together and anything we did extra would be a rehash. Paul's songs were moving away from the rawer "Darling It Hurts" or "To Her Door" thing. So I thought it sounded right.

'Looking at it coldly, it was the right decision and the right time to make it. And it was better to have known before we made the record as it added a lot of focus to that record and we wanted to make it the culmination of what we'd done together. There were some really interesting and different sorts of songs.'

Schofield says he was surprised that Paul hadn't made the decision sooner. 'There was no hit on *So Much Water*. Consciously or unconsciously, we were probably all thinking there'd be a hit off that record because there'd been two or three off each of the previous two albums.'

For Barclay it had been business as usual until the announcement. 'We were rehearsing the songs for the *Comedy* album and Paul just said that this was the last album we'd do together and then we'd do a big tour and that would be it. He gave a little speech and I think we were all right about it because it was at least a year away.'

Long enough away probably that in the back of their minds The Messengers were hoping that Paul would change his mind.

But Paul was already once again thinking of the long game. He was at least eighteen months down the line with his career strategy. There was an album to record, the gap before its release and then the inevitable lengthy touring to promote it.

With the benefit of hindsight, Barclay can see the probable cause of Paul's rationale. The band and songwriter were starting to move in different directions – or more correctly perhaps, Paul was changing and the band wasn't.

'As good as the band was we still had limitations and he was starting to compose songs that we didn't play that well. I thought afterwards, *Why can't we be like Crazy Horse with Neil Young and make a record together and tour every so often instead of ending it completely?* But he just wanted a clean break.'

'At the time of recording *Comedy* I thought that this would be the final album with this line-up,' Paul says. 'And it felt it was right to tell them when I did.

Above: In the studio with Archie Roach and Steve Connolly, working on Roach's *Charcoal Lane* album. Stuart Coupe Collection

Below, from left to right: The gang's together. Manager Stuart Coupe and journalists Toby Creswell, Ed St John and Clinton Walker congratulate Paul at the launch of *Gossip,* Sydney, 1986. Stuart Coupe Collection

Above: The classic Coloured Girls/Messengers line-up – Peter Bull, Michael Barclay, Paul Kelly, Jon Schofield, Steve Connolly. Stuart Coupe Collection

Below: Paul with Ruby Hunter.

Courtesy Mark Hopper Photography

Top: At the Sydney Cricket Ground before a NSW v Victoria State of Origin game. *From left:* Jon Schofield, Michael Barclay, Paul Salmon, Paul Kelly (holding Lily Calderbank, daughter of Lynn Calderbank and keyboardist Peter Bull), Gary O'Donnell and Steve Connolly.
Courtesy Michael Barclay

Middle: Paul and Kev Carmody with Alan Pigram off to the left.
Courtesy Rebecca Howell

Left: Paul onstage with Kasey Chambers at the concert for Joy McKean's 90th birthday. Tamworth, 2020. Courtesy Susan Lynch

SPEED LIMIT 40

MISSION INN 5 BLOCKS

TEXACO

4,260

PAUL KELLY &
THE DOTS

Above: Paul Kelly and The Boon Companions in London. *From left*: Peter Luscombe, Bill McDonald, Dan Kelly, Dan Luscombe and Paul. Courtesy Bleddyn Butcher

Below: Paul (with Siân Darling to his right) and the staff and management of EMI Records receiving gold records for *Life Is Fine*. Stuart Coupe Collection

Top: Paul with his daughters Madeleine and Memphis in New York City, 2017.
Paul Kelly Collection

Middle left: Singing with Madeleine and Memphis, with Charlie Owen on guitar. Paul Kelly Collection

Middle right: Peter Luscombe and Dan Kelly.
Courtesy Leon Morris

Left: Paul with Vika and Linda Bull.
Courtesy Leon Morris

Paul with his current band. *From left to right*: Vika Bull, Bill McDonald, Cameron Bruce, Paul, Peter Luscombe, Ash Naylor and Linda Bull. Paul Kelly Collection

The poet, the singer, the man. Paul Kelly. Courtesy Mark Hopper Photography

'I remember my thinking at the time – and I still agree with it – is that what made bands great or artists great were the limitations. That was what was great about The Messengers. There were certain kinds of music that we liked and certain fierce constraints about what was good and what wasn't. I think the main thing was Steve Connolly. He was so fierce. He hated reggae and I was big into reggae and I could never bring that in. You can hear reggae influences all over *Manila* but that all went sideways. I didn't write songs like that once that band was going.

'So the band had restrictions about it and what they could do. And that's also what made the band great. But I thought we'd done five albums – five records in a pretty short period of time – and I wanted to try other things. I was a solo artist and I got a band together. It was a real band with those guys, but I wanted to try out other things and explore other areas.'

* * *

Although Paul had announced that The Messengers were coming to an end, the band still had to record the album. Alan Thorne remembers the mood in the studio: 'Everyone seemed excited about going back in there. It wasn't that they had a bad experience in the States but they were very comfortable going back into Trafalgar as they'd had a good experience there in the past. *Comedy* was an easy album, simple to do and no problems.

'I think by that time Paul had a level of self-confidence that comes with reaching a certain level of success. I think he had more of a sense of what he was doing and how he wanted to do it. We worked well together and had a good time. I had this attitude of wanting to enjoy myself as well as getting the work done and I think they all felt the same way.'

Thorne recalls that he sensed that the band members were disheartened to hear Paul's announcement about ending his time with The Messengers. 'But it wasn't to the point that it affected anything in the studio.'

For Barclay, however, it felt like The Messengers seemed very fallible at the time. There were signs of them floundering when it came to meeting Paul's expectations in the studio.

'There were songs like "Take Your Time"– it's such a simple song but we could never get it to sit right without a click track and I remember Paul getting quite frustrated by that. He kept saying that it was simple – and it is but we couldn't get it. I often wonder if he just wanted to go and play with people who could nail it in one take. We were a great band. We weren't a slick band, it was a sum of the parts thing.'

Thorne and Paul have not worked together since *Comedy*, but for the producer they were special times.

'Some of the most enjoyable times I ever had in the studio were working with Paul. I have really fond memories of those times.'

* * *

Another factor in Paul's decision to end his time with The Messengers may have been Connolly's increased heroin use. Unfortunately around 1987 Connolly, who until that point had been an avowed hater of heroin, developed a taste for the drug, and soon developed an escalating habit, something that surprised all of his band mates.

While he saw nothing specific in the studio, Thorne was aware that there was increased drug use among some of The Messengers, more with Connolly than Paul.

'Stevie never used anything in the studio, but he'd take breaks and when he came back I could tell he'd been using something. But I never got any indication of Paul straying off in that direction. He'd either stopped or was managing it extremely well.'

Schofield was well aware of the spectre of heroin rearing its head within the band, which in Paul's case he suspects went back to Adelaide days.

'There was lots of pot and lots of heroin around in those days. Anyone with brown eyes will get away with it longer than anyone with blue eyes – you can't see that the pupils are dilated.'

Who had brown eyes in The Messengers?

'Paul and Stevie. Pedro's eyes are hazel and Michael and I have blue eyes.'

Schofield admits using heroin on a few occasions with Paul but says he could count the times on 'one and a half hands'.

Connolly on the other hand had become a serious user.

'At one point I asked him what he was doing and how long he was going to keep doing it. He was starting to turn up two minutes before our gigs. He was living upstairs at the Annandale Hotel. I said, "Why are you doing this?" and he said, "I want to know what it feels like to be addicted to heroin." I thought, *In all the years I've known you that's the only really stupid thing I've heard you say.*'

'Steve's habit certainly didn't help Paul's decision about the band.'

Barclay agrees. 'Towards the end Paul said to him, "I know what you're up to." We had a little band meeting about it in Tassie one day during a tour and he [Connolly] just denied it point blank, and we all looked at him and said, "Who do you think you're talking to?" Paul just looked at him and said that it looked bad for the band and he didn't want Steve pinned onstage. He said he didn't want it around him as he had a weakness for it as well. He told Steve to cut it out.'

Connolly's brother Rohan feels that Steve's move into the world of heroin was facilitated by the influx of money.

'Steve enjoyed the trappings of finally having some money. Certainly he liked to drink decent quality alcohol and used top of the line drugs. But he wasn't extravagant – he never drove and [he] lived in modest abodes. So I think he had a bit of money and wanted to spend it on himself, spoil himself, and heroin was a port of call. I mean, he was so intelligent, and intellectual – so why the fuck?'

Connolly's sister Sharon feels that Steve may have had an undiagnosed depressive illness and heroin was a case of him self-medicating.

The final Paul Kelly and The Messengers live performance came at the end of a run of dates that included big shows in the major cities. It was no secret that this was the end of the line for this combination. But the final show wasn't in Sydney or Melbourne in front of several thousand fans. It was at the comparatively small Batman Fawkner Inn in the centre of Launceston on 18 August 1991.

At the end of the show, the tour manager opened some champagne and handed a glass to each of the band members and Paul. After the show there was more champagne and the next morning – no doubt a little shell-shocked at the realisation that it was actually over – they flew back to Melbourne and on to their homes.

Journalist Dino Scatena was there reviewing the show for *Juke* magazine and recalls the party afterwards, which went much of the night with lots of singing, drinking and smoking. 'Paul was the happiest I'd ever seen him to that point, grinning, floating free,' Scatena recalls.

'It was a less than salubrious way to finish but it was all okay between us and Paul,' Barclay says. 'Although it would have been nice to finish at Selina's in Sydney or somewhere big in Melbourne.'

Jon Schofield adds, 'I thought at least we could have gone out with a concert in Melbourne. That would have been more fitting. We'd done some big shows around the world so to finish there was a bit weird.'

Paul says 'that was just the way the tour was routed. I wasn't thinking we should do this planned farewell in Melbourne or Sydney. Maybe regrettably, but at the time I didn't think about putting this sense of theatre or ceremony around it. If you did it now you'd make more of a song or dance about it. It's thirty years ago. You didn't hype things up so much back then.'

For the first tour after the band separated from Paul, he kept Peter 'Pedro' Bull in the line-up. Barclay believes he wanted to keep a connection with the old band, 'as Pedro was less distinctive than my voice or Steve's guitar'.

To this day, the members of The Messengers continue to derive income from sales of records they contributed to and radio play and other uses of songs they performed on.

Paul has always distributed his money with great generosity, beyond his contractual obligations and what is considered the norm by music industry standards.

'I remember before the whole thing took off,' Barclay says, 'we had a meeting in a café in Victoria Street, Kings Cross, to work out how the money was going to be distributed. At that stage we were playing the Hopetoun for three hundred dollars a week and he [Paul] said that he wanted to have something written down in case something happened. We were all laughing but not long after that we went from the gig at Promises in Sylvania to where money was just flying around and, if it hadn't been written down, where would we have been? We all thought it was fair and nothing to argue about.'

Barclay says that at one stage Paul did question the specifics of the deal. 'Pedro and Schoey didn't care but Steve and I went, "No, we hear this stuff on the radio all the time – we want something from it." We went to lunch and I showed him the letter we'd done back then. He looked at it, folded it up and paid for lunch. He was completely honourable about it. He took some stuff back later but said we would all continue to get a publishing income.'

There is still a good relationship between Paul and Barclay, Schofield and Bull, and they catch up from time to time. Barclay lives with a lingering hope that one day there'll be a call from Paul saying, 'I'm thinking we should do a special show and play *Gossip* in its entirety – are you up for it?'

According to Connolly's brother Rohan, Paul's decision to disband The Messengers was particularly hard for Steve.

'He didn't say much about it but I think there was a definite element of disappointment about how things ended. The whole time that band was together they just had so much fun. Steve loved it, not in a clichéd way, he just loved being a musician on the road and leading the rock'n'roll lifestyle.

'But he never carried on about it when Paul called it quits. There was no "Bloody Paul, why did he break the band up?" stuff.

'Even though Steve didn't say it, I suspect he became increasingly frustrated playing second fiddle to Paul all the time, particularly when he'd been an important part of the sound they'd manufactured.'

'With Steve it wasn't just his solos but his parts within a song,' Paul says. 'We're still playing them, they have lasted a long time. Steve didn't like playing fast. He didn't like shredding or playing a lot of notes. You could almost feel the effort, the sound he would dig out of the guitar.

'Steve had a basic philosophy that if the melody of the song was there, then he didn't want to mess around with it too much, so often his solos were just referencing the melody of the song. Or starting with the melody like on the songs "To Her Door" or "Before Too Long". That was a classic Steve Connolly thing. If it was a good melody he wanted to use it. And then he had his own little way of twisting it around, turning it and making it a new statement.

'Dan Kelly learnt to play from those records, so when Dan plays with me there's a little bit of Stevie and that's really nice. Steve didn't believe that the guitar player should stand out from the band – but that the guitar should serve the song. And he was very involved with how we arranged the songs. He was probably the leading voice in that.'

Connolly did continue making music after The Messengers folded, including playing with his then partner Dee Hannan, and Paul's sister Mary Jo Kelly in folk/Irish influenced Friends and Relations, as well as forming another band The Troubles, and playing with country rock artist Sherry Rich and her band The Grievous Angels.

Towards the end of his life, Connolly formed The Usual Suspects, who played around a dozen shows in Melbourne and recorded ten tracks at Atlantis Studios in October and November 1994. The album was completed and released after Connolly's death in May 1995.

The cause of Steve's death was a bacterial infection, but no one is under any illusion that the condition wasn't made worse by his heroin use. It was a sad end for a musician who had been so integral to Paul's creative world.

'People come together because of a number of things,' says Connolly's sister Sharon. 'They get excited about the things they share with one another, and the way they spark off each other. And when it goes well it goes very well, and then when one of them goes their own way for whatever reason, it can be harder for those who have a lesser profile. The guitarists never have the same profile as the frontman unless they're frontmen as well.

'I think ambition really kicked in for Paul at the end of The Messengers. Steve was equally ambitious. In his own way he was quite hubristic. He was a very proud person but he lacked the killer ambition gene, and the driven ambition that could have built him a career in his own right. Deep down he was never going to be someone who would promote himself very well.'

But to quote David Bowie in 'Ziggy Stardust', 'Boy, could he play guitar.'

CHAPTER 11

EVERYBODY WANTS TO TOUCH ME

'For a country boy I thought they were really tight,
a good band, I can tell you.'
Kev Carmody

IN A POST MESSENGERS WORLD, PAUL WAS A STAR. A SOLO star. He needed musicians but he no longer had any immediate obligations to others. He felt an increased freedom to collaborate with pretty much anyone he pleased. He was Paul Kelly and there was no shortage of songwriters and musicians who wanted a bit of whatever he could insert into their world.

Paul has an inherent creative restlessness – and despite having the ego that is essential to the makeup of any highly creative artist he has the humanity and intuitive smarts to realise that often some of the finest creations are the result of inviting others into your world, no matter how unlikely a successful or productive outcome from such a venture may initially seem.

While never averse to collaborating with others it would be fair to say that Paul's real foray into those pursuits came after he personally received a level of critical and commercial validation for his work with the albums *Post* and *Gossip*.

With the release of the latter he was a bona fide success and now, as well as writing songs for others and hoping that they would be covered by singers other than himself, he was beginning to be in demand as someone to write songs with. Mushroom Publishing would invite him to their songwriting gatherings and pair him with other writers in their stable.

And through this time Paul would open himself up to what he and others could bring to the songwriting process if two writers joined forces, traded ideas and approaches.

After Paul and Fairfax moved back to Melbourne in 1991, he and Steve Connolly produced Archie Roach's debut album, *Charcoal Lane*, after Connolly discovered Roach.

Roach had written a song called 'Took the Children Away' in 1986. It may have been 1987. He's not sure. But soon after he travelled to Sydney to perform it on a television show called *Blackout*.

Connolly saw the show and told Paul he should check Roach out. Paul did. And he liked what he heard.

Paul and Connolly talked. They thought it might be an inspired idea to have Roach sing a couple of songs at their upcoming Messengers show at Hamer Hall in Melbourne.

'I'm working in Fitzroy at a hostel for homeless men,' Roach recalls. 'I got a phone call from somebody from Premier Artists, the booking agency. I was in the office when the phone call came through and they asked if I was Archie Roach. I said I was and then this person said that Paul Kelly was doing a show at Hamer Hall with his band

The Messengers and they were wondering if I'd like to open the show and do a couple of songs.

'I'd heard of Paul Kelly but I didn't know much about him. I needed a bit of convincing that the person on the phone was fair dinkum. I thought maybe it was someone having a go. But I said okay to the show.'

Roach went to Hamer Hall on the afternoon of the show. He had no idea what this Paul Kelly fellow actually looked like.

'It was all new and strange to me. I was taken down to where the dressing rooms and the stage were and I was in the Green Room making a cup of tea and this little bloke popped his head in. He was wearing a black shirt and black jeans and had curly hair. I immediately thought it was security. He asked if I was all right and I said, "Yeah, yeah." Didn't say anything else much and then he said, "I'm Paul," and he said, "Good to have you," and I said, "Thanks, mate." That was it.'

Roach did his sound check and got off the stage. His plan was to head home and get changed and come back for the show but he was told he needed to stay at the venue till show time. He was a bit short of cash and needed to eat. No problems, they said, there's food here. Welcome to show business.

Then it was time to do his songs. Roach laughs recalling that when he did his sound check it looked like a big venue. A big empty venue. Now it was still big – but packed with people.

He walked out and introduced 'Beautiful Child', saying it was 'a song about a fellow who died in jail'. He sang the song and there was little response from the audience. Roach thought this was a little strange but pushed on with his second song.

'I didn't have much stage presence. I said that the next song was about when I was taken away from my family as a little kid and I sang "Took the Children Away". Everything was quiet. And then I walked off and suddenly everyone started clapping. It sounded like rain on a tin roof at night and it built with wave upon wave and I was amazed.'

Roach walked backstage and Steve Connolly introduced himself and told him how great he'd been.

When Paul and The Messengers went on Roach stayed, watching and listening and realising that he knew so many of the songs.

He says he thought, 'Did Paul Kelly write all these songs? They were songs that were always being played on the radio.'

Soon after this show Paul and Connolly went around to Roach's home and talked about recording an album. Roach wasn't so sure about that idea and told them he'd have to think about it. Meanwhile they sat around singing songs from people they all liked, such as Ted Hawkins.

In the end they went into the studio to record what would be the *Charcoal Lane* album with both Paul and Connolly producing. But it was Connolly who took the leading role in the studio environment.

'Paul would throw a few things in. But it was Stevie more. Paul would be there. But what I do remember was Stevie's guitar playing. I'd grown up listening to Duane Eddy and people like that and he reminded me a bit of that, the way he played. I just loved his playing.

'In the studio I took my lead from Stevie – and his guitar.'

Roach was very new to the recording process. He was used to going in, singing a song and that would be it. Then he'd sing another. This was very different.

'This took all day before I even laid down a vocal,' he says. 'It seemed like it took a really long time. A couple of weeks. A lot of the time I was just sitting there listening to Steve and Paul deciding what they liked and what they didn't. I'd just go and have a smoke. This was back in my smoking days. I just thought, *These fellows know what they're doing.* I don't know what I could have added.'

Both Paul and Connolly also play on *Charcoal Lane*. Former Dots bass player Paul Gadsby was brought in for a session, as were Vika and Linda Bull and various other musicians. Paul's sister Mary Jo plays piano on 'Summer of My Life'.

And then Tim and Neil Finn were brought in, both singing on 'Down City Streets', and Tim alone on 'Took the Children Away'.

'I went, *TIM FINN* – on my record.' Roach laughs. 'I was a bit starstruck. I'd known of the Finn brothers since they were in Split Enz.'

Either Paul or Connolly took the album to Mushroom Records and Roach quickly met key record label staff members.

Roach wouldn't actually meet Michael Gudinski until the 1992 ARIA Awards when he won two awards – for Best New Talent and Best Indigenous Release – for *Charcoal Lane*.

'The first time I saw him I thought he was the comedian Steve Wright,' Roach laughs. 'He came up and said, "Good work, son – you start work tomorrow." I'm not sure he knew I was signed to his label.'

The contracts had been sorted out with Mushroom's lawyers with Paul sitting in on the meetings with Roach, who admits he had no idea what was being talked about most of the time.

'It could have been Chinese for all I knew,' he laughs. 'I didn't have a manager so Paul helped me out. They offered me something and Paul said, "They can do something better than that," and stopped me signing it.'

Upon the release of *Charcoal Lane*, Roach went on tour playing shows to promote the album, with Connolly playing as part of his band.

Paul and Roach wrote one song together – 'Rally Round the Drum' which was later recorded by Paul and The Stormwater Boys. Paul also recorded the song with Roach in 2019 for the album accompanying Roach's memoir, *Tell Me Why*.

'We were just sitting around having a yarn and I was telling Paul about my father who was a tent boxer. He was pretty relaxed to write with. It wasn't hard at all.'

* * *

The Messengers' final album, *Comedy*, includes the now Australian classic seven-minute song 'From Little Things Big Things Grow' which Paul wrote with Kev Carmody.

Kev Carmody first heard Paul Kelly in the mid-1980s. Carmody wasn't, and still isn't, a big music listener but if you turned on a radio at the time Paul's songs would begin seeping into your consciousness.

'The ones that got me were the more descriptive ones, songs like "From St Kilda to Kings Cross" which describe the bus trip – because as a Blackfella you could relate to that,' Carmody says. 'You never had enough money to buy a motorcar but you had enough to get on a bus and go on those long damned trips with your nose jammed against the glass. His descriptive capabilities are pretty phenomenal.'

It was after a long hitchhiking trip to Sydney that Carmody actually met Paul.

'I remember when I first went to the big city of Sydney. I got a lift down in a thirty-tonne truck carrying seafood coming from Brisbane and the old driver dropped me off right on Broadway. The fellow I was supposed to meet with was going to show me around the big town.

'So this guy – he was going to record me – takes me to a Go-Betweens concert at the Enmore Theatre and I remember sitting up in the seats in the balcony part, right up high, and he said, "There's Paul Kelly". Paul was sitting there and I met him very briefly that night. Just a hello how are you sort of thing.

'I was quite taken with The Go-Betweens as a band. It was one of the few concerts I'd been to in my life. Until then I'd never really been to concerts except around a bloody campfire.

'I remember that [Paul] wore a leather jacket – and I'd ridden motorbikes all my life. I always had a bike, the old Nortons and the old Triumphs and AJS bikes, and I thought, *Gee, he must have a bloody motorbike.* When we went outside afterwards I was looking up and down the street to see where his bike was, and I said, "You've got a leather jacket – you must have a motorbike," but he didn't have a bike at all. Funny thing – here's a bush bloke in the city assuming that if you wore a leather jacket you had a bike.'

Carmody and Paul continued bumping into each other. The two of them were involved in the Building Bridges Association in 1988, which was an attempt to link the Aboriginal people and the wider community through music.

The association staged concerts that showcased black and white talent at the Bondi Pavilion in Sydney, the first, on 26 January 1988, was in support for the Long March for Justice, Freedom and Hope. A compilation album, *Building Bridges – Australia Has a Black History*, was released in 1989 and included Paul's song 'Special Treatment'. In July that year a Rock for Land Rights concert was held at the State Sports Centre in Sydney featuring Paul and Crowded House.

After Carmody's first album, *Pillars of Society*, was released in 1988, Paul contacted him and asked if Carmody would support him and The Messengers at what used to be the Darling Downs Institute of Technology (now the University of Southern Queensland).

At that show Carmody met all of The Messengers for the first time and immediately fell into their world. He liked the way the band interacted with Paul. 'For a country boy I thought they were really tight, a good band, I can tell you.'

Carmody was quickly embraced by both Paul and the band. He was one of the gang and crammed into the tour bus to go to shows with them as they did more gigs together.

'They had the sort of personalities that, when you first met them it felt like you'd known them forever. You just fitted in with them. There was none of this stand-off business. You were *in*. Travelling with them in the van was a pain in the rear end as it was so cramped. But I had this admiration for them as a band because they were tight and they weren't afraid to do a little bit of solo stuff, throwing stuff into the songs and shows to keep everybody on their toes. Whenever they were around I was just in the fold as it were.'

Aside from Paul, Carmody mostly gravitated to Steve Connolly.

'He had that Irish background in music as well as the rock'n'roll stuff – and the politics.'

Connolly would produce Carmody's 1991 album *Eulogy (For A Black Person)* which also featured contributions from Paul, Peter Bull, Jon Schofield and Michael Barclay.

Paul dropped in and out of the *Eulogy* sessions but it was very much a Carmody/Connolly collaboration. And The Messengers kept coming in to do bits and pieces.

'It was all thrown together bit by bit,' is how Carmody recalls the recording of the album.

A little before there was the camping trip that changed both Paul's and Carmody's lives. Along with Paul's ten-year-old son Declan they headed out into the country.

'I have this old Land Rover. One of those troop carriers for the wife and kids. Paul said he was coming up and that he'd really like to see me. I said we were about to go off for a big camp and that we'd throw everything in the back and off we'd go.

'I remember picking him and Declan up from the bus stop. We went camping at a place called Wivenhoe which is a town outside of Brisbane. It was the first time that the dam there had ever been opened to the public. So we put tents up, got the fire going, and I had the guitars, the banjo and the mandolin. That was when "From Little Things" got started. She was rolled around then, on that trip.'

Carmody and Paul sat around a campfire and dashed off 'From Little Things' at around two in the morning. It was just a casual jam which would evolve into one of the best-known Australian songs of recent times.

'"From Little Things Big Things Grow" owes a lot to "The Lonesome Death of Hattie Carrol",' Paul says, 'go and have a listen to that. Similar melody. Similar chords.'

'I had the title as a potential for a love song like "It's Growing" by the Temptations. It was also a shortening of the Bruce Springsteen song "From Small Things (Big Things One Day Come)". It was only when we started talking about the Gurindji strike that I thought the title would go with this story.'

Carmody says, 'I threw in the chord progression on the mandolin and Paul was a little bit interested and then I swapped it to the banjo and he got a bit more interested and the next thing I said was, "Well, it's a pretty boring bloody chord progression but it'd be a good one to do a story to," and so we started talking about a topic we could write about.

'I told him a few things about my background and of course the big one was the bloody Gurindji Strike. That was huge in our black society. He took to it straight away and you know what he's like – he writes pretty bloody quick, you've got to pull him back.'

The song is based on the story of the Gurindji Strike and Vincent Lingiari. In essence, it describes the events surrounding the Gurindji people and their claim, which was part of a growing Indigenous land rights movement. The protest led to the Commonwealth *Aboriginal Land Rights (Northern Territory) Act 1976* which gave Indigenous people freehold title to traditional lands in the Northern Territory and the power to veto land mining and other developments on those lands.

'We didn't finish it on that trip,' Paul says, 'but we pretty much broke the back of it up there.'

'She was quick,' Carmody says. 'The story was there so it was just a matter of saying, "I don't like this business, that cliché of a snowball in hell – what about a cinder in the snow?" Just turning things around a bit.

'Then Paul went and checked with Frank Hardy and I had a bit of a yarn to Professor Fred Hollows because they were both involved on the ground at the strike, just to make sure everything was okay. Gough Whitlam loved that song.'

In Carmody's mind there was no sense at that point that they had created an iconic Australian song. He thought it was far too long for that.

'Then Paul recorded it but I couldn't because the old man who was the centre of it from an Aboriginal perspective had passed away so there was no way I could record it or be involved with it because he's named in the song. I had to wait two years for the *buramaji*, the respect, before I could do it.'

'I remember playing "From Little Things" for the first time at the Building Bridges concert,' Paul says, 'and it was still new, still fresh and I didn't have it in my head so I had big pieces of A4 paper with the key images written down to help me remember the song – like aeroplane, politicians, sand through the fingers – and I remember thinking the song had really good images. Cinder in snow, I really liked that one, an inverted cliché, "Deportee", the Woody Guthrie song, was in the back of my head, that waltz feeling. Thought there was something in it when [film maker] John Whitteron came up and said he really liked the images in the song – that was how I did my memory sheet because I obviously couldn't write all the words out so I remembered the songs through the images.'

Paul and The Messengers recorded the song for *Comedy*.

'It was a real slow burner. We didn't do a video for it. It wasn't played on the radio. I put it on my record. It just became popular gradually.

'In 1991 I was asked to play at Victoria River for the twenty-fifth anniversary of the Walk Off. I flew on a chartered plane with Robert Tickner, the minister for Aboriginal Affairs at the time, Frank Hardy and Gough Whitlam. I just remember Frank and Gough talking pretty much the whole way but I didn't have much interaction with them. Then I played my song and we went home.'

Two years later Carmody's version appeared on his *Bloodlines* album, with Paul playing guitar, harmonica and singing.

'The version Paul and I did together was actually done for a documentary with Tiddas and Paul and I all together in a studio,' Carmody recalls. 'They wanted a shot of that on the video. I told the sound engineer to flick a switch and see what happens. It was spontaneous.

'We'd only rehearsed it once or twice. I had the banjo and Paul had the guitar and Tiddas were just using their voices. They sent a copy to me when I went back to Brisbane and I said, "The bloody banjo, the sound of it is going in waves – up and down, up and down, can't you level that out somehow?" but they said they couldn't because they had forgotten to switch the banjo mic on.'

'From Little Things' would become a key element in each of the artist's careers. In May 2008, GetUp released a cover version of the song which peaked at number 4 on the ARIA singles chart. Included in this version produced by Tim Levinson of The Herd were samples from speeches by prime ministers Paul Keating and Kevin Rudd, and vocals from both Paul and Carmody, Missy Higgins and other singers.

Paul and Carmody would perform the song at the memorial service for former prime minister Gough Whitlam in November 2014.

'In 2014 when Gough Whitlam died I think one of his sons requested we play the song at the funeral,' Paul says. 'My understanding is that Gough had pretty much planned how the funeral would be. I mean if you plan your own funeral you get the Sydney Symphony Orchestra, you get Noel Pearson to speak.

'I think when I went to Victoria River with him he didn't really know anything about the song. But over time that changed and the family said that it was his request that we sing it.

'It was an amazing experience. Everyone spoke so eloquently. We were on after Noel Pearson and he just spoke brilliantly, just this wave of oratory. He never said Gough's name, it was all "that old man" and I'm sitting there with Kev thinking, "Oh no, we've got to follow this. Who programmed this?"

'Then we walked on and it was actually perfect. Noel had created this wave of feeling. His speech was poetry and then we just followed on with the song – so we surfed Noel's wave. He set up the wave and we surfed it. It was actually the perfect piece of programming. We were pretty nervous – all these former prime ministers up the front – but we'd sung the song so many times before that once we got started it just takes care of itself.

'Circles come around. That song started with images of Gough pouring dirt into Vincent's hands – that famous photo by Mervyn Bishop. That was the start of the song for me – and then to be singing it at his funeral – you never could have imagined it.'

* * *

After 'From Little Things Big Things Grow', Paul also collaborated with Yothu Yindi and Peter Garrett and the remix team Filthy Lucre on Yothu Yindi's now classic song 'Treaty' in 1991. It was a significant year. His daughter Madeleine was born and he also started his life-long personal and professional friendship with the Bull sisters with songwriting sessions around the kitchen table.

'I remember hitting it off with them straight away,' Paul says. 'I don't know how we got to the point of them trusting me to produce their first record but it was a friendship that was easy from the start. I think we all come from strong families and strong ties to family and that struck a chord with us all straight away. It's one of my precious friendships that I have with them and their families.'

The trio had first met in 1988 at Expo 88 when the Bull sisters were in Brisbane to perform one of the earliest live shows they'd done with Joe Camilleri's Black Sorrows. Vika remembers their chance meeting with Paul with some amusement.

'We walked into a Japanese restaurant in Brisbane and there he was having dinner with someone. We said, "Shit, there's Paul Kelly," and went up and introduced ourselves and said hello. He didn't say much – just smiled a lot.'

Vika had been a fan of Paul's since the early eighties, since seeing him on *Countdown*. 'He certainly had a look – that nice curly hair. I also saw Paul Kelly and The Dots play at The Club. It was the best concert I'd ever seen. The place was packed. I might have just turned eighteen so I could get into clubs.'

Linda agrees. 'I remember being fifteen and listening to The Dots. We were fans of his music and he was a good-looking guy … still is.'

After saying hello, Linda says the sisters backed off. 'We got really shy as going up to someone like that is not normally what we would do.

'We just watched him eat.'

Little did the sisters know as they watched Paul chew that they would very soon develop a long personal and professional relationship with him.

Two years later, in 1990, the Bull sisters worked with Paul for the first time. Linda Bull says, 'Paul phoned me at my flat in St Kilda and told me he was producing Archie Roach's album with Steve Connolly and wanted us to sing on it. That was *Charcoal Lane*. It was the first time we'd been in the studio with him. I remember Steve being great and Paul being fantastic too, and Archie of course. I think they knew that Archie was really special. His voice was something else and his songs were beautiful. So they just let us do our thing.

'Because of our work with the [Black] Sorrows we were starting to get known as a unit and asked to do backing vocals. But Paul was the first person to hire us for a session, to sing on the Archie record.

'At that stage we didn't really know Steve. We knew Paul and got to know Steve later, but it was the first time we met him. They seemed to have a great communication and be very close. They worked well together and didn't clash. Steve was in the driver's seat but Paul produced our vocals.'

When Paul relocated back to Melbourne permanently after the end of The Messengers there was more opportunity for the trio's relationship to grow. The Bull sisters were touring constantly with The Black Sorrows, a band who seemed as though they were always on the road. Eventually they decided that they'd like to make an album of their own.

'Paul said that if we wanted to make an album we should think about writing songs and finding our own voice. And he said he'd help us do it. So we would go around to his flat every Thursday to work,' Linda says.

It was a process that tried Vika's patience.

'Paul would just sit there and we would talk and try and get an idea. He just wouldn't give up. He would happily sit there ALL DAY – and wait. He was very patient with us. But I used to wish he would fucking leave. I don't have that patience. Songwriting's not my thing but I think he really wanted to get us to write and he was trying to encourage that so we sat there … all day. And waited.

'And then all of a sudden something brilliant would come out and he'd just write it down. It would be him that would start it. We'd just talk and then he'd go, "Okay," and we'd go from there. It was very intimidating because I thought, *Shit is just going to pour out of my mouth* – which it usually does. *He'll think I'm a fucking idiot.*

'Linda's a little different. She tends to think more, like Paul, so that's why I would often get up and go and make the tea and the sandwiches while those two nutted it out all day and into the night-time.

'We'd sit there. *All day. Into the night.* Declan was a little kid and we'd order pizza as he always wanted pizza for tea.'

'Whenever we could, whenever everyone was home from tours, we'd work methodically on writing songs with each other,' Linda says. 'It was pretty amazing. We knew he was a really great songwriter and at that point we'd done nothing.

'He never forced us to do anything. It wasn't ever a formal, "Right, what are we going to do today?" We'd just tell stories and we'd talk about our family or whatever had happened to us that week, and from that we would start to write.

'The song "Ninety Nine Years" started that way. The idea for the song was something that had happened to us. We'd been out on a date with somebody and we were talking about it and then turned it into a song. Paul would never leave until a song was done. That was a work ethic that we'd never really encountered before. A song would be started and it would be finished. Pretty much every day we met. They were long sessions. We'd start mid-morning and go all day and into the night until we were finished.

'He didn't say much. I remember my husband at the time saying, "He doesn't talk," and I said, "It's because he's listening – that's how he gets ideas."'

Paul says, 'My attitude with getting together to write a song is that, especially with people I don't know – I say that we don't have to end up with a song that day. That's what the publishers want. Songwriting is a form of play so we're going to play together and try and write a song and if we don't finish it then it doesn't matter. We're just trying. And I'm sure I would have had the same attitude with them – *but* part of the fun is that you've got to push on a little. You don't have a bit of an idea and then stop and, much as I love them, they do need a bit of a push. I would probably have been pushing in that sense. I was definitely the driver, getting them to talk and tell stories and edge into an idea and developing it.'

* * *

Although The Messengers had broken up, there was a final release from them and Paul in 1992 – *Hidden Things* predominantly contained songs that hadn't appeared on their previous albums, such as Paul's song about the neglect of Indigenous Australians, 'Special Treatment', 'Rally Around the Drum', a song co-written with Archie Roach, and covers of Woody Guthrie's 'Pastures of Plenty', Joe Geia's 'Yil Lull', Kev Carmody's 'Elly' and James Reyne's 'Reckless'.

In 1991 Paul was approached by Steve Gration from the Magpie Theatre Company in Adelaide to write songs for *Funerals and Circuses*, a group-devised play that dealt with tensions in small-town Australia. The playwright Roger Bennett was invited to shape the play with input from improvisations by all the actors, including Paul who played a petrol pump attendant. Kaarin Fairfax assisted Gration in directing the play, which premiered at the 1992 Adelaide Festival.

Paul also sang 'Hey Boys' with Mark Seymour from Hunters & Collectors, a band Paul and The Messengers had toured with extensively in the 1980s. The song was included in the soundtrack to the film *Garbo*. Neil Finn provided backing vocals for the song.

Finn and Paul had known each other for a long time. In 1985, early in Crowded House's career, Finn recalls meeting some of Paul's family when both of their bands were playing in Queensland.

'I actually have Super 8 film footage of us playing tennis and having a barbecue outside the hotel,' Finn says. 'We did at least a couple of shows together around that time.

'I remember running into Paul on a few occasions in Melbourne because that's just what happened with bands in those days when you were doing the same pubs and the same touring circuit. You would also meet at baggage carousels. That still happens today as everybody flies from city to city.'

Finn's friendship with Paul really began when Paul and The Messengers opened for Crowded House's 1987 American tour.

Now, in the early nineties, they were both living in St Kilda and hung out, often playing tennis in Finn's backyard.

Finn concurs with almost everyone who has ever played sport with Paul that he's extremely focused and even more competitive. Sex and death may be the only things he cites as being important to think about – but winning at any form of sport is right up there too.

'He's very competitive, isn't he? He's quite a fierce competitor on the tennis court. I think on the occasions when we played singles he usually beat me, although I think I might have beaten him once.'

Of all the tennis court encounters they had it's the time Finn was beaten by a heroin-affected Paul that sticks in his brain. 'He'd been using that day – and he still beat me.

'He came over for dinner but before we ate we'd played a game of tennis. I didn't notice anything unusual. It was only when he came to the house and the lamb came out – this beautiful lamb roast Sharon cooked – and he went, "Look, I had some heroin today and I'm not sure I can eat it," and he excused himself and went and sat outside.

'It was kind of bad form as a guest – and he'd just beaten me at tennis which was a bit confounding. I couldn't believe it really, if he hadn't told me I don't think I would have known otherwise because he was quite lucid.'

* * *

Towards the end of 1992 Paul released the solo double album *Live, May 1992* recorded at shows at the Regal Theatre in Perth and the Athenaeum in Melbourne.

By the time this was released Paul and Fairfax and their daughter Madeleine had relocated to Los Angeles, the first of two extended stays in that city during this period.

Paul had been pushing for more inroads into America for a while. In fact the early to mid-1990s was a period when Paul was particularly focused on North America. 'It was a *big* target for Paul,' his manager at the time, Rob Barnham, says. 'He really wanted things to work in America and felt as though to that point it hadn't. He wanted to have an influence there. He wanted Americans to record his songs. He wanted his songs pushed to other artists to record.'

While Barnham was Paul's manager for Australia and New Zealand, Paul also had an American manager, Ken Kushnick.

'I just wanted to try and establish a bit more of a stronghold in America,' Paul says. 'I'd gone backwards and forwards and it was feeling a bit like pouring water in the desert. I thought I'd move there and see if I could build up a profile. It was pretty much my decision. It wasn't driven by a record label. The A & M deal wasn't renewed, so I wanted to find a label and try and build things up – moving there seemed a good idea.'

Soon after relocating to Los Angeles, Paul was introduced to guitarist Randy Jacobs, a former member of Was (Not Was), who shared the same management as Paul in North America.

'Ken Kushnick, who was my manager, told me that Paul needed a guitar player and recommended me,' Jacobs says. 'He sent me a bunch of Paul's stuff and I listened to it and thought it would be fun.

'Paul came over to my house and the two of us sat down and started playing guitar together. We played songs like "Cities of Texas" and "To Her Door".'

Jacobs didn't know too much about Paul. He was aware of The Messengers and the deal with A & M Records but not much else. However the two quickly developed a rapport.

'It's real easy with him,' Jacobs says, 'because it's about songs. My style is rhythm-based so it was easy to fit in. It was funny – he'd say, "Can you do a solo with just four notes instead of twenty-five?" That was the stuff I learnt from him.

'And because of Paul I became a pretty good background singer. When we met I hadn't sung that much because in Was Not Was we had three singers, but with Paul I got back into it.'

Initially the two of them did shows together – clubs and some television appearances in North America. Soon after the end of his relationship with A & M Records Paul was signed to the Vanguard label.

'Paul was trying to make headway as a new artist in America,' Jacobs says, 'but for most of the time the audience he would get was Australian because he was Paul Kelly.

'Some of the songs are decidedly connected to Australia – "Adelaide" and the cricket songs, but there's tons of songs that aren't. I did "Pouring Petrol on a Burning Man" on one of my records with The Boneshakers but I called it "Pouring Gasoline on a Burning Man". I'm actually thinking of doing an album of his songs and calling it *The Book of Paul*. There's a whole bunch of great songs that people outside his domain need to hear.'

* * *

In 1993, Paul and Fairfax's second daughter, Memphis, was born. It was another busy work year, with Paul contributing both songs and vocals to the soundtrack of the ABC television series *Seven Deadly Sins* – a project that brought him back in contact with Martin Armiger, introduced him to Renée Geyer and continued his work and friendship with Deborah Conway.

'It was such a weird pairing,' Armiger said of the sessions. 'Everyone initially said no. Renée said she didn't like Paul's music, and Deborah and Renée were not very easy around each other, they were very competitive.

'This time Paul was much more open to trying things. We were trying to come up with a style. I was basing it on pre-reggae Jamaican music, so ska and sound system stuff, and I had a great funky band – Rex Goh on guitar, Paul Grabowsky on piano and so forth. And I wanted Paul to adapt with me to some of the styles, so we worked together a bit on that, and good on him for trying as I know it was tough for him. But I still couldn't get him to sing like a singer sings. Renée was brilliant. Deborah was brilliant.'

Conway agrees that Armiger was trying to get Paul to push beyond his boundaries then.

'Martin was trying to get him to swing more and be a bit more sexy. To be looser. I was impressed that he was prepared to try.'

The biggest battle in the studio was to get Geyer to sing one of Paul's songs. She wasn't into the idea at all.

'I invited her to sing his song "Foggy Highway",' Armiger said, 'and she flatly refused for the first two weeks. I kept working on an arrangement and a track and then she came in one day and said, "All right, I'll do it," and she did it in one morning at a place in Glebe. She wanted to re-do it but I said to leave it as the rawness was what I wanted. After that they became good buddies.'

'It wasn't that I wasn't keen as I was always a fan of Paul's,' Geyer says, 'but I wasn't sure how I could fit into his world in terms of music. I'd always had unusual tastes given my leanings. I'm an R & B person but I've also always appreciated other forms of music.

'I'm not one of those people where if I like the sound of something I think I'll give it a try. I like to stay where I'm comfortable and do it really well.

'So yes, when "Foggy Highway" was suggested I was wondering how it would work. But I knew that the song was written with me in mind so I thought that at the very least I needed to hear what he was thinking and what he had in mind. When I listened to it I just loved it.

'I developed it into my thing, and he obviously liked what I did with it. I didn't change the melody or the lyrics, but I made it my own in the way I sing it and he liked that. He *loved* it. I think that's where our friendship really started; after that we were very close and have been since then.'

'We all played nicely in the sandpit together,' is how Conway reflects back on the sessions. 'It was during this recording that Renée realised that Paul was a bit of a treasure and cosied up to him. That is where the genesis of the relationship between them began, Paul supporting her with her material and producing for her. She did love him … and she is a difficult woman.'

Anyone who has ever encountered Geyer in full flight would know that she can be a tad unpredictable, and doesn't suffer fools gladly. It would have been with some trepidation that Paul called Geyer in 1994 to explain that he had a song for her – called 'Difficult Woman'.

'He wrote that for me and when he told me about it on the phone, there was probably a thirty-second silence – if not longer – and then I realised that the lyrics were a lot more complex than just an idea about a difficult woman. That would have been too easy.

'We all know I'm a difficult woman so there had to be a little bit more behind it. And he nailed it. It was more about a complicated situation which it normally is with anyone who's considered to be difficult.'

Later in 1994 Paul and Geyer, both at the time living in Los Angeles, started talking about working on an album together.

'He had good ears. He understood my side of what I'm doing. And I knew that I was a fan of his thing. It seemed to make a lot of sense to work together – and he agreed. He said, "Let's give it a go and if it's not working we'll stop it." But it worked. Of course it worked.'

Paul produced the album, along with six of the eleven songs being written or co-written by him.

'It's one of my best records and I acknowledge that *now*, years down the line. I mean, I don't think I would have said it's one of my best records at the time but now I look back and know that it is. I don't even know why. It just is.'

Playing on the album were Geyer's personal band plus some other musicians living in Los Angeles at the time, Geyer remembering the making of the album as being 'a very joyous time'.

Part of the strength of that record – and an aspect of Paul's songwriting that has been constant throughout his career – was his ability to write songs that a woman could sing and live inside comfortably.

'He knows,' Geyer says. 'He's just got an innate sense of how a woman feels. He's not as good when he's got a relationship with a woman. He hasn't always batted a thousand on that level.

'But in general he's a good writer of how a woman is thinking. He seems to have that down until he becomes involved with one. And then he completely loses the plot.

'Which of course is normal because you're too subjective when love comes into it, there's no words. There's no normal. You can't use any knowledge that you would normally use.'

CHAPTER 12

THE NEW SQUAD

'Paul would go, "So you like the old stuff better than the
new stuff?" and they'd scream out, "Yes," and he'd go,
"Too bad."'

Steve Hadley

IN LOS ANGELES PAUL ALSO RECORDED DEMOS WITH SOME
of the musicians who would later become constant figures
in his live band – guitarist Shane O'Mara, drummer Peter
Luscombe and bass player Bill McDonald. They had all
been part of a contingent of travelling Melbourne musicians
and singers, including Paul, Deborah Conway and Archie
Roach, who went to the South by Southwest (SXSW) music
festival in Austin, Texas, as well as playing other showcase
gigs in North America.

Peter Luscombe played his first gig as drummer with Paul
Kelly in March 1993, and embarked on his first tour as part of
the band at the beginning of 1994. Luscombe is the longest-
serving musician who's played with Paul. Between albums and
singles he's performed on twenty-one Paul Kelly recordings.

Luscombe and Paul are close. Closer than Paul has ever been to a band mate since his relationship with Steve Connolly.

Luscombe remembers everything. The other band members will say, 'Ask Peter – he'll remember,' and Luscombe remarks, with a certain sense of pride, that when Paul was writing his own book he'd constantly call Luscombe asking him to clarify dates, times and places.

So of course he recalls the first time he met Paul.

'It was at the old Jump Club and it was an incarnation of The Dots,' he says. 'I just remember that Paul was drinking from a cask of white wine backstage and I said hello and he offered me a drink. He was very cordial.'

Luscombe and Paul moved in similar circles so would run into each other from time to time. The relationship developed when The Black Sorrows – who Luscombe was drumming with – did a bunch of big festival and large venue shows with The Messengers.

Messengers drummer Michael Barclay remembers this time well too, 'Vika and Linda Bull were singing and Peter Luscombe was on the drums. I still remember watching him playing his hats with his feet so he had both hands free to do anything he wanted, and he was *fantastic.*'

'When Vika and Linda were thinking about doing their solo album,' Luscombe says, 'Paul was having these little writing sessions with them and I would drop around. This was 1992. We'd sit around and demo a few ideas on cassette.'

Next Luscombe was part of the quasi house band that accompanied Paul and the other musicians to the SXSW music festival in 1993. The travelling cavalcade played shows in Austin, and later in Orange County at which point Paul decided that he might use this collection of musicians – which also included Bill McDonald, Shane O'Mara and David Bridie – to record some demos.

Over two days in a studio in the Valley near Burbank in Los Angeles they recorded three songs that made it on to the *Wanted Man* album – 'Nukkanya', 'You're Still Picking the Same Sore', and 'Love Never Runs on Time'.

Randy Jacobs co-produced the *Wanted Man* album with Paul and David Bridie, Jacobs having organised the majority of the musicians for that recording, with eleven songs being recorded in Los Angeles and a further two in Australia with Bridie. Paul brought the recordings from those Los Angeles sessions back to Australia, added some parts, including Vika and Linda's vocals, and mixed them.

'"Love Never Runs on Time" was the first session we did for him on one of his records,' Linda says.

'It was actually by chance. We just went into Metropolis to visit him. We didn't go in to sing on that record or that song. We'd been out to dinner and were a bit pissed and he said, "I've just finished this song, do you want to sing on it?" It was late at night.'

In the meantime Luscombe also returned to Australia and decided to leave The Black Sorrows.

Not long after his departure from that band he ran into Paul in St Kilda, taking his washing up to the laundromat. It was soon after Paul, Fairfax and their family had moved back to Melbourne again from LA. Luscombe told Paul he'd just left The Black Sorrows and if he was thinking of putting a band together Luscombe would be interested. Paul smiled but didn't say anything and went about his day.

About three weeks later Luscombe's phone rang. It was Paul asking if he was serious about playing in a band with him. Luscombe was. Paul said he was bringing his American guitarist, Randy Jacobs, out to Australia and doing a four-week tour in January. Was Luscombe interested? Luscombe was.

That tour – with Luscombe and Jacobs being augmented by Peter Bull on keyboards and former Dots member Paul Gadsby playing bass – took in pubs and a few theatres.

At the end of the tour Luscombe told Paul he was up for anything more and Paul said he'd let him know in a few months. Luscombe felt that the dynamics of the band weren't gelling completely the way Paul wanted, and that maybe Bull was revisiting some old playing patterns that were dragging the songs back to the days of The Messengers at a time when Paul clearly wanted to move on from that band.

In the meantime Luscombe went off and played with David McComb on a European tour during which he received word from Paul's manager Rob Barnham that Paul was going out on a big tour in June 1994.

The band that played on that tour was Luscombe, Jacobs, Bruce Haymes on keyboards, Steve Hadley on bass and Graham Lee on pedal steel.

'My country-funk period,' Paul says with a smile.

It was a long tour, on and off for about two and a half months. They did a concert level tour followed immediately by a run of large pub dates. Then, at the end, they recorded the *Live at the Continental and Esplanade* album and some sessions for *Deeper Water*.

One half of *Deeper Water* was recorded with Jacobs as guitarist, the other with O'Mara, who Luscombe considered a logical choice to come into the band.

O'Mara had moved in Paul's orbit well before they actually played together, which was on the SXSW tour in Austin, where, like Luscombe, O'Mara was part of the house band.

Not long after that Rob Barnham called O'Mara asking if he'd like to do an American tour with Paul. He was told he'd be sent a cassette with twenty-two songs on it that he needed to learn.

With Paul living in America at the time, they met in Washington and rehearsed at O'Mara's brother's place – literally running through songs in his bathroom. The two of them headed off in a little van for a run of dates.

'He's easy to work with,' O'Mara says of Paul, 'and knows what he wants. It's the old adage of serving the song. That's the first agenda. Solos are short. Riffs can be proud but you don't mess with the tune.'

O'Mara feels that in those days the band were given less creative freedom than what Paul allows the current players, even though by the time it came to recording *Words and Music* he felt Paul was more receptive to textures and stylistic flourishes than he had been previously.

'I felt that I was hired to play for him. You *were* part of the band but it was *his* band.

'But he's a very sweet man. We had some good times. On tours I shared rooms with him a lot. He's very shy. And he's intense. And fiercely smart. He's pretty determined with what he wants. He is a driven man, one of *the* most driven people I've met.'

O'Mara had various other commitments so there was a revolving array of guitarists – by 1996 Spencer Jones was floating in and out of the line-up, touring with the band and accompanying Paul on an American duo tour, in the same way that O'Mara did from time to time.

This line-up recorded the now iconic 'How to Make Gravy' which was first issued as a track on a Myer Christmas CD raising funds for the Salvation Army and later as a standalone CD. Hilary Brown's father is credited for supplying the recipe in the song.

Hadley remains most pleased of the fact that he plays on 'How to Make Gravy', which he considers has become like an Australian version of The Pogues' 'Fairytale of New York'.

'I was there when he wrote it. It sort of just poured out of him. It was bizarre. We'd been on the road and we always fooled around with songs and ideas on the road and at sound checks.

'Lindsay Field asked him to do a Myer Christmas record but all the good Christmas songs were taken so Paul goes, "Fuck it, I'll write my own," so he wrote "Gravy" – which is not even on a proper Paul Kelly record.

'When I got my head around the story and the way Paul had put it together, I thought, *Oh, there you go, another fucking Paul Kelly classic.* It's become a thing. It's almost like Keith Richards' shepherd's pie recipe. People are making their gravy from Paul's fucking lyrics.

'We shot the video at my place, on the roof on the corner in the stinking heat one day.'

O'Mara, on the other hand, says he had no sense of its enduring quality at the time.

'It's great to be part of that song. It just started as a jam at sound check. Sometimes if we needed to we'd rehearse properly but often at sound check we'd run through bits and pieces and work them up. In this case Paul had nicked a few chords and we just started playing that thing. It *is* an incredible song – just the whole song, the story and the delivery.'

* * *

In 1997, Michael Gudinski thought it was the right time for a Paul Kelly retrospective album. The artist was less enthusiastic.

'I just thought that people needed to recognise the body of work that this guy had achieved,' Gudinski says. 'It took me a long time to talk him into the fucking thing. He didn't want to do it. In his mind I think he thought that the next thing I'd be doing was asking him to do a duets album and then a covers record. Which I would *never* do. *Ever*. But I thought it was a statement on his career and achievement. I mean, *Gossip* only went Top 15.'

Once Paul had agreed to the idea of the collection there was another drama for Gudinski. Paul brought in the photo he wanted to use on the cover – a snapshot of a very young Paul playing beach cricket.

'When he brought the cover in I almost passed out. In truth if you're an artist-friendly person you want to accommodate them as much as you possibly can.

'You work on something for so long and then the guy brings you in this photo … I told him to go and see Pierre [Baroni] in our art department and see if they could work out a package. I think that album is one of the major building blocks of what Paul Kelly is today.'

The '*Songs from the South* collection – Paul Kelly's Greatest Hits' has twenty songs, starting with 'From St Kilda to Kings Cross' and concluding with 'How to Make Gravy'.

Barnham recalls the sudden popularity that accompanied the release of the collection in May 1997. The album sold a staggering number of copies at the time – more than 650,000 copies. But it still didn't make number 1 on the Australian charts thanks to Savage Garden.

'Paul was at number two for at least eight weeks,' Barnham says, 'and then both his album and Savage Garden's dropped at the same time so there wasn't a moment when we could go to number one.'

The album set 1997 up very nicely for Paul. Although he'd been nominated on three previous occasions for Best Male Artist at the ARIA Awards, he would now finally take home the trophy. He was also inducted into the ARIA Hall of Fame.

The next album was *Words and Music*, recorded with the band, which meant both Spencer Jones and Shane O'Mara in the studio doing various parts.

'The thing I remember a lot about that record was the band playing together and just getting a sound,' Luscombe says. 'We'd done a few weeks of rehearsing and the version of "Nothing On My Mind" that appears on that album was the first take of the first track of the first day. I remember that we did five or six band tracks in the first day, so that album wasn't like pulling teeth. It had a real band chemistry and it sounds like it now when I listen to it.'

Paul and the band then hit the road and toured a lot – they went to America and then did some shows in the UK as well as a number of runs around Australia. This was winter/summer touring – theatres in winter, and the pubs in summer. Then, in between all this, Paul would occasionally head overseas by himself or take one or two other musicians.

Sometimes he'd go with just Shane O'Mara or Spencer Jones or as a band. When he went on one duo tour with Shane O'Mara, it left Hadley and Peter Luscombe feeling a little left out. They decided to buy their own tickets and just turned up and did the remainder of the dates with Paul and O'Mara.

Soon after, Paul decamped from Mushroom Records and its publishing division to EMI for recording and Universal Music for publishing.

Paul had an immediate rapport with Tony Harlow, the English record company executive who was running EMI at the time.

'I went to lunch with them the first time they met and I should have gone home after the entree,' Barnham says. 'They clicked and I knew then that he would go to EMI. It was a meeting of minds creatively and on every other front.

'Michael [Gudinski] never thought that we would leave Mushroom, and to be honest nor did I, but we shopped around. We gave Mushroom the option to make offers. Mushroom's recording and publishing offer didn't even come close – Universal offered hundreds of thousands of dollars more for the publishing.'

The biggest bargaining chip Paul had was that, by this stage through Gudinski's generosity and the terms of his deals, he owned or would soon own all the rights to his previous albums – so he was able to offer not only his future recordings and songs but eventually his past catalogue as well.

EMI agreed to give Paul his own label imprint, Gawdaggie Records. The label may have wondered what they'd walked into when Paul delivered his first two albums for his new home. The first, *Smoke*, was a bluegrass album recorded with Melbourne band Uncle Bill, and featuring old and new Paul compositions performed in a bluegrass style. Paul had previously recorded with Uncle Bill on the song 'Thanks A Lot' for the 1997 compilation *Where Joy Kills Sorrow*.

'The idea for that record [*Smoke*] had come from Tim O'Brien's *Red on Blonde*, bluegrass covers of Bob Dylan songs,' Paul says. 'A lot of my songs come from old-time country music. That was part of the DNA of The Messengers with Steve Connolly and Michael Barclay. I realised that a lot of our songs could be done in a bluegrass way and that's how *Smoke* came about.'

The second album with EMI was one of the most intriguing albums of Paul's career – 1999's self-titled *Professor Ratbaggy* album, an excursion into the word of dub, reggae, funk and other sonic excursions. Paul's name wasn't even on the front cover of the album and, to this day, many of his fans probably don't even know about it.

The name Professor Ratbaggy comes from a 1960s Australian television show character, a bumbling but kind-hearted scientist and a comical character who was played by Ernie Carroll on GTV-9 in Melbourne.

Luscombe and Paul had bonded many years earlier over a love of hip hop and rap, and Paul had immersed himself in reggae and dub since at least the time when, as manager, I was making him cassettes of Steel Pulse, The Mighty Diamonds, Toots and the Maytals, and others in the mid-1980s – and he was already very familiar with a lot of its practitioners well before then.

Luscombe recalls his and Paul's hip hop moment, one that harks back to the time Paul was living in Los Angeles in 1993.

'We were sitting outside Canter's Deli getting takeaway burgers and Dr. Dre's "The Chronic" comes on the radio and we're both nodding our heads and I'm going, "I dig this," and he says, "Me too." We really loved the mood and the way it flowed so our love of hip hop has always been there.'

In fact Paul's fascination and love for music outside what he is best known for creating is long-standing – so his immersion into the Professor Ratbaggy project surprised no one who knew him.

Professor Ratbaggy grew out of a band called The Casuals, which was the band Luscombe, Hadley and Haymes played as when they weren't touring or recording with Paul. They had a residency at the Night Cat in Fitzroy and often played with other musicians. 'We asked Paul to sit in, just play guitar and not sing,' Luscombe says. 'He did and had fun, and he said, "Maybe we should write some tunes together."'

Bass player Hadley thinks that the impetus for Paul to involve himself with the Professor Ratbaggy project had its genesis in what Tex Perkins was doing with The Cruel Sea.

'He said to me that he wanted to do something like Tex did with The Cruel Sea and join an instrumental band. That was the vibe. At the time we did our record The Cruel Sea were still kind of big. It was the early nineties and I thought, *What a great idea* – Tex had the surf thing going on with him and we had this sort of whacked-out reggae/funky chicken thing.'

Keyboardist Haymes says, 'He [Paul] wanted to step outside of being Paul Kelly with a capital P and K. He didn't want to be singled out in the band, but of course when you're famous that's what happens. He just wanted to be part of the band and step away from being the great lyricist and frontman. We were a little fruitier, a bit random and a bit saucy. He wanted a bit of that because everyone in his position – from Bob Dylan down – tries not to get cemented into this iconic status. I know Paul fights against that a little. It just ossifies you and you get stuck and you lose a bit of your freedom. This project was a little touch of freedom.'

'The aesthetic or ethos for that Professor Ratbaggy record was to write all the tunes with the band through just jamming,' Paul says. 'Bruce, Peter and Steve Hadley had a little trio and used to play at the Night Cat. Mainly instrumentals. Songs by The Meters and different reggae songs and reggae instrumentals. I got up with them and sang once. Then we got talking and decided to get together once a week and jam and see what happened. That went along for about a year of us playing and coming up with tunes.'

'This was just when he'd signed to EMI,' Luscombe says. 'So we went into a rehearsal space and we had a bunch of ideas, and he had some lyrics and this and that, and then we just did all the tracks. We had this great engineer, Andy Baldwin, who's now living in the States. He totally had the right sensibilities for it sonically.

Baldwin, who had known Paul for many years through working in recording studios in Melbourne, loved the project.

'It was fun because the band are *so* good. They're made for that reggae/dub feeling.

'And Paul is awesome because he loves working with young engineers and I was pretty young back then. He wanted a fresh approach and he shared a lot of records with me that he liked. We talked about Los Lobos and records Tchad Blake had made. Paul loved his sound and so did I so we bonded over that shared sound we were after.

'I remember that Paul would rewrite and change lyrics during the actual recording and even overdubbing time. It was right down to the wire with some things.'

'The opening song – "Please Myself" – sounds like a cassette, and it *is* a cassette,' continues Luscombe. 'That's a recording from the rehearsal. We had this idea that I would play along with the rehearsal tapes when we recorded it and we'd drop in and out of it.

'All that tinny stuff is Paul's cassette recorder. It was one of those records where we were let loose in the studio with a budget and just did what we wanted to.

'That song "White Trash" – I said, "Let's sample that Edgar Winter record and put all those screams in there," so we did it.'

'A song might start with a bass line or someone bringing in a beat,' Paul says, 'and then I would take those tapes away and try and put melodies over the top. That's how that record evolved.'

'When it was done,' Luscombe says, 'Paul presented it and a bluegrass record as his first two albums for his new record company. You can imagine them going, "But I thought we'd signed Paul Kelly."'

Smoke and *Professor Ratbaggy* were released on the same day in October 1999, just after Paul returned to Australia after performances at the Spiegeltent as part of the Edinburgh Festival, along with performances in London and Dublin.

Professor Ratbaggy did twenty or more shows over the year following the release of the album. The show involved electronic samplers and continuous music with no breaks between tunes.

'The whole idea was to keep everyone moving all night. Paul is totally up for stuff like that,' Luscombe says.

Ratbaggy did some shows on the same bill as the usual Paul and band shows – much to the confusion of audiences not in on what was going on.

'We actually supported ourselves a few times,' Hadley says. 'We'd do a Professor Ratbaggy show and then come out as Paul and the band. The audience would all stand there watching us do the Professor Ratbaggy stuff and be obviously wondering what the fuck was going on. Then Paul would go, "So you like the old stuff better than the new stuff?" and they'd scream out, "Yes," and he'd go, "Too bad." Then we'd come out and do all the stuff they were expecting and it was all cool.'

* * *

As the world woke up bleary-eyed to the new millennium and Sydney, Australia, was preparing to host the summer Olympics, Paul, with his marathon vision, was limbering up for the new century.

With regard to his own recordings, the early part of the 2000s saw the *Roll On Summer* EP containing the wonderful observation on the touring life 'Every Fucking City'. EMI must have breathed a sigh of relief when Paul delivered a more typical album in ... *Nothing But a Dream* in 2001, which resulted in good sales, reaching number 7 on the charts and qualifying as a gold album.

That year Paul also found himself performing with one of his major influences. With The Coloured Girls/Messengers he'd opened for Bob Dylan in Sydney when his hero toured in 1986 with Tom Petty and the Heartbreakers. This time Paul did the whole tour with Dylan before heading overseas for solo or duo shows in New Zealand, the UK and Europe, before tackling North America in 2002. He repeated visits to these countries the following year, while his profile suffered no harm back home with the release of not one but two tribute albums to his songs – *Women at the Well* was a collection of female artists singing his songs, whereas *Stories of Me* featured artists such as James Reyne, Catherine Britt, Jeff Lang, Mia Dyson and Dave McCormack.

Paul continued to spread his creative wings, with a seeming emphasis on composing scores for film and television. He contributed to *Silent Partner* and Rachel Perkins' *One Night the Moon* (both in 2001).

One Night the Moon, set in 1930, explores racism. It tells the story of the search for a lost child and the conflict between a white landowner and an Indigenous tracker. The project was conceived by Mairead Hannan, her sister Deirdre, Paul, Kev Carmody, Alice Garner and screenwriter John Romeril.

Paul Grabowsky had become a commissioning editor at ABC Television and decided to commission four music films that would take a different perspective on the way film and music worked together. Instead of the music being – as it usually is – an afterthought, these films would be stories driven by the music and songs. Rachel Perkins, whose credits include *Radiance*, *The First Australians* and *Bran Nue Dae*, was considered as a director. But it wasn't until Paul Kelly had given Perkins a cassette containing some rough versions of songs, including 'This Land is Mine', a song he and Carmody had written together, that Perkins became really interested in the project.

'"This Land is Mine" is a song that gives a version of the story from both the tracker and the landowner's perspectives,' says Perkins. 'After I heard that song I decided I really wanted to make the film. I became very excited about elevating the music in the film process.'

Paul, Kaarin and their daughter Memphis acted in the film and the trio all sing on the film soundtrack. Initially Paul was not at all interested in appearing in the film and took much convincing to become involved in that side of the venture.

'Paul had zero aspirations to be in the film,' Perkins says. 'I did think that having Paul in it would be a drawcard for audiences, but he was resolute that he didn't want to be considered just because of his profile. One of the things that persuaded him to take the role was my belief that it was important that the actors could perform and sing – because the music delivery was so important.

'Despite that, he was still reluctant and insisted on a screen test because he didn't know if he could do it. He had been in the show *Funerals and Circuses* which I had seen, so that gave him a little more legitimacy.

'Paul is naturally shy and when he was doing the screen test he found it difficult to be natural with the other actor we'd put him with. Then I thought that Kaarin was an actor and singer and if she was playing his wife it might be a more natural situation for him. She was terrific and they worked well together so I thought that we should involve their daughter as well.

'In the end Paul inhabited the role, as that of a character who was emotionally a bit shutdown and restrained, but also tough.'

Perkins considers that the involvement of Fairfax was central to Paul's performance.

'Kaarin obviously had lots of experience onstage and onscreen and throughout the whole process she was super encouraging, very sweet and protective of him. I remember Paul was performing when we were editing the film and Kaarin and I went to see him play. She was right up the front dancing and smiling at him.'

Perkins didn't know that cracks in Paul and Fairfax's marriage were deepening, only learning of that situation after the film was completed.

Sadly, after they finished filming, Paul and Fairfax's marriage ended. To say that the rock'n'roll lifestyle is notoriously uncompromising when it comes to relationships is an understatement to anyone immersed in the music industry or possibly any industry involving a seemingly endless 24/7 commitment to success. Paul's unrelenting work ethic certainly didn't help their relationship, and neither did his recreational drug use and predilection for extra-marital encounters.

When they first got together Fairfax didn't contemplate sharing Paul with a legion of his fans. Initially what happened on the road stayed on the road – until it didn't.

'Occasionally letters would arrive or he'd come back from a tour and I'd find condoms in his bag'.

So Fairfax asked questions.

'He wanted us to be like Frida Kahlo and Diego Rivera. I said all well and good for you but I don't want to be cast as her and I'm not sure I like the ending to that story.'

For a long time Fairfax supported Paul, feeling that if she stopped him having experiences it might impact on the songs he wrote or the stories he could tell. So she turned a blind eye to on-the-road shenanigans, selflessly sublimating herself to her perception of his needs.

'It probably makes me stupid,' she laughs.

Ultimately it became a deal-breaker.

Throughout the early period of their relationship Fairfax was also unaware of Paul's other predilection – heroin.

'When I met him I didn't know that was part of his story. He was functional and things seemed good.'

Over time, however, heroin became a constant but irregular part of the equation.

'He would use sometimes. He was not a daily or even weekly user. He was in no way addicted to the drug during that period of his life. Heroin was his go-to thing in down time. He would come home from a tour and score. It was recreational.'

Fairfax and others around Paul can attest, in contrast to the usual image of the user, Paul was at his most animated and amusing when he was stoned. But Fairfax doesn't romanticise the drug, its use or its consequences for the user or those in its range. She had a recurring image of finding Paul dead. One day, she walked into the bedroom after Paul had been using. He'd obviously had too much and was shaking.

'I thought, *What if he dies? – the headlines are going to be that I didn't do enough about it and the children are going to have to live with it forever.* That was the moment I decided to pack my bags and leave.

'Despite the problems I still felt safe when we were married. He wanted to come back to me. He wanted to be in the relationship.'

Fairfax is still on good terms with Paul. She says he is close with his children, now adults who have been forthright about their needs and have read him the riot act. She says he listens to them, he's willing to work through stuff and is kinder because of them.

'When Kaarin and I had the girls she used to say they were really special and I remember arguing with her about that,' Paul says. 'We had Pass the Parcel at a party for one of the kids and Kaarin had this thing that every kid had to get a present and I said, "No, not everyone should get a present because that's the way kids get to deal with loss, disappointment and failure."

'When Memphis and Maddy made their album as Wishful, and Memphis did her first solo record, like everyone, she was hoping to take the world by storm but she didn't. Memphis was disappointed and I said, "You've just got to keep making records." I didn't really make any money until my fourth record, so you've just got to keep making records.'

* * *

Paul kept working through the personal turmoil. The usual band line-up of Hadley, Luscombe, O'Mara and Haymes worked together on the soundtrack to Ray Lawrence's film *Lantana*.

'That worked really well for all of us,' Hadley says. 'I do loads of film music and have done for decades. I did Ray Lawrence's first film, *Bliss*. I was a teenager then I think.

'Ray just asked us to look at the film and if we'd do the music for it. So we went into the studio one day, smoked a joint and played one chord for a couple of hours. Then we played another chord. Paul spent a couple of weeks with Ray cutting it up and putting it in certain parts of the film.'

'We were sort of paying homage to The Necks record *Sex*. That was our inspiration for it. A really simple one-chord piece which we did with their blessing. They were totally cool and it worked really well.'

Paul says, 'The way we did *Lantana* was that we just jammed and then we used pieces of it for the film.'

But O'Mara remembers it as being a time when he had to put his foot down about acknowledgement of his work.

'There was a conversation where some of us said that the credits were *not* "with" – they were "and".'

Eventually O'Mara left the line-up. There were personal reasons in that he felt it was impacting on his marriage to Rebecca Barnard and the band they had together, Rebecca's Empire. Plus O'Mara loved playing with Paul, but didn't feel completely part of what was going on.

'I loved it – but I didn't love it enough to stay. And my personal situation just couldn't sustain the touring. I'd dread being at rehearsal and being given the tour book and realising that I was going to be away for another seven weeks.'

O'Mara's departure opened the door for Spencer Jones to play more as the band's guitarist. That line-up hung in until mid-2003 but then Luscombe sensed that Paul felt that particular combination of musicians had run their course. It was time for a change.

'There had been a lot of touring,' Luscombe reflects. 'And I think there was a feeling from Paul that some people in the band were taking him for granted and there wasn't as much input and involvement from them as Paul wanted. And when you tour you can tire of people's habits.'

In 2004, Paul pulled the plug on the band simply and quickly. Hadley, Spencer and Haymes were all effectively – to use football parlance – put up for draft to other bands at the same time. Only Peter Luscombe remained in the squad for the next season.

Haymes feels like he might have been caught up in the crossfire of change brought on by the hijinx and unpredictable behaviour of Jones and Hadley, particularly on the one American tour they both did together.

'That was a major part of it,' Haymes says. 'On the US tour we did with Spencer and Steve they kind of fucked up a few times and caused a few problems.

'We had to do a live radio show in Philadelphia but Steve and Spencer were left in New York because they got pissed the night before and we ended up having to do it as a trio – just Paul, Peter and me. The bus went without them.

'At the time Paul was ropeable, in his polite sort of way. It really was the most important thing on the tour as it was going out to so many people.

'Basically Steve couldn't be raised. The bus was waiting for us to leave. We were climbing on the wall outside his hotel room, banging on the window, trying to wake him up. We all got on the bus and were sitting there waiting. Poor old Spencer took the bullet. He said he'd go back into the hotel and wake him up. I mean he wasn't in great shape either but he went back upstairs and didn't reappear so Paul just cracked the shits and said, "Right, let's go," and we took off in silence.

'The image I remember most in Philadelphia was seeing these two figures stumbling along the road towards the bus on a really hot and bright day. No sunglasses or anything as they'd left them on the bus.

'Rob Barnham who was managing Paul at the time had organised for Spencer and Steve to get a cab or something to get to Philadelphia which was about two hours away and told them the bus would be parked outside the radio station so they could find the bus. They got out of the cab and were just stumbling up the road looking incredibly hungover.

'Paul didn't say much but I think it was the nail in the coffin for both of them.'

'A few times Spencer and I would get a little bit loose and he'd get a bit pissed off,' Hadley says. 'And so he should – we were stupid fucking silly alcoholics, but overall we always got on great.

'Most people who don't know him think he's really quiet but he's not really. He just doesn't talk if he's got nothing to say. Get him going and he's off.'

Hadley says that during his time with Paul, the singer was extremely moderate with his heroin use and wasn't doing much of it. But when he did do it, it stuck out big time.

'The only time I really saw him pinned or smacked was in the studio or the odd time outside of that – but very rarely in over fifteen years. There was one time I do remember – in Adelaide. He must have had a really fucking serious blast because he was *fucked*. And he actually apologised to all of us. He still did a good show but he was so fucking out of it. That was the only time I saw anything around a show.

'A couple of times late at night we'd be in the studio and particularly when he was doing his vocals he seemed to like to be stoned. You can hear it on a couple of songs – like "Queen Stone" which he wrote with Maurice Frawley. He was pretty whacked doing the vocal for that. You can hear it. I've got a real passion for broken voices. I love it when a singer's voice is really fucked up and you can hear that hurt – that's the real shit …

'And we – by that I mean Paul and me and others – were trying to get Spencer off heroin at that time and it was hard. Paul was pretty good and would say, "Come on, Spencer, stop taking that fucking shit, you're fucked."'

'Spencer was tricky,' Paul says. 'Sometimes he could be really happy, and other times depressed and a bit paranoid.

'I probably got to a point where I wanted to work with people who were low maintenance.'

* * *

By now Rob Barnham was beginning to tire of management and the music business in general. He'd built a close relationship with Paul's family, in particular his mother who now lived in Queensland; she used to phone Barnham weekly when her son was touring overseas to check how things were going.

The pressure on managers is enormous – besides Paul, Barnham had also been involved with the careers of Christine Anu and for a time Alex Lloyd. He had moved his family to Byron Bay and he was tired.

'At the end I was really only managing Paul. But I was burnt out. I used to go out to the farm for a day where there was no mobile reception so I couldn't be contacted. I didn't want to be part of the music industry anymore.'

Paul asked Barnham if he'd hang around as manager until a replacement was found, which in Barnham's mind seemed to take a particularly long time before Paul would eventually settle on Bill Cullen, who took over in 2005.

After a performance by Paul and the band at an A Day On The Green concert, Barnham bade farewell.

CHAPTER 13

WAYS AND MEANS

'It was a real baptism of fire. We had to play *lots*.'

Dan Kelly

THE FIRST THREE YEARS OF THE NEW DECADE HAD BEEN AS active as ever, with change being the only constant. In 2004, Paul put together a new band. Peter Luscombe was the only one who survived the rejigging. First into the regular touring and recording line-up came Bill McDonald on bass.

Luscombe and McDonald had been playing music together for what seemed like forever, certainly a period measured in decades.

McDonald had first encountered Paul Kelly late in the 1980s. He was playing a couple of songs on the ABC TV show *The Big Gig*, a comedy show hosted by Wendy Harmer and featuring the likes of the Doug Anthony All Stars and Flacco (Paul Livingston). Apparently Paul was on it for a comedy sketch but didn't sing.

A couple of years later McDonald had been part of the Australian contingent playing SXSW in Austin with Paul and other Australian artists in America.

McDonald later played on an EP by Paul and subbed for Steve Hadley at an ARIA Hall of Fame function in 1997 when Paul was inducted. So for McDonald, Paul very occasionally flitted into his life in the nineties – and just as quickly disappeared.

Luscombe initially recommended McDonald to Paul for the bass-playing position.

'I think there were a few drugs and drinking problems in the previous band,' McDonald says. '*The Songs from the South* record had come out, which was basically a greatest hits under another name, and I think he wanted to take it up a notch.

'Things were pretty rough initially. We did tours where people couldn't make it, and a bare bones tour ... a little stripped-down thing and we played *everywhere.*'

Next Paul decided to get Luscombe's brother Dan and his own nephew, also Dan, into the band. The two Dans hit it off immediately. They were both fine guitar players and both significantly younger than all the other musicians who played with Paul.

'They hadn't ever played together,' Peter Luscombe says, 'and they didn't really know each other that well – maybe just a bit of a drink here and there – but their chemistry was phenomenal.

'It was like the Keith Richards and Mick Taylor version of The Rolling Stones. There was lots of interplay. It wasn't two guys trying to fit in around each other. And Dan Luscombe also plays piano. So with some songs that didn't need a second guitar he'd play keyboards. Dan Kelly plays a little bit of keyboards as well.'

By this time Dan Kelly was well ensconced in the Melbourne music scene.

Paul's influence on Dan is large, not just in the songwriting sense. Around the time of *Post*, when Paul and

Steve Connolly did their now legendary run in Townsville, they travelled through Brisbane where Dan, who was about eleven at the time, lived.

'I remember Paul and Steve visiting us on their way up to Townsville. They sat outside the house and played "From St Kilda to Kings Cross" and I was like, "Play that song again." It was super exciting. They stayed on our property because my grandmother [Paul's mother] lived on the property next to us and we shared twenty acres.

'I would go home after school and they'd be practising. I distinctly remember Paul sitting in the bath, and Steve playing guitar. I think that's when I went *wow* about the idea of playing music. Up until then I might have been at one sound check – maybe for The Dots.'

Dan was starting his teenage years when "Before Too Long" came out and the ascension of his uncle began. As a result of Paul's increased profile and touring, Paul and his band were around Brisbane on a regular basis and he always came bearing gifts.

'Tapes. Paul would always bring me heaps of tapes – either tapes he'd made up or had bought at shops, or classic record company swag he'd collected. He had everything like the six-tape Atlantic Rhythm & Blues set – or Straitjacket Fits. Sometimes he would give me something and say that I might like it even though it wasn't his thing.'

Dan also recalled going to Paul's shows, particularly watching Paul singing Woody Guthrie's song 'Pastures of Plenty' at the QUT Gardens Point.

'When I was learning to play guitar I must have played *Post* a thousand times. Whenever Steve was up I'd ask him to show me things on the guitar. And then there was *Gossip*.

'My guitar playing is based on what Steve did. I know all his parts back to front. Because Paul has so many songs he can't be expected to remember every single nuance so I am like Paul's archivist ...

'I remember talking to Steve about George Harrison. Harrison is the most tasteful guitarist in history and you can see that in Steve. Steve played in a classic way; it was always simple and tasteful. He had great wide reverb and distorted feedback sounds when he wanted. And then he'd play really borderline country licks.'

So with the spectre of Steve Connolly's playing around him, and an uncle with a burgeoning successful record in *Gossip*, Dan continued improving his guitar skills. And in the background, encouraging him in all sorts of ways, was his mum and Paul.

'Around *Gossip* time I remember Paul calling up and saying that there was a present for me. When I got home there was a Music Man amplifier, the one that he used on *Post*, waiting for me on the verandah. He'd given it to the Weddings, Parties, Anything guys – whose first record I loved too – they were up around my way on tour and Paul said, "My nephew's learning guitar – can you drop this off?"

'Now I had this amp and I was starting to play acoustic guitar but I didn't have an electric guitar. So Paul said, "If you save your money I'll match you dollar for dollar and you can buy an electric guitar." This was around 1987 or '88. I got two dollars a week pocket money and I managed to save one hundred dollars over a year. Paul kept his word and gave me one hundred dollars and we went and bought an electric guitar. It got stolen out of a car on the Gold Coast at the end of Year 12 but by then I was working in a pie shop and could save up enough money to buy another one.

'When Paul toured with The Coloured Girls they'd come and stay at my grandmother Jo's house. They looked so amazing and had these huge booming voices. They would talk about politics – *and* they knew about pig's trotters. It was very exciting being around them. They all knew Irish ballads and sixties songs too. They'd sing "Baby It's You". My mother loved that because she's a ten-pound Pom. I also remember Chris Wilson coming up one time and playing my grandmother's piano. It was like his hands covered the whole piano.'

After Dan finished high school Paul invited him to Sydney to hang around while he and The Messengers finished the *Comedy* album. It was schoolies week and Paul put him upstairs in the Annandale Hotel for two weeks, which meant every day he could walk to Trafalgar Studios and watch the band do their thing.

'They were back with Alan Thorne and doing some final recording and mixing. I think they were trying for that *Gossip* sound. That's where I first met Spencer Jones and Steve took me to Coogee Music and helped me choose a Stratocaster.

'I loved The Coloured Girls. I just thought they were a brilliant live band. They were like superheroes to me. I really couldn't believe it when Steve died. I hadn't seen him for a while and the band had broken up.

'That band was when grown-ups were grown-ups – they were the real deal. And super nice. Michael Barclay got me into The Smiths and said, "You've got to like this band, Dan," and *Lifes Rich Pageant* by R.E.M. They were key bands for me. They weren't retro bands.

'And The Coloured Girls had *the* best leather jackets.'

By 1996 Dan had moved to Melbourne, taking the train from Brisbane and initially living in St Kilda with Paul and Kaarin until he got on his feet, met a few people and found his own share house. 'It was a good change. Brisbane was so hot, I'd finished my university degree and was smoking too much pot and doing nothing.'

Paul was always supportive but Dan was finding his own way and didn't want to be known as Paul Kelly's nephew.

The first time Dan performed onstage with his uncle was back in his home state of Queensland at the Woodford Folk Festival in 1997 when Paul dragged him up to play guitar with him and Lucky Oceans in front of six thousand people. Dan was terrified, the intensity of his terror skyrocketing off the scale when he found out he was required to play a guitar solo.

Through Paul and Kaarin, Dan was introduced to a number of Melbourne musicians, including Maurice Frawley who he played his first Melbourne gig with. Frawley is revered as a singer–songwriter and guitarist and for about a year was one of the players in the earlier Paul Kelly Band.

'Maurice and Spencer were really encouraging,' Paul says. 'They both gave him [Dan] gigs ... They were both very, very generous like that. I know I'm talking about them together but it's hard not to sometimes. They played together so much as well ... Spencer Jones was like a School of Rock – lots of people played with him and learnt how to be in a band, how to travel and tour. Maurice was similar and always very encouraging with the younger musicians coming up behind him.'

Eventually Dan Kelly got his own band together – The Alpha Males. When he joined Paul's new line-up in 2004 it was almost by osmosis.

'We just started rehearsing at Paul's place. Dan [Luscombe] was the classic straight-up sixties riff guy and I probably took on a more textural role. Not always, but that's naturally how it seemed to work, especially when you have three guitars. Dan would play some keyboards as well.'

Dan Luscombe had first met Paul when the guitarist was a teenager and soon after his brother Peter – there's a seventeen-year age difference between the two brothers – started playing in Paul's band around the *Wanted Man* period.

A little later Dan Luscombe was in The Blackeyed Susans who did a tour with Paul.

'After one of the shows I got a letter in the mail from Paul. I didn't know him very well at the time, but we began that tour in Adelaide, playing a show at the Heaven nightclub. A review came out the next day which contained some nice comments about The Blackeyed Susans.

'Paul saw the review, cut it out and put it in an envelope with a little note. I was quite struck by that. He'd woken up and read the review the next morning and wanted to make sure that I didn't miss seeing it. I was touched and thrilled by it. I've still got the note.

'It gave me a little window into the kind of guy he is. He can be very economical with words but that doesn't mean he's not having thought after thought. And kind thoughts. Sometimes he chooses to express them in ways that aren't always conventional.'

Dan Luscombe had been playing with Spencer Jones in The Last Gasp for a couple of years when he heard that Paul was keen to rejig his band.

'I got a phone call from Paul one night at my share house in Carlton and he asked if I'd like to come and have a play.'

At the time Dan Luscombe was not really making any money from playing in The Last Gasp, and was working a couple of cash-in-hand casual jobs and was on the dole. An offer to possibly join Paul Kelly's band would have seemed like a very attractive proposition.

Dan Luscombe called his brother to see what he knew and was told, 'Yeah, if you don't fuck it up I think you're in the band.'

Moving into Paul's band meant he was going to replace Spencer and he did feel guilty about that but Luscombe figured that the writing was already on the wall. If he didn't take over then someone else would. Plus he'd known Bill McDonald since he was four years old, his new buddy Dan Kelly was in the band, and his brother played drums.

'And with Paul's songs. How do you say no to that offer?'

Dan Luscombe went for the gig with Paul and got it. It created a bit of a strain on his relationship with Spencer for a while but that rift mended.

This combination of Peter Luscombe on drums, Bill McDonald on bass, and Dan Kelly and Dan Luscombe on guitars, would later be renamed by Paul as The Boon Companions.

'He just decided to call the band that one day,' Dan Luscombe says. 'It's an old American expression for buddies. Indispensable buddies. I think the term gets used in *O Brother, Where Art Thou?* when a character refers to the others as boon companions. But Paul was aware of it well before that.'

Their first recording with Paul was the *Ways & Means* album. 'Making *Ways & Means* as soon as we did sort of solidified us as a band,' Dan Kelly says.

Bill McDonald describes it as 'we sat down, jammed together and started writing together. He [Paul] must have had a huge backlog of songs. There's a lot of co-writes on the double album, *Ways & Means*.

'I'm very interested in the creative process. I'm effectively a sideman who works with a lot of really incredible people who are band leaders and songwriters of all different stripes and approaches. Paul is just off the scale in terms of professionalism, dedication and craft.

'And the sign of a great leader – which is what he is – is that he just gets the right people together and lets them loose.

'Paul has a highly developed sense of taste which I appreciate in an artist. He's very quick at decision-making – it's yes, no, that's in, that's out. He'll say, "This isn't happening – but we'll give it ten minutes more and if not then it's definitely out."

'Even though he's got the time and the money to spend weeks in the studio, we knock out these records really quickly. Four songs a day sometimes – complete. Vocals, rough mixes, overdubs. It's a good way to work. Why sit around dwelling on it, why sit around double-thinking things? Move on and write another song. Don't write one song, write ten and two of them will be great.'

'We'd get together once or twice a week for a couple of months in Paul's kitchen,' Peter Luscombe says. 'Just sitting around. I'd play a small kit with brushes. There'd be no microphones. Just all of us sitting around and playing. Then we went in and rehearsed properly. We had that classic thing of something like twenty songs and we thought, *Who would be the dream producer for this*? Why, it was Tchad Blake, of course. Paul figured we could get in touch with him via Neil Finn who'd worked with him before. Turns out Tchad had heard Paul's name mentioned by Neil and he was happy to come out and produce a record.'

From Luscombe's perspective recording *Ways & Means* with Blake was just 'one of the best recording experiences you could have – this dream producer and a band who had learnt all the tunes together.

'We were pretty much doing a song a day so there was no pressure. We'd go in there, track it, get it feeling good, record it and do the vocals straight away, and then we'd move on to the next song. It wasn't like we did a bunch of rhythm tracks and then came back and did the overdubs. It was like a completed song, have dinner and then come and do it again the next day. Paul would also often come in first thing in the morning and do his vocal from the track the day before.'

'It was such a fun and productive time,' Dan Luscombe says. 'There were a whole bunch of other tracks that didn't make it. It was a really joyous time.'

When the album was released in 2004 there were more long periods on the road, including dates in the UK and North America, New Zealand and finally Australia.

During this tour Dan Kelly and The Alpha Males were often the opening act.

'It was a funny tour,' Dan Kelly says. 'We would do the Alpha Males show. I was still learning how to be a frontman. Dan [Luscombe] would play as well. Then we'd finish and the other Alpha Males would go, "Great, we can go out and hit the town," but Dan and I would have another two and a half hours to go because Paul's shows are never short.

'It was a real baptism of fire. We had to play *lots*.'

Dan Luscombe remembers the time too. 'When I first joined Paul's band we did a very long seven- or eight-week tour of Australia. Paul is the only person I've ever worked with who can actually do those sorts of tours and get crowds. We were going right through the centre, and Kalgoorlie and north of the centre. It was an incredibly fun time.

'Dan Kelly and The Alpha Males were opening. I was playing in both bands as was Dan, but other members of the band – Christian [Strybosch] and Gareth [Liddiard] – pretty much ran amok backstage every night during Paul's three-hour long set. Every night.

'It was a good time even though at the end of the tour Paul kind of jokingly sacked The Alpha Males in the

Qantas Lounge when we were heading back to Melbourne. Gareth and Chris had somehow gotten the keys to Paul's room and smeared his toothbrush and everything with the complimentary pillow chocolates. It was meant as a bit of a sight gag. Paul's only response was to say, "You're fired," with a smile at the airport the next morning.

'Despite Paul having to put up with some really childish antics for eight weeks, it was a great bonding experience ...'

That year also saw the broadcast of *Fireflies*, an ABC television series which came with a score from Paul and Stephen Rae. Later came a CD entitled *Fireflies: Songs of Paul Kelly* which included performances from Paul, along with The Boon Companions, Professor Ratbaggy, Uncle Bill, plus Catherine Britt, Deborah Conway and Renée Geyer.

Paul's work rate continued to be frenetic. In 2004 he toured in North America with shows in New York, Chicago, Boston, Portland and Los Angeles, backing that up with more extensive touring there and in the United Kingdom and Europe and New Zealand.

'Failure is often more interesting than success,' Paul says. 'In 2004 we were touring England and we got a call from someone representing a French director who had loved the soundtrack to the Ray Lawrence film *Lantana* and wanted us to do the music for a film starring Charlotte Gainsbourg. There was also a short appearance from Johnny Depp.

'We had one day off planned in Glasgow so we watched the film in the London hotel in the morning and then drove up to Glasgow and went and recorded. It was a great little film. We all liked it.

'We played all these different pieces of music and we sent it off with the caveat that it wasn't edited and we could sort that out later.

'[Later] we're in Liverpool, it's really cold and there's about thirty people in the club we were about to play at. Just before we went on, we received an email. "The director has heard the music and he hates it." We all kept saying with a French accent "He hates it. He hates it." But we were gutted.

'We'd poured our heart and soul into this long sixteen-hour recording session on a day off after a long drive. We had our hopes up high – a French movie soundtrack, Charlotte Gainsbourg, Johnny Depp – but, he *hates it.*

'But then again that was the start of the *Stardust Five* record. A lot of the pieces came from there – "Last Orders" is one – where the genesis was in that film stuff. There's stuff you can always do – even with the failures. Keep track of the offcuts.'

To end the year Paul did a show at the Famous Spiegeltent in Melbourne, performing one hundred of his songs, assembled in alphabetical order, over four nights, before repeating that caper at the Sydney Opera House and Brisbane's Powerhouse.

'Around that time I started doing the A to Z shows,' says Paul. 'And Bill Cullen started managing me because I remember him coming along to one of these shows. It was 2005 and those A to Z shows were a real turning point for me because I got in touch with my old songs.

'There are certain songs – popular songs – that people want to hear. It's the age-old thing with performance – to play enough new stuff to satisfy yourself, and playing the songs that people want to hear. And you don't just play the old songs because people want to hear them, the old songs are satisfying for the performer too because they get a response from the audience. A lot of performing is about that feeling that comes back from an audience.

'But the A to Z shows were about doing it all differently. Doing something that you wouldn't normally do. It was one of those middle of the night ideas – "I'll do one hundred songs in alphabetical order by title over four nights." I wrote the press release the next day and committed to it. And then I started working out a song list.

'I had to work really hard at it because I had so many songs, and lots where I couldn't remember how the chords went. So there were a lot of rehearsals. It was a huge mental memory effort.

'It was the beginning of a principle I follow now, looking for new ways to do shows apart from, "I'm Paul Kelly and I've got some known songs and I'm going to play them and a few new songs and here are my band."

'The A to Z shows were perfect because the first night was A to D. The audience is not going to hear "To Her Door" and they know that in advance.

'It felt great. A new path had opened up for me.'

* * *

Paul might have been commander and chief of his band of musicians, but he was also creating a parallel universe, or more practically, another project with a different team. In 2005 he enlisted Mike Albeck, James Gillard, Rod McCormack, Ian Simpson and Trevor Warner – who would be called The Stormwater Boys – for *Foggy Highway*.

'*Foggy Highway* was a follow-up to *Smoke*,' Paul says. 'I just liked the way *Smoke* had come out … I always thought I could definitely do another record like that down the track. Five or six years later – which I thought was ages – we could do it again – and there's got to be a third one but it's been fifteen or sixteen years now. So there may be another one.

'Uncle Bill had broken up by then so I approached Rod McCormack about putting together a band. It included

Ian Simpson who's a gun banjo player. It's his banjo on "From Little Things". We did it at Rod's studio in Terrigal. James Gillard on bass, Trevor Warner on mandolin ... He plays more in a raw style so that made him the perfect foil for that record in my eyes because everybody else was just bang on with everything they did. Mick Albeck on fiddle. I love playing with him. A beautiful feeling and tone. The others were like consummate players – and Rod McCormack plays all those beautiful guitar parts so I didn't have to play that much guitar – that's him on "They Thought I Was Asleep". And Trevor was the grit – which is the way Gerry Hale was – they've got this fire in the way they play.

'We recorded it in five days. I got a motel by the sea, so I had a swim in the morning and then up the hill to record.'

In the middle of 2005 Paul was also involved in putting together *Timor Leste – Freedom Rising*, which involved an array of Australian artists donating songs to raise money for various projects in East Timor.

Paul's elevation received another boost when he performed 'Leaps and Bounds' and 'Rally Around the Drum' at the closing ceremony of the Commonwealth Games in Melbourne in March 2006.

In 2006, Paul's newest edition of his second collection of lyrics – *Don't Start Me Talking*, first published in 1999, was added to the reading list for Year 12 students doing English in the Victorian Certificate of Education (VCE). It would be the start of Paul acquiring a new generation of fans.

Another Paul-related side project emerged that same year. The Stardust Five was Paul's now regular band of Peter and Dan Luscombe, Dan Kelly and Bill McDonald all writing and composing music – very much along the lines of the

Professor Ratbaggy project. And like Professor Ratbaggy Paul's name is not on the front cover of the resulting album.

During 2006 Paul also toured the UK and North America again before ending the year with a two-month A to Z tour which involved four-night stands (twenty-five songs a night) in Sydney, Melbourne and Brisbane.

Around this time Paul came up with the idea of an album of other artists performing their versions of Kev Carmody's songs, the result being the 2007 album *Cannot Buy My Soul*.

'That was all Paul,' Carmody says. 'I had nothing to do with it.'

Once again, in 2007, Paul was involved with composing music for a film, and once again the experience led to unexpected results.

'Richard Roxburgh who was directing *Romulus, My Father* approached me to do the music for it,' Paul says. 'This was after I'd done the music for *Lantana* and *Jindabyne*, another Ray Lawrence film.

'Richard and I started meeting and went up to Maldon where part of it is set and hung out and started getting ideas. We started talking about the music from the Balkans, the area where Romulus's father had come from which had been a melting pot, a crossroads of music. We were sending each other music and talking and we got on really well.

'I started sending him some sketches and it wasn't quite what he wanted so I tried again and it still wasn't what he wanted. We were already under this very tight timeline. That often happens with doing music for films because music is often the last thing – and also it's hard to start work on the music before the film's finished or there's at least a rough cut or something close to it.

'With my sketches I wasn't even close to what he wanted. We thought we understood each other but we didn't and the deadline was getting tight ...'

Paul sent a piece for the start of the movie to Roxburgh but he knocked it back. 'That's when I realised that it wasn't going to work,' Paul says, 'so I told him I didn't think it was working and I was happy if he wanted to find someone else – I could hear the relief. We amicably agreed that he would get someone else to finish off the music. It wasn't like an acrimonious disagreement and we parted on good terms. I was flat for a couple of months, like a minor depression. I just felt like a complete failure.

'Eventually I ended up using that piece of music under what I call the Slim Dusty offcut principle. Slim made one hundred and five records. Every time he went into the studio he'd say, "Are there any offcuts around the place?" – meaning things they'd recorded for the last album that they hadn't used. Everyone else calls them out-takes but Slim called them offcuts – and I've been calling them offcuts too. Dan Kelly is always teasing me about that, saying, "You like using the offcuts, don't you?"'

And indeed Paul almost always finds homes for his songs. Some that he hasn't recorded have been performed by artists such as Jane Clifton ('High Wild Ways'), Karen Marks ('You Bring These Things'), and others. Then there are the songs that have been kept for years – such as 'I Didn't Know Love Could Be Mine', which Paul performed live, but didn't record, with The Dots in the late 1970s which would eventually appear, sung by Vika and Linda on their debut album in 1994.

In 2007, Paul released the *Stolen Apples* album, a collection of songs with biblical themes. 'You know that song "Feelings of Grief" that opens up *Stolen Apples*?' Paul says. 'There's an instrument called a ney – a Turkish instrument – and there's a whole section before the bass comes in. That was the opening music for *Romulus, My Father*.'

When the recording of the *Stolen Apples* album was completed, Dan Luscombe departed the ranks for The Drones. When he told Paul of his decision, Paul's comment was, 'If it was any other band I'd wonder why – but I get it.' During the years Luscombe played in the band, Paul had pushed him to play piano and he took with him an increased interest in playing the instrument.

'He bought me the Roland piano that I still play today,' Luscombe says. 'Early on I said to him that I wasn't really a piano player and he said, "You are now."'

During the course of his touring, both with the band and sometimes as a duo with Paul, Dan Luscombe had the opportunity to observe Paul's work ethic and his almost magnificent obsession with making every moment count.

'I remember watching him go through an X-ray machine at an airport. He was reading a book – *The Iliad* – and reading it right up until he had to pass through the machine. Just before he did, he put the book in the tray, walked through and picked it up on the other side and continued reading.'

Around this time, Dan Kelly – who was playing both guitar and keyboards in the band – started to take off as a solo artist and decided to make that his priority. So Paul quickly found himself two guitarists down.

Peter Luscombe had been putting together a band to play on the Countdown Spectacular tour. Paul happened to be at one of the shows and Luscombe recommended Ash Naylor, who was in the Countdown band, for Paul's band.

'I thought you were going to say that,' Paul said. 'I agree.'

'The next thing I know,' Naylor says, 'I'm having a cup of tea in Paul's kitchen and playing his songs face to face with him. That obviously went well because twelve years later I'm still doing it.'

Naylor can still recall the songs he ran through at his kitchen audition, sitting there playing these songs with Paul who's not renowned for giving away much of what he's thinking. Nervy stuff for anyone.

'I played "Gravy", with my bastardised version of the Spencer Jones guitar line. Then songs from the *Stolen Apples* album, a few songs from *Ways & Means* as well. And of course some of the better-known songs.'

Naylor joined the band and went out on a summer 2007 tour with Paul in what he described as a 'commando unit' – lean and highly skilled. Just four players – Paul, Peter Luscombe, Bill McDonald and Naylor. 'I've been in bands since the eighties in various situations,' Naylor says, 'but in terms of professionalism and experience, joining Paul's band was something I wasn't used to and I had to get used to it pretty quickly.'

They did some Day on the Green shows, a run of pub dates and then the Live Earth concert.

'I remember my first gig being the Torquay pub and Pete saying, "Remember, we love mistakes." And Paul smiled and nodded in agreeance with Pete and I thought, *Well, they've got the right guy if you love mistakes.* I pretty much make a mistake in every song I play. It's all about how you disguise and mask it.'

Paul's band evolved further when Cameron Bruce joined.

Bruce's phone rang one day in 2007. He missed the call but it was a message from Paul Kelly asking if he was interested in coming to Melbourne for a 'bit of a play' – which is thinly disguised musician code for auditioning to be in the band. He figured Paul wanted to keep the keyboard sound in the band now that Dan Luscombe had left. Bruce thinks he came into consideration via a recommendation from Dan Kelly who was a fan of Dave McCormack & The Polaroids, a band that Bruce played in.

Bruce said yes, and was flown to Melbourne where he went to a rehearsal room with Paul and Dan Kelly, Ash Naylor, Bill McDonald and Peter Luscombe.

Paul had sent Bruce a bunch of songs to learn – some things from *Stolen Apples*, a couple of older songs, and a new demo of the song 'Righteous Woman'.

'I found it interesting that he sent me a new song, just a performance on an acoustic guitar, which I guess was for him to see what I'd do with a new song that didn't have any existing parts to it.'

The musicians played together for a few hours, said their goodbyes and Bruce headed to the airport to fly back to Sydney. It was his thirtieth birthday and he had a party to get to. In the cab to Tullamarine the phone rang. Things can move very quickly in Paul Kelly world. There'd been a meeting after Bruce had left the rehearsal room. Would he like to join the band? He would. Happy birthday, Cameron.

A month after the audition at the Bakehouse Studio, Bruce was on tour with Paul. He did a two-week rehearsal then, in what has become a tradition for Paul, a pre-tour performance for a small gathering of friends and family to run through the tour set in front of an audience.

'It's always a tiny show,' Bruce says, 'but it gives us the chance to run through the set in battle mode, which is especially good if you're about to play the Myer Music Bowl or something like that. I think a Splendour in the Grass show was my first gig with the band so it was good to run through the show before that.

'It's like a gig. At rehearsals you're facing each other so it's not quite the same. It's like sport – you can go for a run and train all you like but nothing beats match fitness.'

Bruce also fitted in easily with the band's on-the-road exercise regime, which involves pretty much everyone in the group running, swimming or playing tennis.

'Everyone has their own version of exercise to keep their head straight. When it comes to swimming I'm an ocean guy, some guys like the pool ... You're only onstage for two hours and the rest of the time you're part of a machine that hopefully doesn't get on anybody's nerves.

'There's a lot of time between gigs to fuck up. That's when things can go south. I'm the youngest by many years so maybe it's my responsibility to fuck up.'

On that first tour, Bruce played tennis against Paul in Launceston. Bruce won.

'That day he didn't talk to me till after sound check. Not a word until the gig. I was reasonably new at that stage and I had to ask the other guys. I said, "What the fuck is going on? Paul won't even look at me," and they explained that it was because I beat him at tennis. They said he'd come good eventually. And he did.'

These days, whenever possible, Paul and Bruce play tennis – competitively.

'I run him around a lot but I'm twenty-five years younger. He's fit for his age and also very mentally fit. Sometimes I think maybe I shouldn't go so hard on him because he's older than me – and then I go, *Fuck him*, because I know he wants to win so badly. He's got such a determined streak with everything he does. Everything. And playing sport's just another manifestation of that.'

Ash Naylor agrees. 'Playing tennis with him is like death by a thousand cuts. I played tennis with him in Rushcutters

Bay after that. Walking back he pointed to the house which was where he and Paul Hewson lived. I said, "That would have been a pretty creative house," and he said, "Yeah, a lot of drug taking.'"

Paul's workload and profile ascendancy seemed unstoppable. In 2008 he appeared at the Big Day Out, before heading to Austin, Texas, for an appearance at the SXSW music conference, his first time back there since the early 1990s.

In 2008, Paul also made an appearance on the *Slim Dusty Family Reunion* album.

Slim's daughter, Anne Kirkpatrick, herself a successful and highly respected artist, says someone reached out to Paul and then 'he just turned up at the house – got a cab I think – and walked up the driveway with his guitar – literally sat down in Mum's lounge room with David, Mum and I, and sang his song "Pick It Up and Pass It On" into an old cassette player Mum had on top of the piano. It was just so casual and pretty amazing – such a perfect sentiment for the family album.'

'I met Slim [Dusty] before he died,' Paul says. 'We did at least one or two concerts where he and Joy [McKean] were on the same bill. But the friendship with Joy really started after Slim died. And it's just gotten stronger and stronger over the years. ... I just love her. She's indomitable and tough, and no nonsense. She's a ripper.'

In 2008, Paul and EMI released the second edition of *Songs from the South*, this collection including his song 'Shane Warne', which continued Paul's love of writing songs about sporting figures, particularly cricketers.

At the beginning of 2009 Paul and Dan Kelly opened for Leonard Cohen's national tour of Australia.

'We did ten shows and that was incredible,' Dan says, 'one of the great times. It coincided with the Australian

Open so you play a set in a beautiful winery, then watch Leonard Cohen for three hours, drink the finest wines that Frontier [the promoters] could throw at you and then go home and watch Federer or Nadal on TV. And the next day was another winery and another Leonard Cohen show.

'That was the extremely hot Black Saturday summer but somehow we kept playing where there weren't fires. I remember we played a beautiful winery in Western Australia and we'd done our set and I started getting texts from friends going, "We're okay, we're okay," and I was wondering what was going on – and that's when Black Saturday happened. We flew in the next day and it was just black all around Melbourne.'

It was at this time that Cohen decided to donate proceeds from a show to the fire relief fund.

Soon after Paul appeared – with a cast of thousands – at the Melbourne Cricket Ground for the Sound Relief concert raising money for people affected by the Black Saturday bushfires.

Throughout the whole tour Dan and Paul hadn't actually met Cohen. They'd met and become semi-friendly with a few of the band but had no direct contact with the man himself. It wasn't a slight, just Leonard Cohen being Leonard Cohen.

On the last night of the tour the two were taken to see Cohen.

'He's sitting there in this incredible three-piece suit,' Dan Kelly says, 'and he's got some pretzels on the table, and there was a bottle of wine. That was the night of the fire so we talked a bit about that. I've never seen Paul so nervous. I went to Leonard and asked if he'd like some wine and he said, "No thanks, I had plenty in my youth," and then he offered me some pretzels and I went, "Okay, pretzels with Leonard Cohen – tick."

'I heard that after every show his driver would take him through a McDonald's Drive Thru and he would get one Filet-o-Fish. That was his treat for the day.'

As the year ended Paul received a significant nod from the Triple J radio network when – to commemorate his thirtieth anniversary as a solo artist – a tribute concert was held in Melbourne which was subsequently released as a double CD and DVD.

From Paul's side of things the lead-up to Christmas was a national More Songs from the South tour.

Paul and jazz pianist and composer Paul Grabowsky premiered 'Meet Me in The Middle of the Air', the composer's arrangements of Paul's songs, all of which were connected directly or elliptically with the bible. Also appearing onstage were Vika and Linda Bull and a gospel choir.

'Meet Me in The Middle of The Air' toured nationally but wasn't recorded.

A new decade beckoned. Would Paul slow down? Not a chance. He was *that* Paul Kelly now – more famous than his namesakes in AFL football and political journalism. But there was much more to do. Much, much more.

CHAPTER 14

HOW TO MAKE
GRAVY

'I hadn't written a song for three or four years and I felt
ropey. This idea sounded interesting and scary.'

Paul Kelly

PAUL ENTERED THE NEW DECADE WITH HIS EXPANSIVE AND
idiosyncratic memoir *How to Make Gravy*, which was
published in September 2010.

It was short-listed for the Prime Minister's Literary Award
(non-fiction category) and was co-winner of Biography of
the Year at the Australian Book Industry Awards.

To coincide with the book's publication, the eight-box set of
the *A to Z Recordings* was released and contained one hundred
and five songs recorded on shows between 2004 and 2010.

There was also a sixteen-CD audio book of *How to Make
Gravy* with Paul reading the majority of the text along with
contributions from Judy Davis, Cate Blanchett, Russell
Crowe, Hugh Jackman and Ben Mendelsohn.

Writing the book had been a massive project and had largely consumed him for three years.

'I was on tour in America and I started writing some notes for the box set,' Paul says. 'The first song was "Adelaide" so I wrote a page and a half and then it was one of those light bulb moments – *Oh, if I keep doing this I'll have a book.*

'I came back and thought it would be good for the A to Z recordings and the book to come out at the same time – so I delayed the box set and started writing the book in 2008.

'I remember thinking in that period, between doing those recordings and writing the book, that *Fucking Elvis Costello will come out with an A to Z thing* – but he didn't.

'I made writing the book like an office job – which is not the way I write songs. I decided to write every day. Just sat there and wrote and it was great.

'I really enjoyed writing the book because writing songs is much more elusive. For me writing songs is mostly being bored, and then something happens. You're scratching around, doodling, playing some chords, singing some stuff, and maybe something happens, but usually it doesn't. So writing a book was much more graspable. I said to myself that I'd write five hundred words a day. That'd be my target and pretty much I would get that – or more – every day.

'So for me writing the book was like laying bricks and mortar. You write one sentence after another and you get your first layer of bricks. Then you keep going and you've got a house.

'I had much more confidence that at the end of each day of work I would have something, whereas if you set aside a day to write a song you might get nothing. But it's like fishing. You have to set the time aside, or nothing happens.

I really enjoyed writing the book and I learnt to love the word count function on the computer.

'The book came out in 2010. During the time I was writing it I hardly wrote a song. Maybe there was one or two songs … After the book came out there was more touring with the A to Z shows, which I did with Dan, so by the time it all washed up it was 2012.'

Paul's publisher for *How to Make Gravy* was Ben Ball, who won out over a number of significant bidders, partly, he thinks, because he understood Paul's vision for the book right from the start despite very little of it having been written when the deal was done.

Ball remains proud of his role in the publication of a book that in many ways can be seen to mark the beginning of Paul's now decade-long rise in profile.

'Occasionally a book can show another dimension of somebody and give them an added substance that they maybe always had but it wasn't so obvious. Through the book I think more people came to understand what Paul's about, which they'd always said they understood, but maybe didn't – that he's a storyteller and that he reflects ourselves to ourselves.

'The important thing is that he is a writer. That's not to say that he's not a tune maker and a musician and a singer, but with the book you were invited to look at his work as a collection of words and that is often – not always – more resistant to changes of fashion than other forms of media. It really said to people, what a substantial artist we have here.'

Meredith Rose, who edited the text of *How to Make Gravy*, recalls Paul being extremely easy to work with. 'That's because he's a musician who's used to collaboration. He's not precious but he knows his own mind and will stick to it when he's adamant, but he would also listen to suggestions. So many writers take it personally if you suggest improvements but it's about the work, not the ego, and Paul realises that. He's a natural writer. You either have a writing voice or you don't, and you can't help that as an editor. You can work with structure and tightening but you can't give it a voice – and that was always there with Paul.'

As the A to Z shows ended, so too did Paul's long-term relationship with broadcaster, writer and musician Sian Prior. Prior and Paul had met in 1999 when she launched Paul's lyric book, *Don't Start Me Talking*. They wouldn't become a couple until 2002, by which time Prior had also interviewed Paul for the *Sunday Arts* program on ABC Radio.

Nick Lainas lays claim to having put Paul in touch with Prior. He says, 'Sian took Paul into the classical, opera and literary scene. He wanted to go further in that direction and she took him there.'

When they were together, Prior collaborated with Paul on the songs 'Coma' and 'Shane Warne' on *A to Z*, and she had previously sung with Paul and The Boon Companions on the song 'Los Cucumbros'.

Paul and Prior's relationship unravelled during the filming of the documentary about Paul – *Stories of Me*. As a result Prior asked for her interviews not to be included. She subsequently wrote about their relationship in a memoir entitled *Shy*, in which she chose to refer to Paul as 'Tom'.

Directed by Ian Darling, *Stories of Me* was released in 2012. A candid documentary, it was at times confronting for Paul to watch, something that was evident when he spoke tentatively onstage after its premiere at the Melbourne International Film Festival.

The film is widely available on DVD and spawned two publications, initially *Paul Kelly – The Essays*, a collection of pieces on various aspects of Paul's life and music from people such as authors Martin Flanagan, Sophie Cunningham, Toby Creswell and David Leser, filmmaker Rachel Perkins and others. Later came a digital-only publication, *We're All Here for the Drowning*, a collection of transcriptions from the documentary, edited by Toby Creswell.

* * *

In 2012 Paul began working with James Ledger, who was composer in residence with the Australian National Academy of Music. The idea of involving Paul in a project was first suggested by the Western Australian Symphony Orchestra artistic director, Nick Bailey, when Ledger had been with them in 2007 to 2009.

The timing wasn't great for Paul who was then immersed in writing *How to Make Gravy* and focusing all his energies on the book writing process.

Now with that project completed Paul was available for something new. 'They'd asked me to write a song cycle with James,' Paul says, 'and it was such a scary idea to me and so I thought I should do it because it sounded like a big challenge.'

Ledger and Paul met initially at the Astor Theatre in Perth where Paul was performing an A to Z show with Dan Kelly. Ledger admitted that, while he was very aware of Paul's songs, during the 1980s when Paul was having his initial stream of hit songs he was more immersed in the world of synth pop.

The two agreed that a project was a good idea but neither had any idea what it might be and when Paul sent Ledger an email about their discussions he headed it Fumbling in the Dark.

'I hadn't written a song for three or four years and I felt ropey,' Paul says. 'This idea sounded interesting and scary.'

The two continued exchanging emails, and meeting either at Paul's home in St Kilda or in Perth, where Ledger often was. Both had moments of doubt about whether they could come up with a focused project and there were a number of awkward idea sessions – and some others that were extremely productive.

'I thought rather than trying to write a song cycle I'll see if I can find existing poems around certain themes and put them together and put music to them,' Paul says, 'and that's what we did – and then I realised that I could start with the words first and make a song out of that.'

'Paul hadn't written songs for a while so his first instinct was to turn to poetry,' Ledger says, 'as we tried to get a thread running through this song cycle. And I must say that it was loose threads.

'The experience was a new way of writing music for him, having the words there in black and white in front of him and then setting the words to music. That was completely different from how he had composed before.'

The end result, the album *Conversations with Ghosts*, used poetry by Les Murray, Judith Wright, WB Yeats, Lord Alfred Tennyson and others, along with some new lyrics from Paul.

'The project led us both down a path that neither of us would probably have found by ourselves,' Ledger says, 'and it took us to a very different place that has been quite stimulating.'

The song cycle was performed in Brisbane, Sydney and Melbourne towards the end of 2012 and then a year later in Perth and again in Melbourne.

Paul's work with Ledger was satisfying and productive and the call in 2012 for Paul, an Australian Rules football tragic, to perform 'How to Make Gravy' and 'Leaps and Bounds' at the AFL Grand Final was also a thrill.

When he'd lived in Sydney in the eighties, Paul had played AFL for a while. It's a sport that has been a lifelong passion for him.

'I lived in Edgecliff near Trumper Park,' Paul says, 'and I saw all these blokes training so I asked if I could join them. I was thirty-three! I joined training and then I got picked for a couple of games that season. It just happened by chance because I was living nearby. I got a couple of kicks and handballs on the wing.

'I could have played more football when I was younger I suppose. Later I identified with the Sydney [Swans] player Paul Kelly who wasn't the most skilled player around but he had this incredible drive. I'm not as super skilled as a lot of people I grew up playing with. I think if I'd really, really wanted to and had the drive I could have played football ... for Norwood.' He smiles.

'Paul Kelly, the footballer, and I keep in touch and he'd come to our gigs. He came to a few shows with some of the young Swans. He got very interested in the similarities and differences between what he did as a footballer and what we did as musicians and he asked if he could come to a sound check. It was like us going to watch him train. He found that very interesting.'

When Paul moved back to Melbourne he and Maurice Frawley and a few others started kicking the footy together once or twice a week.

'By 1995 the group, now known as The Kick, was properly organised when performer Brian Nankervis also became involved,' Paul says. 'We meet regularly during the football season. The year after he retired, when Paul Kelly was a runner for the Swans, he and a couple of others came over for a kick. Bob Murphy, Jude Bolton, Richo (Matthew Richardson), Wayne Johnston (the Dominator), Farren Ray – they have all come along. We all get an extra spring in our step when the legends come down.'

Towards the end of the research for this book, Paul invited me to watch The Kick train. 'That's the real me,' he wrote in an email, 'the man who still thinks he's a child.'

* * *

It had been a lengthy gap between studio albums but in October 2012 Paul released *Spring and Fall*.

Greg Walker – who works professionally as J Walker – was called in to record and co-produce *Spring and Fall* with Paul and Dan Kelly. Paul had first contacted Walker after hearing his 2002 album *Happy* (released under his performing name, Machine Translations).

'Paul does what he does with a lot of people who've put out a record that he notices,' Walker says. 'He made contact and suggested we try and write a song together. It was a totally random call.'

For Walker's part the first Paul Kelly album that had really impacted on him was *Post*. 'I think you can hear the slight spectre of failure hanging over that record. I'm interested in that with artists – because obviously he's gone on to have an incredible career. A lot of people get to that point and the pendulum goes the other way. But there's a lot of people who have had a taste of success and it's there for them, but it's by no means guaranteed. It's an interesting point to be at ...

'I'd been around Paul before that as I was playing in a band called King Curly with Steve Appel and we did a tour supporting him.

'Paul loved King Curly. He'd really championed Steve's songwriting. The sort of songs Paul writes and the ones Steve writes are not dissimilar in the sense that they're little slices of Australian life. But my songwriting style is a bit more arty and all over the shop. So when Paul and I tried to write a song together it was a bit chalk and cheese.

'We didn't quite click at the time because I was trying to write a Paul Kelly song. I've learnt that you're better off going into co-writing with no expectations.'

After that they occasionally chatted and loosely kept in touch, but it would be quite a period of time before they worked together again. Paul was busy – naturally – and Walker's production work took off. Then Paul approached him about producing a song.

The two worked on a version of 'Little Bit o Sugar' that was included on the *Won't You Come Around* EP and later re-recorded for the *Ways & Means* album.

What brought them back together was Walker's production of an album for New Zealand artist Tiny Ruins.

'The production was really simple. I'd moved to South Gippsland and I'd started this phase where I was obsessed with recording in old country halls scattered around my area. I couldn't believe there were all these incredible spaces – most of which were designed to have music in them – that were just sitting there empty for three hundred days of the year.

'I recorded the Tiny Ruins album in a hall just up from my house. I ended up doing a series of that style of records, with really stripped-back production. It was a case of putting the artist in a nice sounding space and letting them play their songs, usually with live vocals giving them an honesty to their performance. But there were birds in a cavity in the roof so I didn't go back to that hall again, it was a nightmare.

'The Tiny Ruins record must have tweaked something in Paul and the kind of record he wanted to make with the *Spring and Fall* album. He liked the sound of its sparseness. He got in touch. I'd just discovered another hall up in the hills, a bit further away from me. It was pretty remote and there was no traffic noise. We went and checked it out and it did sound amazing.

'Originally *Spring and Fall* was going to be a duo record with just Paul and Dan. The scheduling of it meant that it was going to be recorded in the winter. If we had the opportunity to do the same thing again now none of us would be up for it because it was such a mission. It was quite a big hall and it was *freezing* cold.

'We had this thing called the Rocket Ship which was this diesel-powered heater. We had to turn it on and off because of the sound it made. It was so loud.'

'We had one of those red jet heaters.' Dan Kelly laughs. 'One of those things where the flame comes up and it looks like the bottom of a harrier jet. We'd put it on for twenty minutes to heat up the hall and then turn it off because it was noisy, and then start tracking. I was recording with half-length gloves on, a beanie, three jumpers and a grey coat. Despite the cold it was pretty great.'

'We were all really committed to the idea of recording in that space,' Walker continues. 'Although we were freezing, the payoff was the really beautiful and warm sound we captured on that record.

'The sound that you hear back reinforces a singer's voice acoustically. It's not like a really big reverb, it's just a warm, fuzzy feeling that singers get in those kinds of spaces and it was just a really beautiful process making that record.

'I was just going to record the two of them but it felt like it needed some double bass so I brought my bass along and we tried that and everybody liked it and suddenly it was a three piece.

'It was one of the most enjoyable records I've ever made. It was a very beautiful process. I think we probably spent two or three weeks up there on and off just chipping away at it and it came out sounding very complete. It didn't need a bunch of overdubs.

'Paul has got the most incredible stamina – vocally but also concentration wise. He can do ten – or fifteen – takes of a track and he will nail take fifteen and be totally present in it which is something a lot of singers can't do. That was something that really stood out to me about the way he works. As long as there's a sense of progress he'll keep doing more and more takes until he gets *the* one.

'Over the three weeks we recorded, Paul and Dan fell in love with the Coal Creek Motel. We stayed there a bit because we had to set the gear up in the hall every time we went to do some recording, then pack it away, and then go back and set it up again.

'Some records work in conventional studios and others don't. Paul was clearly ready to do something different, and to have a bit of an adventure recording.'

* * *

It was nine months after the release of *Spring and Fall* before Paul put together a band (Greg Walker on keyboards and some guitar, Dan Kelly on guitar, Bree van Reyk on drums and Zoe Hauptmann on bass) to play the songs. They played twenty-eight shows in mid 2013.

'It was kind of like Paul's young band as we were all a bit younger than him,' Walker says. 'We played all of that album – and I also had to learn the hits.'

The reason for the delay was a project that had been talked about for some time – a joint national tour with Neil Finn early in 2013.

As always, Finn and Paul had been in each other's worlds for a while. After Crowded House disbanded, Finn and drummer Paul Hester performed together on an episode of the TV series *Hessie's Shed*, the show including a version of Paul's 'Leaps and Bounds' featuring Finn, Hester, bass player Nick Seymour and Paul.

In 2010 Paul and Angus Stone had collaborated on a version of the Crowded House song 'Four Seasons in One Day' (a Tim and Neil Finn composition) for the *He Will Have His Way* tribute album.

In April 2011, Paul and Finn had been the co-headliners at the opening night of the Red Hill Auditorium in Perth. It seemed to be at this point that discussions about a joint tour solidified, being driven largely by Bill Cullen (then managing both Paul and Finn) and agent Brett Murrihy. Both men had been floating the idea with the singers for a number of years.

'Cullen and Murrihy thought that something like that would really resonate and be a great thing to do,' Finn says.

'I think they dropped it in the suggestion box a few times but the timing just wasn't right. And then a month came up that both Paul and I were in between projects. Paul had just recorded another album and I had some time so it was, *Why not? Let's do this thing.* It did seem to capture people's imaginations, much more than I would have anticipated. It was a delight.'

The Goin' Your Way tour was announced in November 2012, ten shows for February and March 2013. The demand for tickets was so great that more dates were announced in January 2013.

The band assembled for the tour was Dan Kelly on guitar, Finn's son Elroy on drums and Hauptmann on bass guitar. Zoe already knew Paul but was nevertheless surprised to get asked to play on this tour.

'I was playing with Lanie Lane. I met Paul when he performed with us on a television show.

'Sometime after the show he sent me an email. I was trekking through the Himalayas with my husband. We had just taken a bit of time off to go travelling. When we got to Shanghai I had reception and I'm reading this email saying, "Hi, it's Paul Kelly – would you be interested in playing bass on a tour with me and Neil Finn?" I had to get [husband] Evan to read it with me as I was going, "Is this for real, what's going on here?"

'As it turned out he didn't remember me from Lanie Lane. He remembered me from the King Curly band I had played in for years. We'd do gigs in Melbourne and there'd be like ten people in the audience, one of whom was always Paul. He loves Steve Appel and so do I. He's an incredible songwriter. Neil Finn was a big fan of Steve's as well.

'I found out that he'd asked pretty much everyone I knew about me. He'd really done his homework. He'd talked to all the backing singers, sound engineers and tour managers I'd worked with. He had *really* asked around.

'I think Paul was nervous because he was having to decide who would play the bass. The rest of the band was all family – Elroy on drums and Dan Kelly on guitar so I was a ring-in and he was deciding for Neil as well so he really wanted to make sure. We did have a jam. He came over to my house and we played a couple of songs and that was it.

'We had two weeks of rehearsals. With Elroy – Neil's son – it was the first big tour he'd done, so he'd done a lot of homework and so had I. I always do, but going into these rehearsals I obsessively learnt everything. And Elroy had done the same thing.

'We'd learnt the songs from the records. And from Neil and Paul – obviously because they'd been playing these songs for years – but they kind of had their new versions of them. In the end we ended up going back to the recorded versions for that tour, maybe because they were singing each other's songs.

'The tour was like magic. We all got along so well and I was just amazed at how chilled Neil and Paul were. We'd all do stuff and hang out and the crew were all part of it. A lovely, lovely magical vibe.

'There was no ego. It was all just about the music.'

The twenty-date tour began on 18 February 2013 at Melbourne's Palais Theatre and concluded at the Sydney Opera House in the Concert Hall on 18 March, the fifth performance of the tour at that venue. The final performance was streamed internationally via YouTube as Neil Finn And Paul Kelly Live at The Sydney Opera House.

The performance was released as a CD and DVD under the title *Goin' Your Way*, the title coming from the chorus of Henry Mancini's classic 'Moon River' which was performed at every concert.

'I think it was me that suggested that song initially,' Finn says. 'I'd learnt it for [my brother] Tim's wedding and it's a song I really like – just the way it's constructed and the sort of song it is. I thought it might suit the end of the night and Paul was fond of it as well, so we did it.'

The concerts featured twenty-nine songs and, as expected, a combination of work from the two artists.

'We put in a wish list of each other's songs that we wanted to do,' Finn says.

'It was a case of finding the way into the songs for each of us and that was quite a prompt as to what songs we'd do and what ones we wouldn't. We wanted to be able to share the vocal duties on some of the songs.

'The other thing that was really important for us was that we had a proper band onstage, one that we really felt we were part of. We didn't want it to be a case of me standing off in the wings waiting for Paul to sing a song and then me walking on to do a song, with a bunch of hot session players behind us. We wanted to be engaged.

'I think we traded emails and Skypes for a couple of months, getting the songs we could do down to a manageable number and honing how we could perform them.

'Then we got together at my studio, to try out what we'd come up with and made a few more tweaks. We actually put quite a lot of thought and preamble into devising a good show.

'I asked Noel Crombie and Sally Milne to design a beautiful backdrop because it seemed that if we were going to do all these great theatres we should have some kind of defining image for the stage and give it a slight theatricality.

'We also thought of using our family members for the band to give it that extra intimacy. He'd used Dan for long periods and Elroy had been playing with me for a little bit and is a great drummer. Liam was doing his own thing and wasn't available, but having him involved was an idea at one point. It all made it feel very down home, comfortable and nice.

'I wanted to play piano on a bunch of Paul's songs because there's some really great piano on them.

'It's great to learn piano on someone else's songs. You actually get inside the mechanics of how other people put songs together. And as anyone who's written a decent song knows, a couple of them come in quick bursts, but most of them require a fair amount of sculpting and patience and coming and going back and forth. What you don't notice when they turn out well is all that process – that gets buried and it just sounds effortless.

'When you start to learn somebody else's songs you see a little bit of the process and you understand the intricacies of what sounds very simple. You think you know the song and then you continually make the same stupid mistake on really easy parts because it's just not in your vocabulary and it's not the way you would have done it. I think that's really good for your brain. It opens you up to altering phrasing and thinking about song structure a little differently.

'With Paul and many of his songs, the weight of the lyric dictates the flow of the songs. I think a song like "How to Make Gravy" – at some point he announced that it was a song without a chorus but I always disputed that onstage and went, "No, it's all the chorus because people know every word of that song." It's amazing.

'Paul's narrative skill is admirable. I haven't been that kind of songwriter. He builds the phrasing around a narrative. The way the melodic phrasing is built around his words is really interesting. He's not pedantic and sometimes his words, the right words, have to be fitted in. I'm usually more interested in getting my words to fit in like clockwork, which limits me, but I've actually been a little better at that in recent times and I give him a little credit for that.'

And what of the possibility of them collaborating on songs at some stage?

'It would have been alluded to at some point, Paul is well down the track in terms of his collaborations. I mean, he's written songs for and with a lot of women and he's worked with Kev Carmody and Archie Roach – and I think he's very good at it.

'We did talk about it for the tour and there was discussion about us maybe writing something together for that. We had one day in Auckland where we knocked around a few things but we didn't come up with anything at the time.

'I've written songs with my brother Tim but very rarely with anybody else. It's a little bit not in my normal canon, whereas with Paul it is. But it's a bit of a wonder we didn't, and maybe we still will. Who knows?'

Paul also remembers the tour well. 'That was just a really, really enjoyable tour. It was a happy tour. Dan Kelly was in the band, and Neil had his son Elroy playing drums.

'The way we approached this was that we'd seen a lot of these tours where the performers were together – but not really together – so we made a conscious decision to really dig into each other's songs. When he sang his songs I was in Neil's band – I'd play piano or guitar and we applied that idea to doing one of each other's songs. I did "Into Temptation", and he did "You Can Put Your Shoes Under My Bed". He had this story about his mother talking about some film star she fancied and saying, "He can put his shoes under my bed."

'We sang harmonies on each other's songs and we'd swap verses and blend into each other as much as possible. What was great for me was learning his songs. You hear these beautiful songs that sound so effortless, almost like they came down from heaven with the music and those melodies. Going inside them is like going into the gears on a watch. The interesting thing about Neil's songs is that there's always little changes going on. Mine have a more traditional structure whereas with Neil one verse will be slightly different from the one before and then there'll be another little bit and something else that's different in the following verse – they have all these little intricacies that you have to study if you're going to play them properly.

'I loved learning his songs and discovering all these beautiful intricacies. They're not following formulas and they're some of the greatest pop songs you'll ever hear.

The exuberance and joy of the tour still evoke fond memories for Paul: 'There were two main highlights for me from that tour – one was singing "Into Temptation", which I've always loved, and really leaning into that song, and the other was playing the opening bars of "Don't Dream It's Over" every night on my own – I can't even tell you the chords, it's some fancy chord with a ninth and a thirteenth. Standing on the stage playing those chords before the band came in was one of the great showbiz highlights for me.'

CHAPTER 15

FROM LITTLE THINGS

'I've always been influenced by Paul's music. I'm inspired
by the way he handles his career and the way he
approaches making records.'
Kasey Chambers

As the years have gone by Paul's confidence has
grown along with his creative restlessness. The urge to
explore and seek new experiences and undertake new
creative endeavours is intrinsic to his being. What next?
What area interests him that he hasn't explored? What if he
tried working with a choir or an orchestra?

When we first met up again as this book was well
underway I joked with Paul that during my interview with
Zoe Hauptmann we speculated, only semi-seriously, that
he had explored so many musical genres that a jazz album
couldn't be far away as that was one musical genre he hadn't
ventured into.

As I said that a gentle smile appeared on Paul's face and he said, 'Well, it's not exactly a jazz album but I did these shows with Paul Grabowsky and we've done a recording …'

It's impossible not to sense that Paul's creative output in future years will involve even more collaboration. There's a definite sense that he's still learning about so many aspects of the writing and composing process and has the humility to realise that, despite all his years of performing, writing and singing, there is still much for him to learn and explore.

Randy Newman once observed that's it's lonely at the top. It's less lonely with others by your side. And often the soundscape is extremely interesting and diverse.

'I've come to realise,' Paul says, 'largely from working with Vika and Linda – that I really like having another voice on a record besides mine. The Triffids did that. So did The Rolling Stones. The Stones would have Keith [Richards] sing a song. The Triffids had Jill [Birt] singing a song. The Velvet Underground had Moe [Tucker] or Sterling [Morrison] sing a song. *The Merri Soul Sessions* – that was different singers, but there's been other songs since that I've liked sung by others. I think it's pretty cool, no matter how much you like a singer. For years and years and years it was just me.'

In 2014 *The Merri Soul Sessions*, which featured Paul's songs performed by Vika and Linda Bull, Dan Sultan, Kira Puru and Clairy Browne resulted in a tour late in that year and extending into 2015.

Paul could, by this point, do pretty much anything he wanted as evidenced by his next two releases – *Seven Sonnets & a Song* saw him musically recreating work by William Shakespeare, and *Death's Dateless Night* was an album of songs by other people that he and Charlie Owen had either performed at funerals or thought would suit such occasions.

Owen had met Paul around 1987 when both were living in Sydney and drinking at the Hopetoun, but it wasn't until both had relocated back to Melbourne after the hazy eighties that the friendship grew deeper. Owen started playing with Maurice Frawley's band The Working Class Ringos.

'Paul loved the Ringos and he loved Maurice's songwriting, and that's how we became friends,' Owen says. 'He used to come and see us regularly and he and Maurice were good friends.'

Frawley had been in The Dots for a short period of time, during which he and Paul had co-written 'Look So Fine, Feel So Low'.

Owen's relationship with team Paul strengthened when Dan Kelly recorded his first single – 'Nasty Streak' – at the home of Owen and his partner Kylie Greer, and the couple released it as a bootleg single. It's a song that Renée Geyer still features regularly in her live show.

Then of course there was that song called 'Charlie Owen's Slide Guitar' written by Paul.

'Maurice and I were supporting Paul and Spencer in Bendigo or somewhere like that,' Owen says, 'and we were all sitting around afterwards waiting for the crew to pack up and Spencer goes, "Paul, play Charlie the new song," and Paul goes, "Okay," and starts playing this song. I thought, *Great, they're taking the piss out of me*, and Spencer goes, "No, Charlie, it's a real song," so that's how the song was delivered to me.

'Because of our friendship and friendship circle we ended up playing at a few funerals together, including Chrissy Amphlett's, and a friend of mine who I'd been working with – Martin Kantor. Martin was the photographer who went on tour with Paul in the States but at the time I didn't realise that connection. When he passed away I asked Paul if he'd come and play with me at Martin's funeral. He did.

'Driving home after the funeral we discussed how there was a poignancy that's unique to playing at funerals, and we thought there was an album in this.

'We'd already worked together on the Maurice Frawley tribute album [*Long Gone Whistle*], but that was more because we were producing it.

'The *Death's Dateless Night* album became about all the songs we've either played together or separately at funerals. We'd played "Meet Me in The Middle of The Air" at Chrissy's funeral, and Townes Van Zandt's "To Live Is To Fly" at Martin's.

'We made the record in my house at Arthurs Seat on the Peninsula. Paul stayed in my next-door neighbour's house which is rented out during holidays.

'For a whole week we were together recording in the lounge room. It was a really good way to do it. J Walker came down to work on it with us.'

'I felt like I was more an engineer on *Death's Dateless Night*,' Walker says, 'as Paul and Charlie both had a really strong sense of what they wanted and what they were doing.'

'I was playing my dead grandmother's piano,' Owen says, 'and we had Maurice's jacket hanging on the back of a chair and Shane's [Walsh – from The Working Class Ringos who also died] double bass was sitting in a corner of the room. I don't think I ever told Paul that I had put all these things around the room but I'm sure he noticed. It made it feel poignant and valid without being sad.'

'One of the songs on *Death's Dateless Night* is "Good Things",' Paul says, 'which was the song that was playing at Maurice Frawley's funeral out in the country. That song was playing through the speakers as he was carried out of the church in the coffin to the hearse. We were all lined up outside the church so I had very strong memories of that song at his funeral. I love the song anyway. And because Charlie played so much with Maurice we really wanted to do a Maurice song.'

The duo also included a few songs – such as LJ Hill's sublime 'Pretty Bird Tree' – not because they'd played it at an actual funeral but because both agreed it would be perfect for such a gathering.

Following the release of *Death's Dateless Night*, Paul and Owen did a tour of churches in Australia, and then shows in the United States and Canada, accompanied by Paul's daughters, Memphis and Madeleine.

At those shows they predominantly performed the album but also other songs from Paul's catalogue that fitted the premise – 'How to Make Gravy' and 'Deeper Water' being two that fitted the bill.

Paul says, 'My daughters Maddy and Memphis sang on *Death's Dateless Night* – "Let It Be" is a song we've sung a bit over the years – we sung it at Kaarin's fiftieth and on other occasions. The version on the record is our family version. I haven't actually sung it at a funeral but I snuck it on the record …

'It was really great fun singing with them [Madeleine and Memphis]. We'd done little bits and pieces together. We sang at the Community Cup with Dan, and various events but this was the first time we'd done a series of gigs together and a tour.

'When we toured it in America during April 2017 they came. That was an even bigger thrill – going with them to places that they'd never been before.

'Singing with family is just a great thing to do. I've done it a lot with Dan. There's just something about the way voices beat together. Maddy and Memphis have an amazing intuitive instinct together. They're beautifully in tune, in a straightforward way. I'm a big fan of unison singing so I often get Vika and Linda to sing parts in unison.'

* * *

Composer James Ledger and Paul kept in contact and in 2015 the composer was commissioned by the Sydney Symphony to write a piece for orchestra and choir that commemorated the one hundredth year since the Anzacs landed at Gallipoli.

On a whim Ledger asked Paul if he was interested in writing something for this. Paul said he was having a year off, but within a week Ledger had received an email from Paul setting out the completed text which would be performed by the choir as part of 'War Music'.

In 2016, after knowing each other for many years, Paul agreed to produce an album, *Dragonfly*, for Kasey Chambers which was released early the following year. As expected, Paul brought his own production stamp to the record.

'I'd asked Paul a few times before this record if he'd produce something for me one day,' Chambers says.

'We work together every now and then. He'd never said no to doing something with me, to producing something – but he also never really committed to it. So I kept asking and asking until I think he realised that the only way I was going to stop asking was if he agreed to do something. Honestly, I think I wore him down.

'I've always been influenced by Paul's music. I'm inspired by the way he handles his career and the way he approaches making records. He's really different from me personality wise. But we really click in the studio. Watching him bring my songs to life and his flavour to them was great. He brought different musicians and an engineer in.

'We did it in Melbourne at Sing Sing Studios. We'd worked there before recording a couple of songs together. It's not like the album sounds like a Paul Kelly record by any means, but you can certainly tell that his influence is there, even on the songs he doesn't play on – because he plays and sings on some songs.'

Paul doing more than just producing the album was something Chambers didn't assume was a given.

'I didn't want to ask and I didn't want to push my luck but then he suggested it. He sent me a message one day saying that he'd been listening to all the songs and was it okay if he tried a few of the harmonies and some of the music on it. I thought that was awesome – and he didn't charge me any extra for it.'

Even with Chambers' long and highly regarded history as a songwriter she still found it completely confronting sending songs to Paul to see what he thought of them. Such is the sense of awe that Paul engenders among even the most experienced songwriters.

'It was honestly one of the most nerve-racking things I've ever had to do in my life. I mean, I'd wanted Paul to produce something for ages and he'd finally said yes, and he'd heard a couple of the songs that I'd played live – "Behind The Eyes of Henri Young" and "Ain't No Little Girl" – and then he asked if I'd send him some more songs, and that's when I went, "Oh my God, I have to send these songs that no one has heard to one of my favourite songwriters in the whole world and get his opinion on them and he's actually going to go through them with a fine tooth comb, going, 'No, this is crap, oh, this one's okay, okay, this one needs work'." I was thinking that this was both the best and worst moment of my life.

'Paul's very honest. He doesn't suffer fools easily and he's not going to piss in your pocket for nothing. He was amazing to work with.

'He's a really beautiful person to be around during that creative process. And he didn't make me cry once – so that was good. I kept expecting that he was going to say something about my favourite song and that I'd be rocking backwards and forwards in the foetal position in a corner for the rest of the session, but that didn't happen.'

Paul persuaded Chambers to record a Woody Guthrie/ Bob Dylan blues–inspired song, 'Talkin' Baby Blues'.

'That was one of the songs I thought wasn't going to make the record. I played it live a lot for a few years, and it was one of the songs I sent to Paul when he asked me for more.

'I said that it was just stupid but he came back and said that it was his favourite song of the new batch and that we had to record it.

'At the end of the session when we'd sort of finished the record and everything seemed done, and we were sitting around with a bottle of Glenlivet Scotch and after we all had one or two or three Paul said he wanted us to go in and do a live version of "Talkin' Baby Blues", and we did and that's how it ended up on the record.'

* * *

As well as working with Ledger, Chambers and all the other artists, Paul was also working on his own material. When he released *Life Is Fine* in 2017 it was his first solo album in five years and EMI Records went to town. Managing Director John O'Donnell worked out that Paul had never had a number 1 album and set about rectifying that with a masterful marketing campaign. The album topped the charts and won four ARIA awards that year.

Life Is Fine was followed by another album, *Nature*, in 2018, which also went to number 1 in the charts. Masterminding the campaign to get Paul's albums to number 1 was O'Donnell, a long-standing fan who had been seeing Paul's gigs since The Dots days.

Having done his first-ever interview as a journalist with Paul, O'Donnell is another person who is passionate about Paul's early albums, particularly *Manila*.

'It's a great record. A great *great* record.

'"Touchy Babe" is fantastic. "Forbidden Street" is stunning. "Clean This House" is a masterpiece. But I think those songs and albums remind him of all the mess in his life at the time. He cannot hear that record and not be reminded of it.'

O'Donnell has thoughts about the ascension of Paul's career since the late 1990s which he describes as 'the doldrum years ... things weren't bad but it was not the renaissance that he's now come to. Paul was playing smaller gigs like the [1350-capacity] Metro in Sydney.'

While agreeing that having Victorian students studying Paul's lyrics didn't hurt, he points out that this wasn't national and that other factors came into play with Paul's career around the mid-2000s, particularly Paul playing the Falls, Splendour in the Grass and Groovin the Moo festivals.

'They [Paul and management] took a third of what they would normally get paid for those festivals. With Splendour a precedent had been set with the Finn Brothers playing there, so I think the organisers were up for it. It was very shrewd planning, to drive these songs home to a younger audience. It was very smartly calculated by Paul and Bill [Cullen].

'For an audience, they don't even know that they know Paul Kelly songs but they're going along to the festivals and the next thing they know they're on someone's shoulders singing along to "To Her Door".

'When I realised that Paul had never had a number-one album, we really went for it with *Life Is Fine* and then followed it up with *Nature*. We had tried it earlier with *Stolen Apples* but had fallen short.'

And of course the third edition of the *Songs from the South* compilation also went to the top of the charts and completed the trifecta.

'It's all part of the rolling thunder that has led to where Paul is now.'

Also in 2017 pianist Anna Goldsworthy approached Paul about doing a project involving words and music relating to nature and animals. Goldsworthy and Paul had initially encountered each other when John Kingsmill suggested that they review each other's recently published memoirs for a project he was working on.

Paul proposed an exchange of letters about writing and memoirs, and this evolved into an extended correspondence before the two met in person at a concert on the Goin' Your Way tour.

Later Paul attended a performance by Goldsworthy and her Seraphim Trio, after which her cello player Timothy Nankervis suggested a collaboration.

'We had to work out if our worlds could meet – and how they could meet,' Goldsworthy says.

'We knew of *Conversations with Ghosts* and what he'd done with James Ledger and came up with the idea of setting poems to music.

'The initial idea [from Timothy] was a zoo theme, pieces about animals, a sort of menagerie. Then both Paul and I embarked on reading a lot of poetry with animals as the theme. The first bunch I collated were all bird poems and I sent those to him. He came back and suggested that maybe we should just stick to birds and the more I thought about it the more I thought it was a lovely idea. Also the themes of flight and migration are rich for music.

'We both almost simultaneously sent each other Emily Dickinson's "'Hope' Is the Thing With Feathers" and Paul was quite wedded to doing Keats' "Ode To a Nightingale".'

The resulting piece includes soundscapes inspired by birds and adaptations of poems by John Keats, Judith Wright, Thomas Hardy, Gerard Manley Hopkins, Emily Dickinson, AD Hope, Gwen Harwood and others.

Thirteen Ways to Look at Birds, performed with singer Alice Keath and the Seraphim Trio (which includes Anna Goldsworthy), had been commissioned by both the Perth and Adelaide arts festivals, and premiered in March 2019 in Adelaide, and in January 2020 at the Perth Festival, followed by performances in Sydney in February 2020.

'I used to have a pretty straightforward answer to how I write songs,' Paul says, 'but over the last six or seven years things have changed.

'My main method of writing songs for many, many years was just singing noises or sounds over a melody and into a tape recorder – sometimes with words attached. I would then generally have the architecture of the song in my mind and know that there'd be a couple of verses and a chorus or bridge or whatever and then I would fill in the words.

'That was my main method for a very long time – and then after working with James Ledger on *Conversations with Ghosts* in 2012 that all changed … the next thing I did after that project was put one of Shakespeare's sonnets to music and that led me to doing other sonnets and making a record of them. That became another way for me to write songs – to look at a poem that I like and try to put music into it. It's a method that's snuck into my so-called normal records.

'My 2018 record, *Nature* – had five poems by other people. The one before that had one – the title track – "Life Is Fine" by Langston Hughes, so it's been another way for me to write songs, and it's also affected the way I write my own words too.

'I still write the old way and doodle away on a guitar or piano and get some words and try and get a tune and try and find some words to fit it – but every now and again I might write a set of words first and then put the music to it.

'It's pretty good after forty years to find a different way to write songs. In a way it's kind of a relief.'

* * *

Change, evolution and growth have been a constant in Paul's life that extends to his personal relationships.

Peter Luscombe has been with Paul long enough to be an observer of his relationship upheavals and feels that Paul tends to deal with emotional dysfunction in his life by not being around, that is by avoiding it, by moving on to the next project, doing the next gig and disappearing on tour. Nick Lainas says when Paul ends something, 'He doesn't look back, that's the end.'

'When he and Sian Prior split up he was on tour with Dan doing the A to Z tour,' says Luscombe, 'that just kept on going.

'When he and Kaarin split up he went to England for a month. We'd just recorded a few tracks for … *Nothing But A Dream* and he went to England for a month to do the rest of the record with Mark Wallace. In that time word had gotten around that he and Kaarin had split up. A Melbourne singer told everybody. I said to him [Paul], "Did you tell [this person] on purpose before you left so that everyone would know by the time you got back?" and he said, "There might have been a little bit of thought that went into that – to take the wind out of the sails." By the time he came back four or five weeks later it was old news. So he wasn't dealing with, "Oh my God, I just found out."'

Luscombe considers that Paul is in a good place with his current relationship.

'I don't think I've ever seen Paul happier. And I reckon it's been in the last three or four years. So you've got to join the dots there. He just seems happy in general. I think he's happy in his art. He gets to do whatever he wants to do – and the success of the last few albums, particularly *Life Is Fine*, really took it to another level.'

Since 2015, Paul has been sharing his life with Siân Darling, an independent artist and activist, although the term 'activist' makes her wince. 'I've inherited the "just do good work and don't draw attention to yourself" attitude from my grandmother. I think she picked it up in Auschwitz. Paul has a similar approach to generous deeds, he does them quietly.' Darling is the co-chair of *Right Now Inc.*, an independent human rights publication and, since 2018, she has been part of Paul's official management team with Bill Cullen, managing specific projects and general strategising. She's full of energy and ideas, wears a take-no-prisoners attitude openly, and is direct and opinionated.

Hard as it may be to believe, Darling insists that she wasn't very familiar with Paul or his back catalogue when they met in September 2014. Darling was playing the part of a bird, a flamingo to be precise, in the production of *Funeral*, during its first season at the Melbourne Fringe Festival. Paul was a guest musician. He showed up. There was banter. He strummed his guitar and played Darling and her dressing room buddies the Bill Withers song 'Lean on Me'. At some point she said, 'I like your nose,' and a few hours later he'd paid the compliment back. There was chemistry.

Darling lost her immediate family when she was nineteen. She says she depends on the natural world for comfort, support and perspective, 'The way one might lean on their family.

'That world is like next of kin. Or perhaps how some experience God – a higher power that's within me, that I'm within. When people get excited over Paul in a fandom way – wanting a photo, to say hello – I think of it being similar to the joy I feel over something in nature, it's like if I saw a wedge-tailed eagle or a kookaburra picking up a black snake.'

Darling wears her politics on her sleeve but insists that Paul isn't political. Instead, she says Paul is an observer and a storyteller and it's the interpretations of his observations and storytelling that inspires and motivates people to take up causes and become advocates for social justice issues, including the First Peoples and the natural world.

'He's able to get people who would not ordinarily think about Indigenous justice to listen to such stories anyway. People who are singing along to fun songs like "Dumb Things" or "Deeper Water" etcetera are at the same time being exposed to stories that are centred on Indigenous justice, like "Maralinga" or "From Little Things", or environmental issues with "Sleep Australia Sleep".'

Released early in 2020, 'Sleep Australia Sleep' tackles the subject of climate change, the tipping point of ecological disaster. Darling says it follows in a long tradition of Paul's songs which she says he calls 'newspaper songs'. They're not protest songs, and they're not political songs. They are songs about things happening around us.

For her part, Darling was the driving force behind the song. 'I'm finding a way to do my job with Paul and occasionally applying it to other issues I care about. My job is to look after Paul but thankfully we have vigorous discussions about shared values that we can work towards. Both of us would love to see poetry taken more seriously in Australia as it is in other countries. Neither of us think highly of the celebrity endorsement approach so it's fun working out the best way to be useful to a cause without relying on that.'

Another project being driven by Darling is a reprise of *Cannot Buy My Soul*, new recordings of Kev Carmody songs. Darling has formed close relationships and gone on to work with two of Paul's friends and co-songwriters, Kev Carmody and Alan Pigram.

While Paul already had the genesis of *Thirteen Ways to Look at Birds*, Darling was also very much involved in the refining of that concept, every day sending him a poem about birds. Like Paul, Darling has a love of poetry, both reading and writing it.

'We have a very long habit of writing each other letters – even if we see each other that day. I send him poems that have relevance to something we are experiencing or discussing. During *Thirteen Ways to Look at Birds*, I sent ones about birds. Then with *Ancient Rain*, the Irish project he did with Camille O'Sullivan, I went on a hunt for Irish poems. I sent him my favourite love poem, "Quarantine" [by Eavan Boland]. He turned it into a song, which is a beautiful song but now this poem, in all its original glory of being words on a page, has been changed. It's lovely that he takes such interest in my passions but it's also confronting when he takes them on, changes them and "paints them Paul" if that makes sense.'

The inspiration, energy and drive Darling brings to Paul's career is more intriguing given her disinterest in his music. She's more concerned with where he fits into people's consciousness and how that can be harnessed for positive change. 'I do marvel at his ability to make people happy with a simple smile or salutation, obviously his songs have made it that way. He's clearly been a passenger in many people's lives as they play his songs through important times. It's a beautiful honour to have, to make people feel so understood, less alone.

'I'm not the biggest fan of his music,' she says without a hint of unease at expressing this opinion publicly. 'I've got a lot of unopened CDs that he's given me. Sometimes I feel a bit cruel that I'm not more easily excited about the actual music. In the house, if he's singing, I often close all the doors between us. He gets it and he knows I value his work I just don't always love the sound of it. There's a lot of music filling up public space these days. I love quiet, you can hear so much in it. Saying that, I'd certainly miss the hum of it throughout the house if it ever stopped. Paul loves singing and I love the joy it brings him and others. He seems so alive when he's singing, especially on stage. Sometimes that fragility in him seeming so alive makes me weep with tenderness. I have the same feeling when he plays football or he's swimming in the ocean. He's so free, so alive, so fragile. In that sense I love his music, for what it can do. We both love poetry and wordplay so we have much fun with that element of his songwriting. As we both work from home, I hear him chipping away at the same songs over and over; writing new ones or practising old ones. It's a little like someone working in a shed with power tools. All kinds of abrasive, repetitive noises and then *voila*, something beautiful or useful appears.

'The sound is growing on me and I sometimes enjoy it, but I look at it mechanically. I like the phrasing in many songs – he squeezes a story into a song. It's a bit like hip hop – I think he's so clever with words. I like hip hop, and so does he. We sometimes cook together with it blasting.'

Darling is usually the first to hear a new song. Paul asks for her opinion and she gives it, sometimes suggesting swapping a word or discussing the right vocalist for a part. 'Often they're perfect as they are without my brutal opinions!'

She involves herself in Paul's creative process in a diverse array of ways. 'At one stage I sent him a poem by Langston Hughes and I challenged him to put it to music – and that became the title track of the album *Life Is Fine*. I taught him the word "petrichor" – it's the smell when water touches dust, the smell of rain hitting dry earth – and that became a song on that album.'

Absentmindedly, Paul forgot to thank Darling on that album, something he had fixed on the reprint. 'I didn't expect to be thanked – I hadn't thought about it until I saw he'd thanked a piano teacher. Then this feeling of injustice fell upon me. It reeked of the "hidden muse" – a concept I don't find flattering. Everyone needs to be acknowledged for their contributions. There's no romance in exploitation. I didn't say anything but apparently my face is an open book. Within a few hours he wrote me a beautiful thank you card and had already fixed his mistake. He writes me beautiful notes and cards. Always a poem,' she says.

Paul's nickname for Darling is Little Wolf and it's the name of a song on his 2018 album *Nature*.

It is clear that Darling stands her ground in the relationship. 'I am more combative, more reactive to feelings. Sometimes he disappoints me and I can't help but confront him to get it out of our way. He loves and looks after me well though; it's consistent, steady, generous and patient love.'

She knows about Paul's past, being his fourth serious partner, and demands simple honesty. She says Paul is in a good and healthy place. 'He's a very simple person – has a few simple pleasures and has shaken some bad habits.'

And, for someone who admits to thinking that 'Randwick Bells' was a song by Jimmy Little, Darling has embraced and influenced the world of Paul in ways that can only be considered positive. The Little Wolf is a powerful force in his creative and personal life.

CHAPTER 16

CHEMISTRY AND COLLABORATION

'Right from the start he said he doesn't want a "yes man" in there. He said he likes to surround himself with opinionated people.'

Steve Schram

THE LINE-UP TO PAUL'S BAND HAS REMAINED THE SAME since Cameron Bruce joined in 2007, with the exception of Vika and Linda Bull becoming full-time members in 2009 and 2010 respectively. Just to keep everyone on their toes, Dan Kelly still comes and goes. Somehow it all falls into place.

It's a line-up that plays and tours well together. They're old friends and have a musical chemistry that – well, it just works. And they tour well; they have that crucial element required for long stints on the road.

'The term Paul uses is The Squad,' Ash Naylor says. 'He used that expression in an interview once. Although it sounds a bit clinical it's actually great because it affords some of us the luxury of being unavailable at times.'

'The great thing about the chemistry of the current band is that everybody knows each other well and we like each other socially,' Peter Luscombe says. 'We find that we hang out. I mean, when we're not touring with Paul, Bill and Ash and I play a lot together.'

But when the call from Paul comes that's where they go. They're never totally sure when that might be but the calls have kept coming.

'Paul selects people he wants to be around and who can do the job,' Luscombe says. 'Everyone in this band walks onstage every night with an absolute love of what they're doing – and a total regard for Paul's material.

'Bill [McDonald] and I often talk about this. Paul doesn't need us. He can do this without us. He can go onstage without us. But I like to think we bring something to it with the chemistry we have and the love we have for his songs and the respect we have for him as an artist. Paul brings out things in us, and encourages great performances from the band because he allows everybody to do what they do and trusts what we can bring to it. He's played with us long enough to know that we're there to serve the songs.

'The thing that struck me most when I first started working with Paul was how secure he was in his own skin as an artist. And because of that he trusts. I feel that I'm trusted by him. With other people I've found that they won't give you the reins because if you do something good it won't be theirs. Whereas Paul has this thing where he wants input. He likes to be pushed. But he'll let you know when he doesn't agree with something.

'If he doesn't like something he'll just say, "Have you got anything else?"'

Paul also increasingly involves Luscombe in the process of developing a song. They've been together so long that he trusts his judgement.

'Sometimes he'll send me something and go, "Do you reckon this is anything?"' Luscombe says. 'Maybe it's just a rough recording. It was like that with the Adam Goodes song. He asked if I reckoned it was anything and I told him that it had warmth and was moving.

'There's a trust there. Sometimes I think it's a case of him not being convinced about something. But if Paul's convinced about a tune then I trust him. He's hearing something in it.

'We've had songs where we've gone back to them – and back and back – and eventually it's a case of, "Okay, let's leave this one for a while." But usually you can tell straight away. In some ways his songs play themselves and you're just trying not to get in the way. My role is to go, "Okay, we've just put the most comfortable pair of slippers on that song."'

Bill McDonald thinks that the creative relationship between the current band members hasn't changed a bit since they started. Throughout this period they've predominantly worked with the sound engineer Steve Schram, who also often finds himself in a co-producer's role.

'We've had a long relationship with him. He works a lot at Soundpark Studios, which is where we go after working through things at Bakehouse Studios. Bakehouse is a great studio that's made completely from dumpster material, apart from the gear obviously. The building is a big open space and we can all sit together – apart from the drum booth – and look at each other and play together.

'We rehearse at Bakehouse Studios and when it comes time to record we just go to Soundpark and play the new songs or songs that we've rehearsed. We do it all old-school –

like The Beatles. When we're recording we'll do twenty takes and Steve Schram will be saying, "No, you haven't got it yet," or we might get it in one or two takes. And then he'll say, "That's it – you're never going to get it any better than that." All the band play together at once. Occasionally we'll do a fix-up but ninety-five per cent of the time what you hear is an entire band take. We don't use click tracks or anything like that. We just wait until we get a good take.

'Paul still works the same way he always has since I've been in the band. Sometimes he will walk in with a completed song that's done and dusted. Sometimes he'll go back to older stuff. We've dug up songs that he's had for twenty-five years and he's never felt right about. Sometimes it will just click and feel right. Other times we'll give it a try and he'll still think it's not right.'

Cameron Bruce also enjoys the fact that recording with Paul is done quickly and with the whole band together. And the fact that they rarely do overdubs.

'We just hang in there until there's a good band take. If it's not working and it's really feeling like a fight to get it then Paul hits the off switch and we just stop playing. To me that's just like saying that this song isn't ready to be born yet. Not to get too spiritual about it, but it's another force going "not yet". That's how I read it.

'There's a practical element too. You're paying for a studio and you might not get anywhere for days with a song, but it doesn't matter because he's already got enough songs. It's not like he's relying on *that* song. He's always got another song. And it's rare that it happens anyway – maybe once or twice since I've been in the band.'

Steve Schram jokes that he's 'the only guy to give Paul a number one', in reference to the success of the *Life Is Fine* and *Nature* albums, both of which Schram produced. The two first worked together on *The Merri Soul Sessions*, and as Schram says, 'He keeps inviting me back.' In terms of their interaction, Schram says that Paul is very focused.

'Paul knows what he likes, he knows what he wants and he has very good ears for parts working together. But right from the start he said he doesn't want a "yes man" in there. He said he likes to surround himself with opinionated people.

'The way we do it is very live. We do all Paul's vocals live with the band. There's rarely an overdub. Backing vocals usually go down live. So we move very quickly and he relies on me to pick the take and hear when things are or aren't working. At the end we're trying to make it translate out of little speakers. When you're in with the band performing it's a bit harder to know if it's working or not. But that's the job of everyone in the band. We all assume the same role, so he's open. Everyone can throw in their two cents' worth and when someone does – because they're a talented bunch – they're usually correct.

'Sometimes we get stuck – which means we spend two and a half hours hunting down a song, whereas usually it's an hour. It's *fast*. Usually two or three songs a day – completed.

'And there's not a lot of pre-production. One, maybe two, rehearsals before they go in just to get the songs down.

'Sometimes Paul will bring in a demo and everyone will start playing, and we hunt that one down. Everyone is *really, really* good. It's like a tornado tears through the studio. We will cut takes together – just like The Beatles did.'

Schram says that these days Paul doesn't plan to make a specific album and will just book a week or ten days of recording.

'Aside from *Merri Soul*, Paul has never booked the studio to make an album. He just comes in to record. He records in batches and he has "offcuts" left over – I think that's an expression he picked up from Slim Dusty. And often he puts the offcuts together.'

'We know the parameters,' McDonald says. 'It's Paul who's going to be singing the songs. Even if a song doesn't work at that time that's not the end of it. It's just put away. Nothing is ever wasted. Ever.

'Paul's actually talked about making a record called *Offcuts*. In England on tour we learnt new songs between gigs, on the bus, anywhere. It'd be, "Let's try this," and then the song would be recorded from the desk at sound check and filed away.'

In a live context McDonald knows his role and sticks to it. As he says, 'At my age to be making original music – *great* original music, with a *great* songwriter, well, it's a fucking miracle.'

Before Paul and his band go out onstage to honour those songs they go through the same ritual backstage night after night, show after show.

'We have a Brother Pete,' McDonald says. 'Luscombe makes a drink for everyone. It's usually vodka and Sprite. Dan Kelly used to make his version of a British Invasion, which was vodka and Red Bull. And of course there's a Virgin for when various people aren't drinking.

'And virtually always there's a little sing together, a run-through of a song or two.'

When they walk onstage there's a remarkably consistent band who rarely have a show that's below par.

'Our worst show is still pretty good and it would not be obvious for the audience to see that it wasn't happening. For some reason someone might be having a bad night or there might be sound issues. But it's very rare and it would be hard for anyone outside the band to notice.'

Over the years one dictum has become a given with members of Paul's band: Do Not Mess With Steve Connolly's Guitar Parts. In fact, do not even be tempted to mess with them. Even slightly. Dan Kelly recites that dictum and will tell you, like many others, that Connolly's guitar playing was remarkable, and now sacrosanct and untouchable. 'Occasionally Shane O'Mara would be tempted to have a little whittle and it was like, "Hey, dude, don't do it."' Dan laughs.

'I have accidentally played some of the lines the wrong way – but never intentionally. It's like when Ash plays a solo in "Before Too Long" ... I don't know if he's ever fucked it up but Paul just quietly wanders up and says, "Don't fuck up," just to fuck with him, at the start of the song. The simplest ones are often the hardest.'

Peter Luscombe also has a deep admiration for Connolly's work. 'He's left a legacy that every guitar player worth their salt respects,' he says. 'You can't not play those lines. You can't not play that melody. You can't not play that solo. Every guitar player struggles to play his solo in "Before Too Long". It's like it's *his* thing.'

Similarly, for Bill McDonald, there's no suggestion that he will take liberties with some of the Paul classics. Not for a moment.

'We don't mess with the old songs. I learnt "Before Too Long" note for note – just like Jon Schofield played it. It's a case of honour the song. They mean something to people so you don't fuck around with that.'

Cameron Bruce also respects the gospel of The Messengers performances when it comes to his own playing.

'Steve Connolly's playing was so melodic. You can hum the solos and they're the ones you don't fuck with because they're not really solos, they're well-written parts. It's the same way that you wouldn't change the cello in a Beethoven symphony. It's a written part. There are other parts that are more textural that you can play around with. There's little bits of stuff in "How to Make Gravy" for instance, that's a more textural thing.'

'I think,' Paul says, 'like most recording artists, I don't listen to my records after they are completed. That probably comes as a surprise to other people. Lots of people know my records much better than I do. It's an intense period when you're making a record, and you know the songs and parts inside out. But once an album is made that's it.

'Over the years however I have learnt that fans listen to records over and over and when they call out for songs they're calling for the recorded version. They know every guitar break, every drum fill, and all the nuances of a song. That's all gone for me. What stays with me is just the song. The singing starts to change, the versions of the song start to change with whoever is in the band. For a long time I moved away from trying to play my songs in the way they were recorded. But when I started playing with Dan Luscombe and Dan Kelly, they wanted to play the songs the way they'd grown up listening to them. They had the feeling that those songs were carved in stone. You might think that new band members would want to do their own version, to make it their own, but no. Dan [Kelly] said he wanted to honour the original recordings, what he heard on record when he was thirteen and learnt to play guitar to.

'So at that stage I started going back and honouring those early recordings. And now when we play "Before Too Long", for instance, it's quite similar to the original recorded version. I went a long way around and came back to the early recordings. After listening to the records to get a reference point for playing, I really discovered how distinctive and inventive Pedro's parts were, so I wrote to Pedro and told him.'

The two present-day guitarists Naylor and Dan Kelly frequently perform on the same albums.

'We kind of nut it out,' Naylor says. 'After all these years you get to the point where you realise you're serving the song, and not your ego. That's what your own records are for.

'It's like with Jim Moginie and Martin Rotsey in the Oils and when Marty Willson-Piper and Peter Koppes were in The Church. You find a way to complement each other without stomping on each other's parts. But, at the same time, you're not there to showcase your own guitar playing, you're there to make the song come to life. That's something you learn over time.

'Playing my guitar parts is like reading from an English textbook, whereas learning to play Dan's parts is like trying to read a surrealist novel in French.

'With some of the recent songs, like "With the One I Love" – I feel like I am in my natural habitat. I grew up playing in bands in the mid to late 1980s. I loved bands like The Smiths and R.E.M. and that grinding alternative sound. That's something I'm very familiar with. The Tom Petty and the Heartbreakers kind of feel. That was the approach we took with that.

'At the centre is Paul's vision and his ability to encourage everyone to contribute. He makes you feel that your input is valued.'

That encouragement to contribute is something that every member of Paul's current band respects and values. But they all know when to defer to the songwriter and band leader. Peter Luscombe refers to him as the FSG – which simply stands for the Final Say Guy.

And amid all the talk about guitar players Naylor feels it's important for people to recognise what a fine guitar player Paul is. It's something that's not usually drawn attention to, with discussion usually about his lyrics first, his voice second and anything else is dust.

'Paul has a very distinctive way of playing guitar. You put any guitar in Paul's hands and it sounds like Paul. He had a guitar break down on the American tour and he borrowed my Strat and, guess what? It sounded like Paul. So that's pretty cool. I get a kick out of seeing him with one of my guitars.'

Dan Kelly is also clearly in awe of his uncle and recognises the genius in the apparent simplicity of his songs and playing style. 'Everything is elemental with Paul. Get the rhythm right. Sing it loud and strong. Eat your pasta with garlic. That doesn't mean any of it is unsophisticated. But his whole vibe is always elemental.

'Sometimes it's intimidating. Paul very rarely makes a mistake. Kasey [Chambers] is like that too. They're like classic sixties singers. Everything is just *there*. I have to do forty takes to get my vocals right against a wall of guitars but he just drives it right in and parks it out front.'

Naylor sits very comfortably in Paul's band. He has his own band as an outlet for his own songwriting so there's no feelings of frustration and unfulfilled aspirations there. He's one of Paul Kelly's guitar players and he's good with that.

'When I'm playing in Paul's band I feel like my role is defined, and I've defined it for myself as a guitar player – I'll also do backing vocals if required. That said, you've got Vika and Linda and Cameron Bruce who are all fabulous singers so my role as a guitar player is pretty contained – and I like that role. I never feel the need to step out of that. Paul's kinda got the lyric thing covered.'

At the core of the band in Naylor's opinion is the relationship between Paul and Luscombe.

'Their right hands just seem totally in sync. They're so used to each other. A lot of the machinations of the band centre around that relationship and the feels they come up with. They have a relationship that has endured since the early nineties, through all the changes both musical and personal, and all the different situations that have occurred and I think that speaks for itself.'

Luscombe is one of the few band musicians that Paul socialises with on a fairly regular basis. They will often have dinner together and have had a football tipping competition that has been going for a decade and a half.

Although they are technically the newest band members, Vika and Linda Bull have also become close to Paul, both personally and in the business of creating music, because of their long-standing relationship.

'We always ask Paul to be involved with our things. He's always interested in our projects and helping us develop as artists. And on the other side of things, if he's doing a record then we work with him.

'It's crossed over like that and it's now got to the point where we're like family, and we go on holidays together.'

One of many things Vika likes about working with Paul is that he's straight up with her and the rest of the people he plays with. There's no subterfuge, no confusion as to what's going on.

'Being like that is very gutsy of him. He's always been very upfront and honest and open. You can't hate him for that. You might be upset about it but you go, *Well, at least he was straight with me – and he had the decency to look me in the eye and say, "That's the way it's going to be."* He doesn't owe anybody anything.'

One instance of this was when Vika and Linda had sung the song 'Bound to Follow (Aisling Song)' for the *Nature* album but their voices were replaced with Kate Miller-Heidke on the released version.

'Paul actually wrote a note to us both saying that he'd got Kate to re-do it and that he hoped we didn't mind. It was like, "No, she's perfect for the part." We're not opera singers and he wanted an opera singer for that part. But it was good that he let us know as we had recorded it for the album so it wasn't like when we heard the album for the first time we would have gone, *That's not my voice.*'

Linda also respects Paul's directness and clarity about what's going on.

'One of the great things about Paul, for someone who doesn't really speak, is that he's a very good communicator. You never feel like you've been ripped off or talked about behind your back.'

Such was the case when Paul decided – after a little pressure from his record company – to sing the song 'With the One I Love' on his *Nature* album. The version of the album he submitted to EMI Records had Linda singing that song but label boss John O'Donnell felt strongly that it needed to have Paul's voice.

'Paul called and told me what had happened. He was straight up and said the record company would prefer it if he sang it. It was a radio thing. He'd done *The Merri Soul Sessions* with other people singing his songs and it was like, "We want to hear Paul singing his songs, that's the hit song – we want him to sing it." My attitude was, "If you can get it on the radio, go for it."'

In the studio and onstage Vika considers that Paul is demanding – but in a way that she respects.

'He expects the best. We have to be on our game. Especially live.

'I like Linda's voice and Paul's voice and the way we sound when we sing together. It's like a family group, like The Carter Family or The Staple Singers.'

Linda has her theories about why the relationship with Paul is now so close and has lasted so long.

'I don't think it's all about music. I think it's about his understanding of family. It's important to him and it's important to us too. I think he respects our lives as working mums. He gets that and often I think he works around that. I think that's a big part of our closeness.'

At this stage of Paul's career, while not taking anything for granted, Cameron Bruce says he'll be surprised if the core line-up changes again.

'It's like Crazy Horse – you just keep coming back to it. And it's an easy band. No one's on drugs or drinking so much that they forget to turn up to sound check. Everyone's pretty nice and normal and professional.'

* * *

As well as playing with his band (the squad), Paul continues to collaborate with many artists, many of whom would jump at the chance to work with him again, including Kev Carmody.

'I reckon it'd be great. When we write together we hardly ever look at each other. Recently he came and stayed for a few days before Bluesfest, the guitar came out and we worked on a few ideas. It's more than likely that in a couple of years something might come up, and he'll say he's recording it. Last time I just started off with a couple of chord progressions and we put a title on it – "Jesus and the Gypsy". Paul took to the title straight away.

'When we are together and he's jamming on the guitar and doing something and I'm jamming on my guitar and doing something and all of a sudden it comes together and one of us will go, "That feels pretty good," and then we'll start working that music. For example I'll throw something in and say, "What about 'Jesus and the Gypsy'?" and then bang bang bang from him. He's pretty quick at putting rhyming stuff down the side. He puts that in fairly well right away and then we just fill in the rest. It's totally random. There's no thesaurus. No rhyming dictionary. Bugger that.'

James Ledger would also jump at the opportunity to work with Paul again.

'It would be wonderful. He's inspiring to work with, and has a great work ethic. If he says he'll do something, he does it. I mentioned to him about the possibility of him singing at my wife's fiftieth birthday four years before the actual day – and he kept it in his head and of course he did sing at her birthday.'

William 'Billy' Miller from The Ferrets also frequently works with Paul these days. Miller has known Paul since the late 1970s when they both had flats in the same building in Punt Road. Miller remembers he was underneath Paul's balcony, the one that looked in the direction of the Nylex clock tower that features so prominently in the lyrics to 'Leaps and Bounds'.

Paul and Miller are both fanatical about Test cricket and so for the past six or seven years Paul travels to Miller's home on Boxing Day, usually bearing ham and other supplies, and the two settle in for the first day of the Test and remain glued to the screen for the remainder of the day's play.

The two had begun a songwriting collaboration during another cricket-watching session.

'I was at Paul's place one night about six years ago watching a Test in South Africa so it was really late at night. Play stopped suddenly because of a rain delay.

'I'd never written a song with Paul before but as soon as it started raining and play stopped we both jumped on the acoustic guitars, which were all around the room, and within thirty minutes we had our first song. We wrote three that night,' Miller says.

One of those – the first of the songs they collaborated on – was 'Don't Let a Good Thing Go' which was sung by Dan Sultan on *The Merri Soul Sessions* album.

'On another night we wrote another two or three songs – or at least started them, and they all ended up on *Life Is Fine* – "Firewood and Candles", "Rock Out On the Sea" and "Rising Moon".

'That night a friend of Paul's came around. He'd just broken up with his girlfriend and was really morose. At one stage he talked about having her over for dinner and how he got firewood and candles. We both just jumped straight on the guitars, I hit an A Minor and *bang*. Then he mentioned feeling like a rock out in the sea, and *bang* again. It was an amazing night.'

'Firewood and Candles' won the APRA Song of the Year in 2018.

The relationship continues today with Paul and Miller constantly firing texts of lyrics and MP3s with song snippets backwards and forwards to each other.

'It's such a spontaneous thing. That was the initial template and now the minute he walks into my place he's on the upright piano because he loves his piano playing, and we're jamming straight away.

'We're always coming up with bits and pieces and Paul stores them all away. Billy McDonald, who plays bass in my band as well as Paul's, told me that Paul will put something away and it might stay there for fifteen years, but it will eventually be used.'

* * *

Another artist working with Paul over the last few years is internationally acclaimed pedal steel guitar player Lucky Oceans. He has played with Paul since the late 1980s when he played on *Under the Sun*, contributing to 'Big Heart', 'Don't Stand So Close to the Window' and 'To Her Door'.

'Paul knew how to design this musical thing for the time, which was then called pub rock – and what a dynamic interaction he had with that band [The Coloured Girls]. But his music is timeless. His eighties music doesn't sound eighties – it transcends the era it was made in.'

Oceans makes a good point. Whereas the majority of recordings made in specific eras sound like products of their time, there is nothing that ties Paul's albums to a particular era beyond the people playing on them and the occasional lyrical reference to a time and place. Sonically there is nothing of that eighties drum sound or other studio trickery that locates so many recordings in that time.

Oceans is not alone in admiring Paul's willingness and happiness to help out other artists, no matter what their experience is, and also his way of making a song out of just about anything.

'In 1990 I invited him over to collaborate when I had hardly ever written a song. I told him I had an idea about lawnmowers in a garage and how they started working on each other, repairing themselves, and he started singing "the machines are fixing themselves". He can make something out of the worst piece of crap around. That's what he can do, take little things like that and make them into a work of art.

'His persistence is huge and his belief that something can be done is inspiring. Paul has raised the bar for every other songwriter in Australia and that's been an amazing thing.

'Everyone who collaborates with Paul comes out of the experience richer, with the feeling that, yes, you *can* make that song a little better. He offers hands-on advice about exactly *how* to make a song better. And he's extremely generous with everyone.'

The most recent project Paul worked on with Oceans was *Purple Sky*, Oceans' album of interpretations of songs by country great Hank Williams which features Paul singing 'I Can't Help It (If I'm Still In Love With You)' and the lesser known 'Alone and Forsaken'.

'With that album I was floundering, I'd lost my purpose, and Paul brought me back to it and got me back on track.' Ultimately Oceans says, 'I don't think anyone else other than Paul Kelly has written so many songs that define and describe the Australian experience.'

* * *

One of Paul's most recent collaborative experiences was with Paul Grabowsky, whom he first worked with in 2010 on 'Meet Me in the Middle of the Air'.

For the past few years, Grabowsky has curated and performed a series of shows in a purpose-built concert venue at Mount Barker summit in the Adelaide Hills. Grabowsky's focus is on chamber music but for the past four years these shows have been interspersed with vocal performances from artists like Kate Ceberano, Lior, Megan Washington, Vince Jones, Lisa Gerrard, Archie Roach – and Paul.

'Paul agreed to do a couple of shows,' Grabowsky says. 'We worked out the songs, and rehearsed them, and then Paul said we should record the show and be objective about the whole thing. So we committed to doing a proper studio recording.'

The recording is *Please Leave Your Light On*, which is simply Grabowsky's piano and Paul's voice. No guitars. No other instruments. The songs, all bar one, are for the most part ballads and avoid some of Paul's obvious hit tunes and well-known songs.

The album includes a reading of 'You Can Put Your Shoes Under My Bed', Paul changing the word 'spastic' to 'elastic' as he was uncomfortable singing the original lyrics from the song.

'I transcribed the songs,' Grabowsky says, 'paying particular attention to his vocal phrasing, such as where he puts the actual notes, and how best to transpose them into a piano world. It was a case of stripping the guitars away and reimagining them as songs accompanied by piano.

'I think Paul loves this project because I never play the songs exactly the same way twice and he says it's a bit like a high-wire act and he has to be very on his toes.

'He's such a consummate musician and so consistent in the level that he's able to deliver at. He has a phenomenal memory for all the songs that he's written. You know you're working with a master when you're working with someone like this.'

Grabowsky and Paul have similar work ethics. They're intense, focused, and constantly thinking of projects that will stimulate them.

'Paul's restless and like all great creative spirits he's always thinking about what to do next.'

Neither dismiss future collaborations if the idea presents and it feels right to both of them.

'It's all about trust and Paul has a lot riding on these things. He's Paul Kelly and he doesn't want to get up there with some klutz who's going to make him look or sound less than Paul Kelly.

'For me, working with Paul has been an opportunity to take those songs somewhere different without changing their essence. What I've been trying to do is extract what the essence is – he's a great songwriter so you're working with very fine material.

'There's an intensity with Paul. Nick Cave has it too, and it's palpable. This is a guy who's in it for the long game and if it doesn't kill him he'll be there for the duration.'

CHAPTER 17

THE WORK

'Paul was able to weave poetry and specialness out
of a sign on the top of a disused Melbourne factory.
He's *that* good.'

John Watson

PAUL'S INFLUENCE ON SONGWRITERS AND CREATIVE
individuals both in Australia and overseas is significant.

Towards the end of 2019, in addition to the latest update
of the *Songs from the South* album, Paul chose over three
hundred of his favourite poems which were published in an
anthology entitled *Love is Strong as Death*. The collection
sold extremely well, and probably exceeded sales for all
poetry books combined in that year.

Nikki Christer, the publisher of the poetry collection,
had bid for Paul's memoir as well as having known him
through a wide circle of friends such as writers Richard
and Martin Flanagan.

'Paul was a poet before he was a songwriter and I
always knew that he has a love of poetry, and he talks

about poetry in his memoir so it was just something that seemed so blindingly obvious. And what a joy – to find the poems that have meant the most to you over the years and find new ones. I knew he would enjoy that process.'

Well not exactly. Initially Paul had said no to Christer's suggestion, but a few months later he came back to her. 'The idea had obviously percolated in his mind.'

Then Christer watched as Paul chose poem after poem. 'I told him we could only include his "must have" so I thought two hundred poems and that just grew. But I think you can read it as a narrative and that's one of its great strengths. And to introduce people to poetry who have been put off it by the way they've been taught it at school.

'Poetry is about emotion and who better to present emotion to us than Paul, that's what he's been doing with his songs for years.'

The acclaimed and highly respected Australian poet Robert Adamson (who is represented in the collection) had written the foreword for Paul's first collection of songs, *Lyrics*, published in 1993. Paul subsequently provided a quote for the cover of Adamson's 2004 autobiography, *Inside Out*.

Paul and Adamson didn't actually meet until they bumped into each other at a Sydney Writers' Festival about a decade ago. Adamson has been listening to Paul's songs since he first heard *Post*. 'I remember comparing him to Jackson Browne in terms of how crafted his lyrics were. They're both much more careful than Dylan's in terms of technique and being polished.

'Around "Deeper Water" and "How to Make Gravy" he was doing these Raymond Carver–esque songs that are beautifully written. I noticed that back with "From St Kilda To Kings Cross" as well.'

In 2009 Adamson approached Paul about submitting some poems for the annual anthology *Best Australian Poems*.

'I wrote to him and said his songs were like poetry and asked if he did write poetry. He sent me two – "Thoughts in the Middle of the Night" and "One More Tune" – which I included as they read as well as anything in the anthology.'

The acclaimed American musician and fiction writer Willy Vlautin has stated that *So Much Water So Close To Home* was what prompted his move into writing fiction, particularly the song 'Everything's Turning to White', based on the short story by Raymond Carver.

'My brother had *Gossip*, the Australian version – the double record, which was hard to get in the US, and he turned me on to it. He knew I'd like it and I did. Man, I became a huge fan overnight. I think I was seventeen or so, when my brother got *Post* which was even harder to get, and then soon after *Under the Sun* came out on a US label.

'I just couldn't believe how great the songs were, the lyrics. I've always been drawn to lyrics and there was something about his songs that really made sense to me. They were often story-based and stories that I understood, working-class stories. But there wasn't a macho bent to them like Bruce Springsteen had taken with "Born in the USA" at the time. It seemed in the US a lot of story-orientated writers were heading in that direction. But Paul was different. They were simple and smart, with such great melodies …

'Over the years I've tried very hard to write like Paul Kelly. There's such a wisdom to the lyrics, compassion, such craft. It's hard to explain, maybe a sort of working-class elegance to them. Also a decency and that's a tricky word to say about rock'n'roll, but there was this feeling that he gave me back then that made me want to be like him and be like the songs he wrote. I wanted to write the way he wrote and I wanted to be sound enough mentally to write songs like that. To me he wrote more like a novelist than a self-destructive punk rocker. He's a true craftsman.'

As Vlautin's music career developed and he toured America with Richmond Fontaine, he was fortunate to open for and meet Paul.

'Before I opened for Paul I first saw him play in Portland in the late nineties. He was solo and travelling with a guitar player. He was so damn good. He was thirty miles from where Raymond Carver was born but he wasn't playing "Everything's Turning to White" so I told the friend I was with that if he'd call out for that song I'd buy him drinks all night. I was really shy back then and couldn't do it, but my friend did. I could tell it pissed off Paul but eventually he played it and goddamn it was amazing. Since then I've met him and watched him play a number of times. He's the way you'd hope when you listen to him: humble, cool, a bit wild-eyed, but always funny and kind.'

* * *

Michael Gudinski is proud of the fact that he still has a strong connection with Paul – his Frontier touring company has put him on shows with Leonard Cohen ('by this stage he'd become much more savvy and could sing'), and Bob Dylan, plus Frontier is the promoter for the annual How to Make Gravy show.

'I have no bitterness that Paul's not on the label anymore. I'm proud of him. None of us would have expected this level of success. He made mistakes, we may have made a couple.' He smiles. 'And he had his own issues that, to be honest, I wasn't aware of. The Gravy shows will get bigger and bigger. And for him I love that it's not about the money. I'm sure he loves the money but he won't let money cloud the big picture.

'Paul doesn't lack for confidence anymore and he's very caring and sharing of his time and experience. He seems very comfortable in the role that he's in. There're very few acts that can stay relevant, not so much in terms of hit records but in terms of great music.

'I think there's a lot more left in Paul in terms of great music, collaborations and vision.'

* * *

John Watson, who first saw Paul in Townsville and then went on to be a band manager for Cold Chisel, Midnight Oil, silverchair, Missy Higgins and Gotye, is perfectly positioned to describe Paul's career trajectory. When he moved to Sydney in the mid-1980s Watson was also in a band – The Spliffs – who opened for Paul and The Coloured Girls on a number of occasions.

'Paul is just on the back end of that generation of artists that came through, out of the pubs in the late seventies. He's not so much younger but his career is a little younger. He arrived in the limelight a little later than Midnight Oil and Cold Chisel and so forth but he was part of that generation of artists who had to compete for the attention of the same group of audiences – if you're not going to be good tonight by the end of the second song people are going to leave and they're going to walk one hundred yards down the road and when they get there they might see The Angels or the Divinyls or INXS or Rose Tattoo.

'That competition was tough. These were seriously very good rock'n'roll bands who all got very good in different ways at reaching out and grabbing you by any part of your anatomy that they could possibly get a firm grip on to ensure that you didn't look anywhere else. If you think about the presence of Peter Garrett or Jimmy Barnes or Chrissy Amphlett, or in their own ways Angry Anderson or Doc Neeson or Michael Hutchence – these were people who learnt in the strongest possible way how to maintain control of a room.

'Paul's built from different cloth. He's not seeking to dominate by theatricality – or by over-theatricality. But he's still seeking to weave a web and, through his storytelling and through his demeanour onstage, he had his own way of commanding the attention of a room. He was smart enough to work out, as he got up into bigger and bigger rooms, how to maintain that control.

'Part of what made Chris Wilson so compelling when The Coloured Girls and The Messengers became that beer barn band on the back of *Under the Sun*, that vintage of the band – which my band supported a number of times – was that Chris Wilson was a *powerful* presence onstage, an almost Clarence [Clemons] and Bruce [Springsteen] dynamic which helped Paul who might otherwise have been a little introverted or quiet to dominate a beer barn in the same way as the other artists who were around then.'

Watson is acutely aware that Paul's career path hasn't exactly followed the textbook.

'There wouldn't be many careers that have got a start then gone away – and gone away for a while – and then come back.

'*Post* was '85 and "Billy Baxter" was in 1980. That's a *big* gap. The audience that came to him around *Post* and then *Gossip* is an audience that doesn't have anything to do with the earlier period. I mean there might have been a few people at the Hopetoun who remembered but ninety-eight per cent of that audience is just taking him on face value because they like "Before Too Long" and "Leaps and Bounds".'

Watson has no issue with any suggestions that Paul's career has been a carefully planned, nurtured and image-conscious one – no matter how much Paul would seem to eschew notions of image.

'That's what all artists do. As per the Springsteen Broadway show where he says, "Yeah, I'm THAT good." People like you and I get into it going, "This is magical – I want to understand the magic." But you get closer and closer to it until at some point you realise that there is a deception at the core of it – and that can take the shine off things for a while and in some cases permanently, but if you keep moving beyond that and see it as a craft, there's a genius in it.

'I'll give you the perfect example – The Beatles song "Penny Lane". If you go and stand at the shelter in the middle of the roundabout [in Liverpool] it is the most bog ordinary, grey, bland, uninspiring nondescript, unpoetic place you could imagine. It is the north of England in all its dour greyness.

'But how good is Paul McCartney? He turned that location into this place that has lived in all of our imaginations – this technicolour landscape with all these magical people and, yes, at one level that's a magic trick and a deception and a ruse, but on another level it's transcendent and it's everything that you would want art, entertainment and craft to be. It takes the mundane and everyday and turns it into something else. You don't always want an artist to hold up an exact mirror. If you want to see exactly how things are all you've got to do is look around you, but if you want to see things in a different way, a heightened way, then that's what these craftspeople are capable of doing.

'One of the dangerous parts of being an artist is letting people see how the sausage is made. In the first instance it can diminish the work – you mean "Penny Lane" wasn't that pretty, but if you can get out the other side and go, "It wasn't pretty but I love the image of it and it has made it pretty for me – and, wow, how good was he to make that theatre. That's how good he was."

'To my mind that knowledge shouldn't sully – it should enhance. If you're a fan of this person and the illusions they create, how good are they?

'Paul was able to weave poetry and specialness out of a sign on the top of a disused Melbourne factory. He's *that* good.'

* * *

David Fricke has been Paul's biggest international media supporter since the early 1980s when he initially heard Paul's work with The Dots.

Fricke visited Australia for the first time around 1983 working on a story for *Musician* magazine. During that process he immersed himself in Australian music and was embraced by the likes of Mushroom Records who gave him *Talk* and *Manila*.

'I didn't think of Paul as a singer–songwriter. I thought of him as a band guy and the tracks I heard by The Dots I thought were interesting and kind of cool but I'm not sure that it was the kind of moxie that I was getting from the Oils and Chisel and in a psychedelic way from The Church or the classic stuff that I was getting into like Skyhooks or The Loved Ones.

'Paul was in this interesting, weird kind of limbo where what he was doing was kind of new wave, kind of Springsteen-ish, but it wasn't fish or fowl so I really had trouble connecting with the songs. Then I heard *Post* and went, "Oh, this guy is on another level."

'I won't say getting rid of the band [The Dots] was a good idea but it actually brought his voice to the fore. It not only freed him but it freed the music to be heard in a much more cooler way so you really heard what he could do as a singer.

'Paul's got a very odd voice. It's a little nasally, it doesn't have that robust, weirdly street opera-like style that Springsteen has, and it's more normal than Dylan so in a way his voice is a little deceptive because you don't think of him as a strong singer, but next to the song you can't imagine any other voice singing it.

'Then you start hearing the story told by not just the storyteller and the guy who wrote the story, but in some way by the guy who lived it. Even if it is in his imagination there was some kind of personal and historical authority behind the tale as he developed it and told it.

'When he started with The Messengers and all the other contexts I've seen him in, I started to realise that he's always at the centre of it, but the only way you heard it the first time was with everything else out of the way on *Post* ...

'You don't write the songs to fit the band, but that's what Paul did – he built The Coloured Girls/Messengers around himself and *Post* allowed him to do that.'

Fricke has seen pretty much every incarnation of Paul's bands from The Coloured Girls on and agrees that they were possibly the best band he's played with. Which doesn't mean they were necessarily the best musicians to share a stage with Paul, more that they were the right band at the right time as Paul forged his own identity as an artist.

'They set the tone and the standard and gave him the platform to grow as a writer. *Post* was an important introduction, and those initial records – *Post*, *Gossip* and *Under the Sun* were where he really established his voice and style and authority as a singer and songwriter ... He started with *Gossip* which was a great double album and then honed it down and focused it on the next records and that gave him the authority and the confidence to go anywhere he wanted. To go back to bands, to go solo, to do weird projects, to play in duos, collaborations – whatever he wanted to do he was able to follow that. In a way you have to build all that up, and build that kind of padding. It's like you're building a diving pool. The platform is ready; you fill it with water, and now you can jump.'

Fricke discounts the constant references to Paul as either the great songwriter of Melbourne or Sydney.

'That's just geography. He's extrapolating things that go beyond geography ...

'What I saw was a guy who really wants to drink up the life of where he is, and in his case it's going to be processed and digested, it's going to come out in his writing. It may not come out in specific references, it may come out in something that's completely integrated and in a way where you can't imagine any other voice singing it. I love coming out of the subway late at night in Times Square, when it's all wet and cool, and thinking how much it reminds me of walking around Kings Cross.

'It's Paul's perception and his ability to take those experiences and put them into a universal context, one that can resonate beyond his own experience. His songs are running around in my head at an intersection that I can go to any day.

'Paul creates ways for you to get into his songs. And it may be experiences that are entirely foreign to yours – like "Other People's Houses". I heard him sing that in 1990 at a club in Manly in Sydney. The room was really quiet and he sang this song.

'I don't know anything about cleaning other people's houses. It's not what my parents did, they struggled in their own ways – but man, the connection with that song and the way he sang it was so powerful. In some ways it was like he was singing like people from different races would, as more often than not it's blacks or Latinos or Asians – immigrants trying to get a leg-up – who do those jobs. And here's this little kid following his mama. I had to wait forever for it to come out on record. It was on *Hidden Things* and I go, "Seriously, you hide this – this is one of his greatest songs."'

Fricke is quick to dismiss any suggestion that Paul still dreams of 'making it' on a global stage. He thinks that has already been accomplished.

'In a sense he has made it, and he's made it in a way that's a lot deeper and a lot more meaningful than other artists who come to this country [the United States] from outside, the ones who come here and really nail it and are massive, massive, massive and then they're gone. You're never big forever – no one is. And for Paul, to be able to come here as much as he does and command an audience that respects him and wants to hear the new songs, wants him to grow – you can't beat that.

'Springsteen, Neil Young, Bob Dylan, Joni Mitchell – all of the archetypes are what you could say Paul is in the lineage of – but that group is the anomaly, it is not the norm, and it's the wrong recognition to strive for.

'What you want to strive for is to be heard – and to be heard consistently and in a way where other artists who are your peers respect you, and you can come into [another country] and the people coming to the shows are both old friends, and people who are bringing new friends, or people coming because they've just heard something.

'Paul is Australia's Slim Dusty, Dylan, Springsteen and Neil Young combined. He can be all Australian and still have a connection with people outside of Australia.

'Paul is a survivor. I'm not just listening to songs from *Gossip* or songs from *Under the Sun* or songs from *Hidden Things*, or even *Deeper Water*. I'm listening to the new things where he's singing Shakespeare or collaborating with other artists.

'"How to Make Gravy" may possibly be my favourite Paul Kelly song.

'It's not so much a song about Christmas as it is a song about longing. It transcends holiday. It transcends setting. And what he does is narrow all those big things down into simple interactions.

'You have Gravy Day in Australia. Springsteen can't do that – he had to borrow July 4. With Dylan no one goes "Happy Like a Rolling Stone" day.

'It shows he's connecting with people in a very intimate way but on a large scale.'

Indeed, Paul's public profile has grown and grown to the point where he's now a more significant live drawcard than he's ever been before. He's done that while becoming a hip and cool figure who appeals to an extremely broad range of people.

Unlike so many other artists of his age Paul's audience keeps rejuvenating. While he has many long-standing fans who keep attending his concerts, they're likely to be standing next to a bunch of kids who weren't even born when *Gossip* was released.

Part of what has kept Paul's currency appealing and relevant to a younger audience is astute positioning. Paul has transferred his endlessly inquisitive interest in new music into his concert bills. He is the guy who supports and encourages new, up-and-coming contemporary Australian music.

For the How to Make Gravy 2019 tour the opening acts were Thelma Plum, Marlon Williams, Courtney Barnett and Kate Miller-Heidke. He keeps promoting and surrounding himself with new and relevant music and artists.

There was a key moment when this seismic audience change occurred, particularly in Victoria, but its impact spread quickly.

'I can pinpoint when I felt a noticeable escalation in the crowd response and crowd numbers,' Ash Naylor says. 'It was around when we played Splendour in the Grass in 2007, which was around the time that Paul's lyric book was part of the VCE curriculum reading list.

'So a lot of the songs were in the consciousness of a lot of younger people whose parents probably had the records.

'I remember George Negus introducing us at a festival. He said, "The Yanks have got Bob Dylan and we've got Paul Kelly," and the place erupted. It was something akin to Beatlemania, like an aeroplane's jet engine noise. It was phenomenal.

'At the heart of it is the calibre of the material. People want something with substance, and they get it. Throughout it all, Paul has never been a nostalgia act. I suspect there's a portion of Paul's current audience who still buy records but he's also got the kids who are into streaming too.

'And the songs are relatable. People obviously have to be able to relate to the lyrics in some way to get into the shows and songs. He has this way of getting to the point without being too prosaic, and still evocative. It's a skill and it's what he does. He's a writer and he works on it.'

Deborah Conway's theory about Paul's longevity is that 'He just never stops working. It's an amazing amount of energy that he invests into what he does. He's completely driven. I think he's hugely ambitious. *Hugely* ambitious. And more so as he gets older. There's that feeling that time is running out and he needs to get his body of work out there. It's like he wants to wring every possible ounce of whatever he can out of this life. These things are incredibly admirable.

'There's a determination in him that is belied by his quiet and gentle demeanour. People don't see it immediately but there's a steely core. One of the things that I admired about Paul when I first met him was that he never said yes to anything he didn't want to do. He'd always stick to his guns. He was quiet – but very firm.'

'He's in the army of song,' Bill McDonald says. 'And he must have had that in him from the get-go because he takes it so absolutely seriously.'

'Paul is incredibly determined,' Dan Kelly says. 'There's something about his personality type. If he was in my garden he'd have to look up Wikipedia or some reference to find out what a plant was or what birds he saw, or the history of the area. He *needs* to know. It's a strong curiosity that drives him on. And Paul has an interest in classical education. I have my theories about that too. It creates a different sort of musician.

'That old-school inquisitive thing, wanting to know about Greek mythology. You didn't get taught that at school in the eighties. But it comes through via your Paul Kellys or Richard Flanagans who have a different kind of thinking. And then there's family positional stuff, just like it is with everybody. The later you are born in the family the more determined you get and it's a pretty determined family. Everyone quietly goes and does their thing …

'Paul is strong willed. If he's unhappy with your performance – and that's going to happen from time to time – and there's something he wants rectified, he never mentions it after the show. He might not even mention it at all, but the next time at sound check he will always go, "Let's run that one – let's run it again," and you know what he's doing. You can't tell musicians after a show that they've fucked up. They'll just get their backs up and go, "Fuck you." Next day at sound check is a new day and it's just, "Let's get this right."'

So it's Paul Kelly, chief, commander and leader of the squad?

'He does command that thing,' Dan Kelly says. 'It could be terror but it's not. As Spencer [Jones] said, "He makes you love him."'

CHAPTER 18

LEAPS AND BOUNDS

As I reached the end of writing this book I had two songs running through my head – neither of them by Paul. I could hear Kris Kristofferson in 'The Pilgrim, Chapter 33', singing about a guy who's a poet and a picker, and how this character keeps on changing for better or for worse and searching for something he's never found. I kept thinking about Paul and whether he is satisfied with his work. I figure the answer is probably yes, but his verve would always be energetically telling him that a lot more has to be done.

Over more than four decades Paul's built an enviable body of work. The restlessness that enlivened him as a youth on his first adventure after leaving high school, opening him up to a world of people, possibility, stories and songs, continues to pervade his creative working life. Paul probably hasn't told me about all of them, but while researching this book I've heard about many upcoming projects.

There's talk of a Christmas album, with several songs already recorded, including a version of The Band's song 'Christmas Must Be Tonight'. An album of reinterpretations of songs by Australian artists is mooted, as is a collaboration with Gareth Liddiard and Fiona Kitschin from The Drones. As this book goes to press Paul is planning to release a selection of the songs and poems he's been posting on his social media pages during the COVID-19 lockdown, under the title *Forty Days*. He's also given assistance to Siân Darling, who's overseeing the updated edition of the Kev Carmody tribute album *Cannot Buy My Soul*, due out in August 2020; briefly discussed with Charlie Owen the idea of an album of songs that could be sung at wakes, and even proposed to rework portions of this book into an album of songs. Okay, I made the last one up.

As his history would attest, anything seems possible. Paul is in the rare position where he can explore any creative bent he decides upon, and he clearly has no shortage of ideas.

The other song I had running through my head – not so much for the lyrics but simply the title – was Lou Reed's 'Growing Up in Public'. Paul has spent his adult life as a well-known figure. While there are benefits to that, the burden of constant scrutiny and judgement is not hard to imagine. Paul's songs, personal life and observations have been chronicled, dissected and reflected upon by a countless number of people. For many, Paul's songs have soundtracked their lives and just hearing an opening line, chord or chorus will take them to a particular time and place. But more than that, many use Paul's songs and stories as yardsticks for human decency. They can identify either through their own experience or through their relationships with others the stories of injustice, the imperfect, the flawed – the stories of being human. They can relate to or hold as an ideal the cheeky and elevating songs of love and joy.

Paul is undoubtedly a voice of an Australian generation and among his work are many songs that will be listened to, sung and celebrated long after he has left us. They both reflect and impact on our world and how we see ourselves. Sometimes they mirror, sometimes they guide. Sometimes they applaud, sometimes they chastise. Could an artist ask for anything more?

Over the course of writing this book I was reminded many times of songs of Paul's that I'd always loved; many that I'd been witness to the creation and evolution of. I listened again to records that possibly I should have paid more attention to when they first came out, and found things in them that I hadn't expected. Sometimes the song and the listener take time to find each other in ways that are meaningful.

During that trip I developed an enhanced appreciation for what Paul has created, and will continue to build on. I realised that Paul Kelly is an inexhaustible figure – musically, intellectually, personally. He creates without much thought as to what the audience might think. Of course he wants the creations to be loved. That's natural. He knows that while some will embrace certain projects, others will not, but he's good with that. Because he has such a wide body of work he can reach and connect with a vast array of people.

The mark of any true artist, no matter what the field or medium, is that they find ways to create and keep creating work. Of course they want an audience to engage with it all, but the principal consideration, the statement, is the work itself.

I've realised more than I ever did that Paul works extremely hard at what he does. There may be happy accidents that get a song started but after that it's hard graft, revision, thought and refinement, all of which contribute to making the finished song sound so damn effortless and natural.

It's hard to imagine Paul not writing songs or creating music or waking up one morning and thinking of a new artistic avenue to explore. Like so many of the artists he reveres, it's reasonable to think that he will keep performing those songs and new ones for a long time to come. Like Bob Dylan, Paul is a song and dance man, and that's what song and dance men (and women) do.

Sometimes, in the moments between the songs, I have thought back to the story of the audience member who approached the band in the empty room at Mittagong RSL on that December night in 1985. I wonder if she and her friends ever gave Paul a second chance and developed into Paul Kelly fans. At the 2019 How to Make Gravy concert in the Domain in Sydney I found myself looking out at the audience and wondering if she was out there. Or maybe, just maybe, she was somewhere else and still considers Paul and his band to be the worst she's ever seen.

I suspect that either way Paul would just smile at the thought and be pretty comfortable with whichever way it has turned out.

ACKNOWLEDGEMENTS

As always with a project of this magnitude there's a huge array of folk to thank. And with that comes the cold fear of forgetting someone important. If you're that person please accept my apologies.

Paul Kelly gave infinitely more than I expected throughout the whole process, constantly volunteering opportunities to chat, answering questions and suggesting areas and subjects to explore. I can only hope I have done him justice.

Siân Darling and Bill Cullen also both totally embraced what I was attempting and never once made it feel like I was wearing out their patience. Thank you both.

My long-term publisher Matthew Kelly, a self-confessed Paul Kelly tragic, worked with me in the early stages of the project before handing me over to the extremely accomplished, professional and super-understanding Vanessa Radnidge. Among many things Vanessa suggested some fundamental restructuring to this book for which I'm eternally grateful.

Jacquie Brown took on the painstaking work of fine tuning, finessing and keeping track of the myriad changes to text, structure, photos and a whole host of things I probably don't even know about. Thank you.

They say a good editor is everything. I've been blessed with not only a good editor – but a *great* one in Deonie Fiford, who took my manuscript apart and stitched it back together with surgical skill that frequently had me gasping.

And when Deonie commented in the manuscript that one of her favourite of Paul's albums was *Spring and Fall* I realised that not only was she a superb editor but a serious fan of the subject.

Over more than eighteen months I conducted many many interviews – as often as possible in person. I'd like to thank: John O'Donnell, John Watson, Martin Armiger, Michael Barclay, Christopher Barnett, Rob Barnham, Billy Baxter, Ron Blake, Robert Adamson, Alan Brooker, Tim Brosnan, Ron Brown, Michael Gudinski, Rachel Perkins, Vika Bull, Linda Bull, Joe Camilleri, Kev Carmody, Raphael Lee (Fred) Cass, Kasey Chambers, Deborah Conway, John Dowler, Chris Dyson, Kaarin Fairfax, Neil Finn, Sally Ford, Alex Formosa, Huk Treloar, Cameron Bruce, David Fricke, Willy Vlautin, Paul Gadsby, Renée Geyer, Nikki Christer, Anna Goldsworthy, Paul Grabowsky, Steve Hadley, John Lever, Bill McDonald, Zoe Hauptmann, Bruce Haymes, Michelle Higgins, Michael Holmes, Randy Jacobs, Dan Kelly, Mary Jo Kelly, Sheila Kelly, Nick Lainas, Chris Langman, James Ledger, Don Walker, Ben Ball, John Lloyd, Dan Luscombe, Peter Luscombe, Tom and Ian Stehlik, Anne Kirkpatrick, Greg Martin, Lucky Oceans, Shane O'Mara, Charlie Owen, Greg Perano, Billy Pommer, Irene Karpathakis, Steve Earle, Archie Roach, Jon Schofield, Meredith Rose, Steve Schram, Terry Darmody, Andy Baldwin, Chris Thompson, Alan Thorne, Tony Thornton, Yanni Alexander (nee Stumbles), Greg Walker, Philip White, Chris Worrall, Richard Guilliatt, Jeannie Lewis, Sharon Connolly, Rohan Connolly and Billy Miller.

The quotes from Peter Bull came from interviews conducted for the National Film and Sound Archive by John Bannister. Thank you both.

For all sorts of wonderful and useful assistance big shout outs to: Ian McFarlane, Stephen Vineburg, Dino Scatena, Hugh Gibbons, Rebecca Howell, Greg Champion, Danny Goldberg, Simon Drake, Caroline Kung, Gerard Schlaghecke, Michael Roberts, Graham Lee, Jill Shelton, Vince Simonetti, Joy McKean, David Laing, Terry Darmody, James Anfuso, David N Pepperell, Chris O'Hearn, John Wotton, Larry Buttrose, Ailee Lynn Calderbank, Toby Creswell, Greg Noakes, Mark Muir, Meryl Gross, George Enrique Munoz, Deb Martin, Patrick Emery, Ian Darling, John Kingsmill, Greg Fleet, Stuart Spence, Max Crawdaddy, Bernard Zuel, John Kane, Peter 'Skip' Beaumont-Edmonds, Brecon Walsh, Bleddyn Butcher, Leon Morris, Wendy McDougall, Michael McMartin, Dennis Atkins, Ian Greene, Mark Dodshon, Sian Prior, Jen Jewel Brown, Greg Phillips, Clinton Walker, Donald Robertson, Steve Lippincott, Juno Gemmes, Marcus Schintler, Zac Brown, Murray Bramwell, David Messer, Gary Hunn, Kylie Greer, Wendy McDougall, Ian Greene, Mark Hopper, Andrew Southam, Greg Phillips and Michael Armiger.

When we met, Susan Lynch told me stories of her teenage years, with a portable record player next to her bed, listening to Paul's classic eighties album – and of course with no knowledge of my involvement with Paul and those records. Then while walking one night she suggested I get serious about pursuing this book. Since then she's supported and assisted me and spent hours and hours (and hours) discussing its contents, researching, reading every version of the manuscript, helping with the format, making changes and suggestions. It's a much better book because of her efforts – and I'm a much better person for having her in my life. Thank you Susan.

INDEX